SCOPE AND CATEGORIES OF HUMAN RIGHTS

SCOPE AND CATEGORIES OF HUMAN RIGHTS

Editor

Jyotsna Tiwari

ISHA

ISHA BOOKS

DELHI-110033

Scope and Categories of Human Rights

ISBN: 81-8205-384-6

Rs. 750

Published in 2006 in India by
Isha Books
D-43, Prithviraj Road, Adarsh Nagar, Delhi-110033
E-mail : ishabooks@hotmail.com

Laser Typesetting at: Master Computers, Delhi
Printed at: Salasar Imaging System, Delhi

Preface

Human rights are based on humankind's increasing demand for a life in which the inherent dignity and worth of each human being are accorded respect and protection. They allow us to develop fully and use human qualities, intelligence, talents and conscience and to satisfy spiritual and other needs. Their denial is not only an individual and personal tragedy but also creates conditions of social and political unrest, sowing the seeds of violence and conflict within and between societies and nations.

All societies possess notions of justice, fairness, dignity, and respect. Human rights, however, are but one path to implement a particular conception of social justice. In the past two decades, the revolutionary force of the demand for human rights has become unusually clear. Across the globe, regimes that had cynically manipulated the language of human rights have been sent packing by a citizenry that insisted on taking human rights seriously.

With the continuing spread of political liberalization and democratization, an ever-growing number of governments are being pressured at home and from abroad to live up to these commitments. In today's world, a consistent pattern of gross human rights violations is widely perceived to undermine a regime's national and international legitimacy.

The scope and categories of human rights are comprehensively narrated in the present volume. Students, teachers and researchers, policy-planners, and human rights activists will find this book most useful.

Editor

Contents

Preface *v*

1. The Right to Freedom of Thought, Conscience and Religion 1
2. The Scope of Health Behaviour and Health Education 16
3. Health and Human Rights 34
4. Human Rights Law and Freedom of Association 91
5. Connecting Mental Health and Human Rights 126
6. Human Rights and Conflict 148
7. Economic Social and Cultural Rights 181
8. Human Rights Education in Universities and Colleges 214
9. Human Rights and HIV/AIDS 225
10. Defining the Scope of Business Responsibility 278
11. ICTs in Support of Human Rights, Democracy and Good Governance 287

Bibliography 316

Index 318

1

The Right to Freedom of Thought, Conscience and Religion

Article 18 of the Universal Declaration of Human Rights: "Everyone has the right to freedom of thought, conscience and religion; this right includes freedom to change his religion or belief, and freedom, either alone or in community with others and in public or private, to manifest his religion or belief in teaching, practice, worship and observance."

Article 18 of the International Covenant on Civil and Political Rights:

1. Everyone shall have the right to freedom of thought, conscience and religion. This right shall include freedom to have or to adopt a religion or belief of his choice, and freedom, either individually or in community with others and in public or private, to manifest his religion or belief in worship, observance, practice and teaching.

2. No one shall be subject to coercion which would impair his freedom to have or to adopt a religion or belief of his choice.

3. Freedom to manifest one's religion or beliefs may be subject only to such limitations as are prescribed by law and are necessary to protect public safety, order, health, or morals or the fundamental rights and freedoms of others.

4. The States Parties to the present Covenant undertake to have respect for the liberty of parents and, when applicable, legal guardians to ensure the religious and moral education of their children in conformity with their own convictions."

Article 8 of the African Charter on Human and Peoples' Rights:

> "Freedom of conscience, the profession and free practice of religion shall be guaranteed. No one may, subject to law and order, be submitted to measures restricting the exercise of these freedoms."

Article 12 of the American Convention on Human Rights:

1. Everyone has the right to freedom of conscience and of religion. This includes freedom to maintain or to change one's religion or beliefs, and freedom to profess or disseminate one's religion or beliefs either individually or together with others, in public or in private.

2. No one shall be subject to restrictions that might impair his freedom to maintain or to change his religion or beliefs.

3. Freedom to manifest one's religion and beliefs may be subject only to the limitations prescribed by law that are necessary to protect public safety, order, health, or morals, or the rights or freedoms of others.

4. Parents or guardians, as the case may be, have the right to provide for the religious or moral education

of their children or wards that is in accord with their own convictions."

Article 9 of the European Convention on Human Rights:

1. Everyone has the right to freedom of thought, conscience and religion; this right includes freedom to change his religion or belief and freedom, either alone or in community with others and in public or private, to manifest his religion or belief, in worship, teaching, practice and observance.

2. Freedom to manifest one's religion or beliefs shall be subject only to such limitations as are prescribed by law and are necessary in a democratic society in the interests of public safety, for the protection of public order, health or morals, or for the protection of the rights and freedoms of others.

The right to freedom of religion is further guaranteed by:

— Article 5(d)(vii) of the International Convention on the Elimination of All Forms of Racial Discrimination;

— Article 14 of the Convention on the Rights of the Child;

— Article 9 of the African Charter on the Rights and Welfare of the Child; and

— Article 4(i) of the Inter-American Convention on the Prevention, Punishment, and Eradication of Violence against Women.

International human rights law prohibits discrimination on the ground of religion. Article 18 of the International Covenant on Civil and Political Rights, pointed out by the Human Rights Committee, the right to freedom of thought, conscience and religion guaranteed by article 18(1) of the International Covenant "is far-reaching and profound; it encompasses freedom of thought on all matters, personal conviction and the commitment to religion or belief, whether manifested individually or in community with others." Furthermore, "the freedom of thought and the freedom of conscience are protected equally with the freedom of religion and belief."

It is noteworthy that article 18 "does not permit any limitations whatsoever on the freedom of thought and conscience or on the freedom to have or adopt a religion or belief of one's choice. The Human Rights Committee also importantly underlines that, on the basis of articles 18(2) and 17 of the Covenant, "no one can be compelled to reveal his thoughts or adherence to a religion or belief."In other words, every man or women has the right to keep his or her religion or belief an exclusively private matter in all situations.

The Human Rights Committee further states that "article 18 protects theistic, non-theistic and atheistic beliefs, as well as the right not to profess any religion or belief. The terms 'belief' and 'religion' are to be broadly construed. Article 18 is not limited in its application to traditional religions or to religions and beliefs with institutional characteristics or practices or practices analogous to those of traditional religions.

The Committee therefore views with concern any tendency to discriminate against any religion or belief for any reason, including the fact that they are newly established, or represent religious minorities that may be the subject of hostility on the part of a predominant religious community."The Human Rights Committee further observes "that the freedom to 'have or to adopt' a religion or belief necessarily entails the freedom to choose a religion or belief, including the right to replace one's current religion or belief with another or to adopt atheistic views, as well as the right to retain one's religion or belief.

Article 18.2 bars coercion that would impair the right to have or adopt a religion or belief, including the use of threat of physical force or penal sanctions to compel believers or non-believers to adhere to their religious beliefs and congregations, to recant their religion or belief or to convert." The Committee adds that "policies or practices having the same intention or effect, such as, for example, those restricting access to education, medical care, employment or the rights guaranteed by article 25 [i.e. the right to participate in government] and other provisions of the Covenant, are similarly inconsistent with article 18(2). The same protection is enjoyed by holders of all beliefs of a non-religious nature."

Article 8 of the African Charter on Human and Peoples' Rights is brief. It merely stipulates that "freedom of conscience, the profession and free practice of religion shall be guaranteed" and that "no one may, subject to law and order, be submitted to measures restricting the exercise of these freedoms." It is noteworthy that this provision is silent on the question of freedom of thought and also on the freedom to adopt or change a religion or belief according to one's own convictions.

The right to freedom of conscience and religion as protected by article 12 of the American Convention on Human Rights is in many ways similar to the freedoms guaranteed by article 18 of the International Covenant. However, in the Convention freedom of thought is not linked to these freedoms but to the right to freedom of expression set forth in article 13. The right to freedom of conscience and religion under article 12 of the American Convention also includes "freedom to maintain or to change one's religion of beliefs", a freedom that is strengthened by article 12(2) of the Convention, according to which "no one shall be subject to restrictions that might impair his freedom to maintain or to change his religion or beliefs."

It follows, a fortiori, that no one may be subject to "coercion" - the term used in article 18(2) of the Covenant - for purposes of either preventing a person from, or obliging a person to, maintain or change his or her religion or beliefs. In other words, a person's religion or beliefs must at all times be fully voluntary. Freedom of conscience and religion as protected by article 12 of the American Convention is included in the list of non-derogable rights in article 27(2) and must therefore be guaranteed also "in time of war, public danger, or other emergency that threatens the independence or security" of the State party concerned (art. 27(1) of the Convention).

The Inter-American Court of Human Rights pointed out that "the right to freedom of conscience and religion allows everyone to maintain, change, profess and disseminate his religion or beliefs," adding that this right is one of the foundations of democratic society, which, in its religious dimension, "constitutes a far-reaching element in the protection of the convictions of those who profess a religion and in their way of life".

Article 9(1) of the European Convention on Human Rights guarantees "the right to freedom of thought, conscience and religion; this right includes the freedom to change [one's] religion or belief." In terms very similar to those used in article 18(1) of the Covenant, article 9(1) of the European Convention also protects the freedom of every person, "either alone or in community with others and in public or private, to manifest his religion or belief, in worship, teaching, practice and observance".

The right to freedom of thought, conscience and religion is far-reaching and covers all matters relating to one's personal convictions. It protects not only religious people but also, for instance, atheists, agnostics, sceptics and the indifferent. The right to freedom of thought, conscience and religion also implies that every person has the unconditional right to have and adopt a religion of his or her choice. This freedom includes the right to change one's religion. Every person has the right not to be coerced or otherwise compelled to maintain, adopt or change a religion.

The right to freedom of thought, conscience and religion, including the freedom to have, adopt or change religion according to one's choice, are protected unconditionally, although freedom of conscience does not imply a right to refuse all obligations imposed by law. No limitations may be imposed on the freedom to adopt or change a religion of one's choice. Under the International Covenant on Civil and Political Rights and the American Convention on Human Rights, freedom of thought, conscience and religion cannot be derogated from in any circumstances.

Freedom of thought, conscience and religion is a cornerstone of a democratic society/a society respectful of human rights. Article 18(1) of the International Covenant guarantees the freedom to manifest one's religion or belief "either individually or in community with others and in public or private" and the freedom to do so "in worship, observance, practice and teaching". As noted by the Human Rights Committee, it is thus a freedom that "encompasses a broad range of acts.

The concept of worship extends to ritual and ceremonial acts giving direct expression to belief, as well as various practices integral to such, including the building of places of worship, the use of ritual formulae and objects, the display of symbols, and the observance of holidays and days of rest. The observance and practice of religion or belief may include not only ceremonial acts but also such customs as the observance of dietary regulations, the wearing of distinctive clothing or head coverings, participation in rituals associated with certain stages of life, and the use of a particular language customarily spoken by a group.

In addition, the practice and teaching of religion or belief includes acts integral to the conduct by religious groups of their basic affairs, such as the freedom to choose their religious leaders, priests and teachers, the freedom to establish seminaries or religious schools and the freedom to prepare and distribute religious texts or publications. The Committee strongly recommended that these provisions be abolished since they were not in conformity with article 18(1) and (3) of the Covenant.

Article 8 of the African Charter on Human and Peoples' Rights is the most laconic of the provisions considered "the profession and free practice of religion", adding that "no one may, subject to law and order, be submitted to measures restricting the exercise of these freedoms." According to article 12(1) of the American Convention on Human Rights, the right to freedom of conscience and religion includes "freedom to profess or disseminate one's religion or beliefs either individually or together with others, in public or in private".

Under article 9(1) of the European Convention on Human Rights, the right to freedom of religion includes "freedom, either alone or in community with others and in public or private, to manifest [one's] religion or belief, in worship, teaching, practice and observance". According to article 9 of the European Convention, "freedom to manifest one's religion is not only exercisable in community with others, 'in public' and within the circle of those whose faith one shares, but can also be asserted 'alone' and 'in private'; furthermore, it includes in principle the right to try to convince one's neighbour, for example through 'teaching', failing which, moreover, 'freedom to change (one's) religion or belief', enshrined in Article 9, would be likely to remain a dead letter.

Among the freedoms guaranteed by article 18 of the International Covenant, only the freedom to manifest one's religion or beliefs may be restricted. According to article 18(3), this freedom "may be subject only to such limitations as are prescribed by law and are necessary to protect public safety, order, health, or morals or the fundamental rights and freedoms of others". The Human Rights Committee emphasizes that this provision "is to be strictly interpreted: restrictions are not allowed on grounds not specified there, even if they would be allowed as restrictions to other rights protected in the Covenant, such as national security.

Limitations may be applied only for those purposes for which they were prescribed and must be directly related and proportionate to the specific need on which they are predicated. "The Committee importantly adds that limitations on the right to manifest one's religion or beliefs "must not be applied in a manner that would vitiate the rights guaranteed in article 18". Lastly, the limitations must not, of course, "be imposed for discriminatory purposes or applied in a discriminatory manner". In resorting to limitations on the right to manifest one's religion or beliefs.

According to article 9(2) of the European Convention on Human Rights, "freedom to manifest one's religion or beliefs shall be subject only to such limitations as are prescribed by law and are necessary in a democratic society in the interests of public safety, for the protection of public order, health or morals, or for the protection of the rights and freedoms of others." The grounds enumerated cover in substance those found in the other two treaties.

There is thus an important convergence on the major issue of limitations on the freedom to manifest one's religion or beliefs. However, article 9(2) of the European Convention adds the condition that limitations for the reasons invoked must be necessary "in a democratic society". The necessity test must therefore be made in the light of the needs of a society based on a democratic constitutional order.

Article 18 of the International Covenant must be read in conjunction with article 20, according to which the following acts "shall be prohibited by law":

— any "propaganda for war" (art. 20(1)), and

— any "advocacy of national, racial or religious hatred that constitutes incitement to discrimination, hostility or violence" (art. 20(2)).

It follows that the manifestation of religion or beliefs must not at any time be used as a tool for the encouragement of war or for advocacy of hatred. The Human Rights Committee confirms that no derogation made pursuant to article 4(1) of the Covenant "may be invoked as justification for a State party to engage itself, contrary to article 20, in propaganda for war, or in advocacy of national, racial or religious hatred that would constitute incitement to discrimination, hostility or violence".

The fact that States parties are legally bound to outlaw war propaganda and religious incitement to discrimination, hostility and violence implies that they also have a legal duty to ensure that this prohibition is respected in practice. Every person has the right to manifest his or her religion either in private or in public and either individually or in community with others. The manifestation of one's religion or beliefs may cover such activities as worship, observance, practice, teaching, evangelization and rites.

The right to manifest one's religion may be subjected to limitations, provided that such limitations are prescribed by law imposed in order to protect a legitimate aim, namely public safety, (public) order, health, morals or the rights and freedoms of others, and necessary in order to protect the legitimate objective. At the European level, the notion of a democratic society plays a pivotal role in determining the necessity of measures limiting a person's right to manifest his or her religion or beliefs.

According to the Human Rights Committee, "the liberty of parents or legal guardians to ensure that their children receive a religious and moral education in conformity with their own convictions" under article 18(4) of the Covenant "is related to the guarantees of the freedom to teach a religion or belief stated in article 18.1". This means, inter alia, that article 18(4) of the Covenant "permits public school instruction in subjects such as the general history of religions and ethics if it is given in a neutral and objective way", but that "public education that includes instruction in a particular religion or belief is inconsistent with article 18.4 unless provision is made for non-discriminatory exemptions or alternatives that would accommodate the wishes of parents and guardians.

Article 12(4) of the American Convention guarantees the right of parents and guardians, as the case may be, to provide for the religious and moral education of their children or wards that is in accord with their own convictions. Although article 9 of the European Convention contains no similar guarantee, the second sentence of article 2 of Protocol No. 1 to the Convention states that: "In the exercise of any functions which is assumes in relation to education and to teaching, the State shall respect the right of parents to ensure such education and teaching in conformity with their own religious and philosophical convictions."

According to the European Court of Human Rights, this sentence, which is an adjunct to the fundamental right to education guaranteed by the first sentence of the article, "is binding upon the Contracting States in the exercise of each and every function - it speaks of 'any functions' - that they undertake in the sphere of education and teaching, including that consisting of the organisation and financing of public education".

The provision "aims in short at safeguarding the possibility of pluralism in education, which possibility is essential for the preservation of the 'democratic society' as conceived by the Convention. In view of the power of the modern State, it is above all through State teaching that this aim must be realised. "Article 2 of Protocol No. 1 thus "enjoins the State to respect parents' convictions, be they religious or philosophical, throughout the entire State education programme" and it does not therefore "permit a distinction to be drawn between religious instruction and other subjects".

However, the second sentence of article 2 of the Protocol "does not prevent States from imparting through teaching or education information or knowledge of a directly or indirectly religious or philosophical kind. It does not even permit parents to object to the integration of such teaching or education in the school curriculum, for otherwise all institutionalised teaching would run the risk of proving impracticable." The same provision "implies on the other hand that the State, in fulfilling the functions assumed by it in regard to education and teaching, must take care that information or knowledge included in the curriculum is conveyed in an objective, critical and pluralistic manner.

The State is forbidden to pursue an aim of indoctrination that might be considered as not respecting parents' religious or philosophical convictions. That is the limit that must not be exceeded." Under the International Covenant on Civil and Political Rights and the American Convention on Human Rights, parents or legal guardians have the right to ensure that the religious and moral education of their children is conveyed in accordance with their own convictions. It is, however, compatible with the International Covenant to impart public school instruction in subjects such as the general history of religions and ethics provided that this is done in a neutral and objective manner.

Under the European Convention on Human Rights, the Contracting States are legally bound to ensure that in each and every function that they undertake in the field of education and teaching, the religious or philosophical convictions of parents or legal guardians are respected. This means that States have to take care to impart information or knowledge in an objective, critical and pluralistic way and that they are forbidden to pursue an aim of indoctrination.

The recognition of a religion as a so-called State religion or a religion that is simply an official or traditional religion or a religion professed by a majority of the State's population can easily imply that other religions are discriminated against. However, as noted by the Human Rights Committee, this situation "shall not result in any impairment of the enjoyment of any of the rights under the Covenant, including articles 18 and 27, nor in any discrimination against adherents to other religions or non-believers".

It would, for instance, be contrary to the non-discrimination provision in article 26 of the Covenant to adopt "measures restricting eligibility for government service to members of the predominant religion or giving economic privileges to them or imposing special restrictions on the practice of other faiths". The Committee points out in this connection that article 20(2) of the Covenant provides "important safeguards against infringements of the rights of religious minorities and of other religious groups to exercise the rights guaranteed by articles 18 and 27, and against acts of violence or persecution directed towards those groups".

Lastly, the Committee stresses that "if a set of beliefs is treated as official ideology in constitutions, statutes, proclamations of ruling parties, etc., or in actual practice, this shall not result in any impairment of the freedoms under article 18 or any other rights recognized under the Covenant nor in any discrimination against persons who do not accept the official ideology or who oppose it." The Human Rights Committee has emphasized that States parties to the International Covenant on Civil and Political Rights have a legal duty to ensure that there is no discrimination against adherents of different religions or non-believers.

Although the right to conscientious objection is not expressly guaranteed by the International Covenant, the Human Rights Committee "believes that such a right can be derived from article 18, inasmuch as the obligation to use lethal force may seriously conflict with the freedom of conscience and the right to manifest one's religion or belief. When this right is recognized by law or practice, there shall be no differentiation among conscientious objectors on the basis of the nature of their particular beliefs; likewise, there shall be no discrimination against conscientious objectors because they have failed to perform military service.

The Human Rights Committee has accepted that the right to conscientious objection can be derived from article 18 of the International Covenant on Civil and Political Rights. This right is not unconditional and the Committee may be reluctant to re-examine decisions taken by the national authorities in this regard. However, when the right to conscientious objection is recognized in national law, there must be no discrimination between the persons concerned on the basis of their particular beliefs.

2

The Scope of Health Behaviour and Health Education

Today, the range of health education and health behaviour change strategies are nearly limitless. Health professionals and health education specialists may counsel people at risk for AIDS about safe sex; help children avoid tobacco, alcohol, and drugs; help adults to stop smoking; help patients to manage and cope with their illnesses; and organize communities or advocate policy changes aimed at fostering health improvement.

Health education professionals work all over the world in a variety of settings including schools, worksites, voluntary health organizations, medical settings, and communities. They are challenged to disseminate the best of what is known in new situations. They may also forge and test fundamental theories that drive research and practice in public health, health education, and health care.

A premise of Health Behaviour and Health Education is that a dynamic exchange between theory, research, and practice is most likely to produce effective health education. Perhaps never before have those concerned with health behaviour and health education been faced with more challenges and opportunities than they are today. Kanfer and Schefft observed that "as science and technology advance, the greatest mystery of the universe and the least conquered force of nature remains the human being and his actions and human experiences." The body of research in health behaviour and health education has grown rapidly over the past two decades, and health education is recognized increasingly as a way to meet public health objectives and improve the success of public health and medical interventions.

The science and art of health behaviour and health education are eclectic, rapidly evolving, and reflective of an amalgamation of approaches, methods, and strategies from social and health sciences. They draw on the theoretical perspectives, research, and practice tools of such diverse disciplines as psychology, sociology, anthropology, communications, nursing, and marketing. Health education is also dependent on epidemiology, statistics, and medicine.

There is increasing emphasis on identifying evidence-based interventions and disseminating them widely. This often requires individual health education and health behaviour professionals to synthesize large and diverse literatures. Many types of professionals contribute to and conduct health education and health behaviour (HEHB) programs and research. Health education practice is strengthened by the close collaboration among professionals of different disciplines, each concerned with the behavioural and social intervention process, and each contributing a unique perspective.

Psychology brings to health education a rich legacy of over a hundred years of research and practice on individual differences, motivation, learning, persuasion, and attitude and behaviour change. Physicians are important collaborators and are in key positions to effect change in health behaviour. Likewise, nurses and social workers bring to health education their particular expertise in working with individual patients and patients' families to facilitate learning, adjustment, and behaviour change, and to improve quality of life.

Other health, education, and human service professionals contribute their special expertise as well. Increasingly, there will be partnerships with genetic counsellors and other specialists in this rapidly developing field. The major causes of death in the United States and other developed countries are now chronic diseases, such as heart disease, cancer, and stroke.

Behavioural factors, particularly tobacco use, diet and activity patterns, alcohol consumption, sexual behaviour, and avoidable injuries are among the most prominent contributors to mortality. The resurgence of infectious diseases, including foodborne illness and tuberculosis, and the emergence of new infectious diseases such as antibioticresistant infections, HIV/AIDS, Hepatitis C, and human papillomavirus (HPV) are also largely affected by human behaviours.

Substantial suffering, premature mortality, and medical costs can be avoided by positive changes in behaviour. Most recently, there has been a renewed focus on public health as a result of anthrax exposure due to terrorism. During the past twenty years, there has been a dramatic increase in public, private, and professional interest in preventing disability and death through changes in lifestyle and participation in screening programs.

Much of this interest in disease prevention and early detection has been stimulated by the epidemiologic transition from infectious to chronic diseases as leading causes of death, the aging of the population, rapidly escalating health care costs, and data linking individual behaviours to increased risk of morbidity and mortality. More recent developments, such as the AIDS epidemic, have also contributed.

Even as epidemiologists' efforts to better specify the links between diet, lifestyle, genetic predisposition, and environmental factors and disease approach the limits of science, they continue to generate headlines and influence public policy. Landmark reports in Canada and the United States during the 1970s and 1980s heralded the commitment of governments to health education and promotion.

Increased interest in behavioural and social determinants of health behaviour change spawned numerous training programs and public and commercial service programs. Data systems now make it possible to track trends in risk factors, health behaviours, and healthy environments and policies in the United States and, in some cases, to tie these changes to disease incidence and mortality. Indeed, there have been positive changes in several areas. A major accomplishment has been surpassing the targets for reducing deaths from coronary heart disease and cancer.

Blood pressure control has improved and mean population blood cholesterol levels have declined. Alcohol-related motor vehicle deaths and deaths due to automobile crashes and drowning have continued to decrease. Fewer adults are using tobacco products, and more are engaging in moderate physical activity. More adults are meeting dietary guidelines for consumption of fruits, vegetables, and grain products and for dietary fat as a percentage of calories.

Rates of HIV/AIDS have levelled off and transfusion-related HIV infections have decreased markedly. The proportion of women age fifty and older who have had breast examinations and mammograms has exceeded the goal of 60 percent in forty-seven states. The United States has made progress toward the goal of reducing health disparities for more than half the objectives identified in Healthy People 2000. Major litigation against the tobacco industry and a multistate settlement have resulted in increased restrictions on tobacco advertising and enforcement of laws against selling tobacco to minors.

The collective efforts of those in health education and public health have indeed made a difference. While this progress is encouraging, much work remains to be done in these areas. Not all the news is favourable, though. More adults and children are overweight. Diabetes is increasing in near-epidemic proportions. More adolescents are sexually active. After major increases in seatbelt use in the early 1990s, rates have declined slightly and remain at 67 percent, well below the target rate of 85 percent. One-fifth of children under three years old have not received a basic series of vaccinations for polio, measles, diphtheria, and other diseases. Sixteen percent of adults under sixty-five years of age have no health insurance coverage.

More than 70 percent of adults over age fifty have not been screened for colorectal cancer. Ethnic minorities and those in poverty still experience a disproportionate burden of preventable disease and disability, and for many conditions the gap between disadvantaged and affluent groups is widening. Changes in the health care system provide new supports and opportunities for health education. Respect for patients' rights is now recognized as fundamental to the practice of medicine.

Moreover, there is increased attention to issues of shared decision making. At the same time, patients' access to information about their health care institutions and providers remains limited. Insurance carriers and managed care systems can impose barriers that impede patients' exercise of their rights to make treatment decisions. The advent of managed health care and health care financing reform pose new challenges as the drive for cost containment affects the entire health care system.

While increased accountability often results in cost savings and fewer unnecessary services, little is known about its effects on the health of patients and the overall quality of care. Clinical prevention and behavioural interventions may grow in importance under managed care when their cost-effectiveness is demonstrated and recognized, but the climate of fiscal constraint will probably slow adoption of efficacious behavioural strategies in the short run.

The rapid emergence of new communication technologies and new uses of older technologies, such as the telephone, also provide new opportunities and dilemmas. A variety of electronic media for interactive health communication (for example, the internet, CD-ROMs, personal digital assistants) can serve as sources of both general and individualized health information, reminders, and social support for health behaviour change.

E-health strategies are becoming an important part of the armamentarium of strategies for those in health education and health behaviour. New technologies have the potential to cause harm through misleading or deceptive information, promotion of inappropriate self-care, and interference in the patient-provider relationship. Interactive health communications provide new options for behavioural medicine and preventive medicine and are altering the context of health behaviour and health education as they unfold and as their effects are studied.

In the fields of health education and health behaviour, the emphasis during the 1970s and 1980s on individuals' behaviours as determinants of health status eclipsed attention to the broader social determinants of health. Advocates of system-level changes to improve health called for renewal of a broad vision of health education and promotion. These calls for moving health education toward social action heralded a renewed enthusiasm for holistic approaches rather than an entirely new worldview.

They are well within the tradition of health education and are consistent with its long-standing concern with the impact of social, economic, and political forces on health. Over the past fifty years, outstanding leaders in health education repeatedly stressed the importance of political, economic, and social factors as determinants of health.

The view of health education as an instrument of social change has been renewed and invigorated during the past decade. Policy, advocacy, and organizational change have been adopted as central activities of public health and health education. Most recently, experts have explicitly recommended that interventions on social and behavioural factors related to health should link multiple levels of influence, including the individual, interpersonal, institutional, community, and policy levels.

According to Griffiths, "health education attempts to close the gap between what is known about optimum health practice and that which is actually practiced."

Simonds defined health education as aimed at "bringing about behavioural changes in individuals, groups, and larger populations from behaviours that are presumed to be detrimental to health, to behaviours that are conducive to present and future health."

Subsequent definitions of health education emphasized voluntary, informed behaviour changes. In 1980, Green defined health education as "any combination of learning experiences designed to facilitate voluntary adaptations of behaviour conducive to health. The Role Delineation Project defined health education as "the process of assisting individuals, acting separately or collectively, to make informed decisions about matters affecting their personal health and that of others".

Health education evolved from three settings: communities, schools, and patient care sites. Health education includes not only instructional activities and other strategies to change individual health behaviour but also organizational efforts, policy directives, economic supports, environmental activities, mass media, and community-level programs. Two key ideas from an ecologic perspective help direct the identification of personal and environmental leverage points for health promotion and education interventions.

First, behaviour is viewed as being affected by, and affecting, multiple levels of influence. Five levels of influence for health-related behaviours and conditions have been identified. They are (1) intrapersonal, or individual factors; (2) interpersonal factors; (3) institutional, or organizational factors; (4) community factors; and (5) public policy factors.

The second key idea relates to the possibility of reciprocal causation between individuals and their environments; that is, behaviour both influences and is influenced by the social environment. Health education covers the continuum from disease prevention and promotion of optimal health to the detection of illness to treatment, rehabilitation, and long-term care.

Health education is delivered in almost every conceivable setting-universities, schools, hospitals, pharmacies, grocery stores and shopping centers, recreation settings, community organizations, voluntary health agencies, worksites, churches, prisons, health maintenance organizations, migrant labour camps, advertising agencies, the Internet, people's homes, and health departments at all levels of government.

Health promotion is a term of more recent origin than health education. As defined by Green, it is "any combination of health education and related organizational, economic, and environmental supports for behaviour of individuals, groups, or communities conducive to health". For example, the Ottawa Charter for Health Promotion defines health promotion as "the process of enabling people to increase control over, and to improve, their health . . . a commitment to dealing with the challenges of reducing inequities, extending the scope of prevention, and helping people to cope with their circumstances . . . creating environments conducive to health, in which people are better able to take care of themselves".

While some may argue that greater precision of terminology can be achieved by drawing a clear distinction between health education and health promotion, to do so is to ignore long-standing tenets of health education and its broad social mission. Clearly, health educators have long used more than "educational" strategies. In fact, the terms health promotion and health education are often used interchangeably in the United States.

In some countries, such as Australia, health education is considered a much narrower endeavour than health promotion. Nevertheless, although the term health promotion emphasizes efforts to influence the broader social context of health behaviour, the two terms remain closely linked and overlapping, share a common historical and philosophical foundation, and are often used in combination.

The term health education is to be understood in the historical sense, as a broad and varied set of strategies to influence both individuals and their social environments, to improve health behaviour, and to enhance health and quality of life. The central concern of health education is health behaviour. It is included or suggested in every definition of health education and is the crucial dependent variable in most research on the impact of health education intervention strategies.

Positive informed changes in health behaviour are typically the ultimate aims of health education programs; if behaviours change but health is not subsequently improved, the result is a paradox that must be resolved by examining other issues, such as the link between behaviour and health status or the ways in which behaviour and health are measured.

Informed decision making is a desirable endpoint for problems involving medical uncertainty, and studies suggest that shared decision making may lead to improved patient satisfaction and health outcomes. Likewise, environmental or structural interventions to change presumed social environmental determinants of health behaviour are intended to improve health by changing behaviour.

Thus, efforts to improve environments, policies, and so on should ultimately be evaluated for their effects on health behaviour; if policy changes but it does not lead to measurable changes in behaviour, it may be either too weak, too short-lived, or only a limited determinant of behaviour. In the broadest sense, health behaviour refers to the actions of individuals, groups, and organizations as well as their determinants, correlates, and consequences, including social change, policy development and implementation, improved coping skills, and enhanced quality of life. Kasl and Cobb define three categories of health behaviour as follows:

— *Preventive health behaviour*: Any activity undertaken by an individual who believes himself to be healthy, for the purpose of preventing or detecting illness in an asymptomatic state.

— *Illness behaviour*: Any activity undertaken by an individual who perceives himself to be ill, to define the state of health, and to discover a suitable remedy.

— *Sick-role behaviour*: Any activity undertaken by an individual who considers himself to be ill, for the purpose of getting well. It includes receiving treatment from medical providers, generally involves a whole range of dependent behaviours, and leads to some degree of exemption from one's usual responsibilities.

During the past century and more specifically during the past few decades, the scope and methods of health education have broadened and diversified dramatically. Today, health education can be found nearly everywhere.

The settings for health education are important because they provide channels for delivering programs, provide access to specific populations and gatekeepers, usually have existing communication systems for diffusion of programs, and facilitate development of policies and organizational change to support positive health practices.

Six major settings are particularly relevant to contemporary health education: schools, communities, worksites, health care settings, homes, and the consumer marketplace.

— *Schools*: Health education in the schools includes classroom teaching, teacher training, and changes in the school environment that support healthy behaviours. To support long-term health enhancement initiatives, theories of organizational change are used to encourage adoption of comprehensive smoking control programs in schools. Diffusion Theory and the Theory of Reasoned Action have been used to analyse factors associated with adoption of AIDS prevention curricula in Dutch schools.

— *Communities*: Community-based health education draws on social relationships and organizations to reach large populations with media and interpersonal strategies. Models of community organization enable program planners both to gain support for and to design suitable health messages and delivery mechanisms. Community interventions in churches, clubs, recreation centers, and neighbourhoods have been used to encourage healthful nutrition, reduce risk of cardiovascular disease, and use peer influence to promote breast cancer detection among minority women.

— *Worksites*: Since its emergence in the mid-1970s, worksite health promotion has grown and spawned new tools for health educators. Because people spend so much time at work, the workplace is both a source of stress and a source of social support. Effective worksite programs can harness social support as a buffer to stress, with the goal of improving worker health and health practices. Today many businesses, particularly large corporations, provide health promotion programs for their employees. Both high-risk and populationwide strategies have been used in programs to reduce the risk of cancer and cardiovascular disease.

— *Health Care Sites*: Health education for high-risk persons, patients, their families, and the surrounding community and inservice training for health care providers are all part of health care today. The changing nature of health service delivery has stimulated greater emphasis on health education in physicians' of-fices, health maintenance organizations, public health clinics, and hospitals. Primary care settings, in particular, provide an opportunity to reach a substantial number of people. Health education in these settings focuses on preventing and detecting disease, helping people make decisions about genetic testing, and managing acute and chronic illnesses.

— Homes: Health behaviour change interventions are delivered to people in their homes, both through traditional public health means-home visits-and through a variety of communication channels and media such as the Internet, telephone, and mail. The use of strategies such as mailed tailored messages and motivational interviewing by telephone makes it possible to reach larger groups and high-risk groups in a convenient way that reduces barriers to their receiving motivational messages.

— *The Consumer Marketplace*: The advent of home health and self-care products, as well as the use of "health" appeals to sell consumer goods, has created new opportunities both for health education and for misleading consumers about the potential health effects of items they can purchase. Social marketing, with its roots in consumer behaviour theory, is used increasingly by health educators to enhance the salience of health messages and to improve their persuasive impact. Theories of Consumer Information Processing (CIP) provide a framework for understanding why people do or do not pay attention to, understand, and make use of consumer health information such as nutrient labels on packaged food products.

Recipients of Health Education

For health education to be effective, it should be designed with an understanding of the recipients, or target audiences, and their health and social characteristics as well as their beliefs, attitudes, values, skills, and past behaviours. These audiences consist of people who may be reached as individuals, in groups, through organizations, as communities or sociopolitical entities, or through some combination of these. They may be health professionals, clients, people at risk for disease, or patients.

There are four dimensions in which the potential audiences can be characterized: sociodemographic characteristics, ethnic or racial background, life cycle stage, and disease or at-risk status.

Sociodemographic Characteristics and Ethnic or Racial Background: Socioeconomic status has been linked with both health status and health behaviour, with less affluent persons consistently experiencing higher morbidity and mortality. The recognition of differences in disease and mortality rates across socioeconomic and ethnic or racial groups has led to increasing efforts to reduce or eliminate such health disparities. For example, it has long been known that African Americans die at earlier ages than do whites. As of 1998, life expectancy for African American males was 67.6 years compared to 74.5 years for white males. The difference is slightly less for African American women, 74.8 versus 80 for white women, but still alarmingly discrepant.

A variety of sociodemographic characteristics such as gender, age, race, marital status, place of residence, and employment characterize health education audiences. These factors, while generally not modifiable within the bounds of health education programs, are useful in guiding the tailoring of strategies and educational material and identifying channels through which to reach consumers. Printed educational materials should be appropriate to, and, ideally, tailored to the educational and reading levels of particular target audiences and be consistent with their ethnic and cultural backgrounds.

Life Cycle Stage: Health education is provided for people at every stage of the life cycle, from childbirth education, the beneficiaries of which are not yet born, to self-care education and rehabilitation for the very old. Developmental perspectives help guide the choice of intervention and research methods. Children may have misperceptions about health and illness, such as that illnesses are a punishment for bad behaviour. Knowledge of children's cognitive development helps provide a framework for understanding these beliefs and ways to respond to them. Adolescents may feel invulnerable to accidents and chronic diseases.

The Health Belief Model is a useful framework for understanding the factors that may predispose youth to engage in unsafe sexual practices. Older adults may attribute symptoms of cancer to the inexorable process of aging. Beliefs such as this must be considered in designing, implementing, and evaluating health education programs.

Disease and At-Risk Status: People who are diagnosed with specific diseases often experience not only symptoms but also the distress associated with their prognosis and with having to make decisions about medical care. Thus, while they may benefit from receiving health education, their ability to attend to new information may be compromised at critical points due to their illness. Because of this, the timing, channels, and audiences for patient education need to be carefully considered.

Successful patient education depends on a sound understanding of the patient's view of the world. For individuals at high risk due to family history or identified risk factors, health behaviour change interventions may have heightened salience when linked to strategies for reducing individual risk. Even so, strategies used to enable initial changes in behaviour, such as quitting smoking, may be insufficient for maintaining behaviour change over the long term even in these persons. Models and theories of health behaviour can suggest strategies for relapse prevention for high-risk individuals.

Over the past two decades, research programs have been established to identify and test the most effective methods for achieving health behaviour change. More precise quantification of personal health behaviours and improved health outcomes has grown from partnerships between behavioural health scientists and biomedical experts. During this period, findings from some major health behaviour intervention studies have become available and have provided important insights for the field.

In the late 1970s and early 1980s, three large community cardiovascular disease intervention studies were begun in California, Minnesota, and Rhode Island. Each study addressed smoking, hypertension, high-fat diets, obesity, and physical inactivity-all widespread risk factors that many practitioners were tackling. The multicomponent risk reduction programs in these trials used mass media, interpersonal education programs for the public, professionals, and those at high risk.

Community organization strategies were used to create institutional and environmental support for the programs, and theory-derived program planning strategies emphasized community participation. In the 1990s, all three studies reported their findings for risk factor changes. They each found favourable secular trends in control sites and modest or nonsignificant intervention effects on risk factor reduction. While randomized, controlled trials provide the most rigorous test of health behaviour interventions, the past decade has been marked by an increase in carefully designed evaluation research in health education that combines quantitative and qualitative methods.

Overall, there has been a growing trend toward evidence-based health education and health behaviour as the findings of numerous large health behaviour intervention studies have been published. The U.S. Task Force on Community Preventive Services aims to define, categorize, summarize, and rate the quality of evidence on the effectiveness of population-based interventions for disease prevention and control; to provide recommendations on these interventions and methods for their delivery based on the evidence; and to identify and summarize research gaps.

The challenge of understanding and improving health behaviour is a central challenge for health policy today, and is "one of the most complex tasks yet confronted by science. To competently address that challenge, the . . . research community must simply do more and do it better" in certain key areas of behavioural research. A coordinated and focused effort will be essential to resolving many of the most vexing health issues facing our society. The integration of the best available knowledge from theory, research, and health promotion and education practice can help advance that agenda in the next decade.

3

Health and Human Rights

Since the creation of the United Nations over 50 years ago, international responsibility for health and for human rights has been increasingly acknowledged. Yet the actual links between health and human rights had not been recognized even a decade ago. Generally thought to be fundamentally antagonistic, these two worlds had evolved along parallel but distinctly separate tracks until a number of recent events helped to bring them together.

Conceptually one can point to the HIV/AIDS pandemic, to women's health issues, including violence, and to the blatant violations of human rights which occurred in such places as the Balkans and the Great Lakes region in Africa as having brought attention to the intrinsic connections that exist between health and human rights. Each of these issues helped to illustrate distinct, but linked, pieces of the health and human rights paradigm.

While the relationship between health and human rights with respect to these and similar issues may always have made sense intuitively, the development of a 'health and human rights' language in the last few years has allowed for the connections between health and human rights to be explicitly named, and therefore for conceptual, analytical, policy, and programmatic work to begin to bridge these disparate disciplines and to move forward. In the last few years human rights have increasingly been at the centre of analysis and action in regard to health and development issues.

The level of institutional and state political commitment to health and human rights has, in fact, never been higher. This is true within the work of the United Nations system but, even more importantly, can also be seen in the work of governments and non-governmental organizations at both the national and international level.

The importance of the HIV/AIDS pandemic as a catalyst for beginning to define some of the structural connections between health and human rights cannot be overemphasized. The first time that human rights were explicitly named in a public health strategy was only in the late 1980s, when the call for human rights and for compassion and solidarity with people living with HIV/AIDS was embodied in the first World Health Organization (WHO) global response to AIDS.

This approach was motivated by moral outrage but also, even more importantly, by the recognition that protecting the human rights of people living with HIV/AIDS was a necessary element of the worldwide public health response to the emerging epidemics. The implications of this call were far reaching. Framing this public health strategy in human rights terms-although initially focused on the rights of people living with HIV/AIDS rather than on the broad array of human rights influencing people's vulnerability to the epidemic-allowed it to become anchored in international law, thereby making governments and intergovernmental organizations publicly accountable for their actions towards people living with HIV/AIDS.

The ground-breaking contribution of this era lies in the recognition of the applicability of international law to HIV/AIDS issues and in the attention this approach then generated to the links between other health issues and human rights-and therefore to the ultimate responsibility and accountability of the state under international law for issues relating to health and well being.

The series of international conferences held in the past decade under the auspices of the United Nations system have also been of critical importance in helping to clarify the links between health and human rights. While all of these conferences, ranging from the World Summit for Children held in 1990 to the World Conference on Racism held in 2001, are relevant to health and human rights concerns, the two most crucial in articulating the health and human rights link were the 1994 International Conference on Population and Development and the 1995 Fourth World Conference on Women.

These conferences brought together policy-makers, activists, and representatives from local, national, and international agencies, as well as government representatives. The negotiated documents resulted in the first concrete links between health and human rights in international consensus documents and helped to focus attention to the dual obligations of governments regarding both health and human rights

In recent years there has been a substantial increase in attention and resources devoted to implementation of health and human rights within virtually all United Nations development agencies and programmes, due in large part to these international conference processes. All of the organizations and agencies of the United Nations have, albeit to varying degrees, begun to consider the relevance of human rights to their work in the health field.

The 1997 Programme for Reform put out by United Nations Secretary-General Kofi Annan, however, has been most crucial in moving the United Nations system's conceptual attention to human rights towards implementation and action within their own work. The Programme for Reform designates human rights as among the core activities of the United Nations system. The human rights are to be understood to cut across the four substantive fields of the United Nations' work: peace and security, economic and social affairs, development co-operation, and humanitarian affairs. Each of the agencies with responsibility for health currently has policy documents at various stages of elaboration which concern health and human rights, and technical staff responsible for the integration or implementation of human rights into at least some aspects of their work, a situation that would have been unimaginable even a few years ago.

1. The United Nations International Children's Emergency Fund (UNICEF) has restructured its policy and programmatic framework around the Convention on the Rights of the Child.

2. The Joint United Nations Programme on HIV/AIDS (UNAIDS) recognizes human rights as a theme relevant to all aspects of its policy and programme work; where the importance of contextual factors that increase vulnerability to HIV/AIDS is recognized, including existing discrimination against certain groups, and where human rights are cited as core values and guiding principles for the mission of UNAIDS.

3. A Memorandum of Understanding now exists between the United Nations Development Programme and the Office of the High Commissioner for Human Rights.

4. The United Nations Development Programme Human Development Report for the year 2000 has an explicit focus on human rights, and the WHO is currently preparing its first strategy on health and human rights.

Likewise, the bodies of the United Nations system with responsibility for human rights are also paying increasing attention to health-related concerns. This is most easily seen in the recent attention to HIV/AIDS and reproductive health by the human rights treaty monitoring bodies. However, this commitment extends to the recent appointment of two health-related focal points in the Office of the High Commissioner for Human Rights: one responsible for integrating HIV/AIDS issues into the work of the human rights bodies and structures, and the other serving as a general liaison for all health and human rights issues.

Governments are also increasingly recognizing the relevance of human rights to their health and development work, and calling for technical assistance in the field of human rights. This is true in developing and industrialized countries alike. In Nepal, a comprehensive workshop was recently held on tuberculosis and human rights. An open debate in South Africa recently focused on the human rights implications of a proposed new regulation concerning AIDS reporting and AIDS-status disclosure to third persons.

In Colombia, the Convention on the Elimination of All Forms of Discrimination Against Women is being used as a framework for mobilization around much of the work in family planning. Within the United States, President Clinton issued an Executive Order in commemoration of Human Rights Day in 1998 that obliges the United States to respect and implement fully its obligations under the international human rights treaties to which it is a party and to 'promote respect for international human rights in our relationships with all other countries'.

As a result, all United States federal agencies, including those with health-related responsibilities, have been directed to re-examine their policies and strategies from the perspective of international human rights standards. Non-governmental organizations, such as Amnesty International and Human Rights Watch, are also increasingly considering the implications of the health and human rights connection for their own work.

Non-governmental organizations that focus on health or development issues, many of which previously saw human rights as having little relevance to their work, are increasingly using not only the rhetoric of human rights but also its method of analysis to help shape their interventions. One prime example is the recent decision of the International Council of AIDS Service Organizations (ICASO) to name the promotion of human rights in the context of HIV/AIDS as one of its fundamental organizing principles.

In addition, human rights non-governmental organizations are expanding their formerly tight focus on civil and political rights to pay increasing attention to economic, social, and cultural rights, including the right to health. These developments are helping to shape new forms of advocacy and to put increased pressure on governments to take responsibility for the health of their populations.

The current challenge is to ensure that the increased rhetorical attention to rights translates into policies, national legislation, and actions that will effectively impact on the underlying conditions necessary for health, as well as the ways in which health policies, programmes, and services are conceptualized and delivered.

Academics and researchers are also increasingly finding the links between health and human rights to be of critical importance in expanding their domains of work. Academic centres with an explicit focus on the links between health and human rights are beginning to appear in a number of places, some with a focus on specific substantive issues, and others concerned with health and human rights more broadly.

In the last several years, institutions around the globe have begun to offer courses in health and human rights, international conferences on health and human rights have been held in a number of locations, and professional health journals such as The Lancet, the Journal of the American Medical Association, and the American Journal of Public Health have devoted space to exploring health and human rights issues. The first course on health and human rights was offered at the Harvard School of Public Health in 1992.

Since then, courses on health and human rights have been increasingly offered in countries such as the United States, France, Sweden, Brazil, South Africa, and Zimbabwe. Efforts are currently under way to document existing courses on health and human rights. Understanding the implications of linking health and human rights is of increasing importance to policy-makers, government officials, and activists-indeed, to anyone concerned with health issues, human rights issues, or the links between the two.

While human rights thinking and practice has a long history, the importance of human rights for governmental action and accountability was first widely recognized only after the Second World War. Agreement between nation-states that all people are 'born free and equal in dignity and rights' was reached in 1945 when the promotion of human rights was identified as a principal purpose of the newly created United Nations.

The United Nations Charter established general obligations that apply to all its member states, including respect for human rights and dignity. Then, in 1948, the Universal Declaration of Human Rights was adopted as a common standard of achievement for all peoples and all nations. The basic characteristics of human rights are that they are the rights of individuals, which inhere in individuals because they are human, that they apply to people everywhere in the world, and that they are principally concerned with the relationship between the individual and the state.

In practical terms, international human rights law is about defining what governments can do to us, cannot do to us, and should do for us. For example, governments obviously should not do things like torture people, imprison them arbitrarily, or invade their privacy. Governments should ensure that all people in a society have shelter, food, medical care, and basic education.

The Universal Declaration of Human Rights can well be understood to be the cornerstone of the modern human rights movement. The preamble to the Universal Declaration of Human Rights proposes that human rights and dignity are self-evident, the 'highest aspiration of the common people', and the 'foundation of freedom, justice and peace'. 'Social progress and better standards of life' including the 'prevention of barbarous acts which have outraged the conscience of mankind', and, broadly speaking, individual and collective well being, are understood to depend upon the 'promotion of universal respect for and observance of human rights'.

Although the Universal Declaration of Human Rights is not a legally binding document, nations have endowed it with a tremendous legitimacy through their actions, including invoking it legally and politically at the national and international levels. Portions of the Universal Declaration of Human Rights are cited in the majority of national constitutions drafted since it came into being, and governments often cite the Universal Declaration of Human Rights in their negotiations with other governments, as well as in their accusations against each other of violating human rights.

Under the auspices of the United Nations, more that 20 multilateral human rights treaties have been formulated since the adoption of the Universal Declaration of Human Rights. These treaties create legally binding obligations on the nations that have ratified them, thereby giving them the status and power of international law. Countries that become party to international human rights treaties accept certain procedures and responsibilities, including periodic submission of reports on their compliance with the substantive provisions of the texts to international monitoring bodies.

The key international human rights treaties, the International Covenant on Economic, Social and Cultural Rights (UNICESCR) and the International Covenant on Civil and Political Rights (UNICCPR), further elaborate the content of the rights set out in the Universal Declaration of Human Rights and contain legally binding obligations for the governments that ratify them. Together with the Universal Declaration of Human Rights and the United Nations Charter, these documents are often called the 'International Bill of Human Rights'.

Building upon these core documents, other international human rights treaties have focused on either specific populations (for example, the international Convention on the Elimination of All Forms of Racial Discrimination, the Convention on the Elimination of All Forms of Discrimination Against Women, and the Convention on the Rights of the Child, or on specific issues. There are also regional human rights treaties, which essentially concern the same sets of rights but are only open for signature by states in the relevant region, such as the African Charter on Human and Peoples' Rights, the American Convention on Human Rights, and the European Convention on the Protection of Human Rights.

Only the Asian region does not contain such a treaty. Additionally, there are numerous international declarations, resolutions, and recommendations which, although not strictly binding in a legal sense, express the political commitment of governments to promote and protect human rights and provide broadly recognized norms and standards relevant to the topic at hand. In the past decade, the series of international conferences held under the auspices of the United Nations have, to a great degree, helped give recognizable content to many of the rights contained in the various human rights treaties. Out of each of these conference processes has come a declaration and programme of action reflecting the consensus of the nations of the world.

Though technically 'non-binding' commitments, these documents demonstrate that there is a consensus of the world community that international human rights treaty norms encompass the relationship between health and human rights, including reproductive rights, and that there are steps that ought to be taken at the local, national, and international levels to advance these concerns. While these conference declarations and programmes of action represent nothing more than the political commitments of the governments present at their inception, the fact that they are then adopted at the next session of the United Nations General Assembly gives them a degree of formal standing.

Although the declarations and programmes of action from the 1994 International Conference on Population and Development (ICPD) and the 1995 Fourth World Conference on Women (FWCW) have been of particular relevance, the 1993 World Conference on Human Rights and the 1995 World Summit for Social Development have also helped explicate the relevance of the health and human rights framework to government action.

Individually and collectively, these documents have been of critical importance in helping to elaborate provisions relevant to vulnerable groups, women's human rights, and broader concepts of health and human rights. Those commitments have helped to create new approaches for considering the extent of government accountability for health issues, as well as for determining the content of health issues using a rights framework.

In so doing, these conference documents are helping to clarify the evolving meaning of the relationship between health and human rights and the steps needed for implementation.

Human Rights and Health Perspectives

The specific rights that form the corpus of human rights law are found in the international human rights documents. While it is possible to identify different categories of rights, it is also critical to rights discourse and action to recognize that all rights are interdependent and interrelated, and that individuals rarely suffer neglect or violation of a particular right in isolation.

For historical reasons, the rights described in the human rights documents have been divided into civil and political rights on the one hand and economic, social, and cultural rights on the other. Civil and political rights include the rights to liberty, to security of person, to freedom of movement, to vote, and not to be subjected to cruel, inhuman, or degrading treatment or punishment or to arbitrary arrest or detention. Economic, social, and cultural rights include the rights to the highest attainable standard of health, work, social security, adequate food, clothing and housing, and education, and the right to enjoy the benefits of scientific progress and its applications.

Although the Universal Declaration of Human Rights contains both categories of rights, these rights were artificially split into two treaties due to Cold War politics, with the United States championing civil and political rights, and the former Soviet Union those rights considered to be more economic, social, and cultural in nature. Since the end of the Cold War, acknowledgement of the indivisibility and interdependence of rights has, once again, become commonplace.

The Convention on the Rights of the Child, the first human rights treaty to be opened for signature after the end of the Cold War, is the only one so far to include civil, political, and economic and social rights considerations not only within the same treaty but within the same right. Health and government responsibility for health is codified in these documents in several ways. The right to the highest attainable standard of health appears in one form or another in most of them.

While the rights to information, education, housing and safe working conditions, and social security, for example, are particularly relevant to the health and human rights relationship, specific reference must be made to three rights: the right to non-discrimination, the right to the benefits of scientific progress, and the right to health.

The principle of non-discrimination is key to human rights thinking and practice. Under international human rights law, all people should be treated equally and given equal opportunity. Within the international human rights framework, discrimination is a breach of a government's human rights obligations. Adverse discrimination occurs when a distinction is made against a person which results in their being treated unfairly or unjustly. In general, groups that are discriminated against tend to be those that do not share the characteristics of the dominant groups within a society.

Thus, discrimination frequently reinforces social inequalities and denies equal opportunities. Common forms of discrimination include racism, gender-based discrimination, and homophobia. Each of the major human rights treaties specifically details the principle of non-discrimination with respect to race, colour, sex, language, religion, political or other opinion, national or social origin, property, birth, and, as it is called, 'other status'.

Governmental responsibility for this right includes ensuring equal protection under the law, as well as in relation to such issues as housing, employment, and medical care. The prohibition of discrimination does not mean that differences should not be acknowledged, only that different treatment must be based on objective and reasonable criteria.

Although the international human rights documents do not explicitly prohibit discrimination on the basis of health status, the United Nations Commission on Human Rights has stated that 'all are equal before the law and entitled to equal protection of the law from all discrimination and from all incitement to discrimination relating to their state of health'.

Closely allied to many of the issues relevant to health is the right to 'enjoy the benefits of scientific progress and its applications', recognized explicitly in the ICESCR, Article 15. This right includes governmental obligations for the steps necessary to conserve, develop, and diffuse science and scientific research, as well as freedom of scientific inquiry. The implications of this right for health issues have been explored recently with respect to access to drugs for the developing world, to name one important example.

In fact, this right is increasingly being cited by activist groups, non-governmental organizations, and others concerned by the large and growing disparities and inequities between wealthier and poorer populations regarding access to antiretroviral therapies and other forms of HIV/AIDS care. In addition, the relevance of this right to concerns about the development of vaccines that adequately respond to the specific needs of all populations, both in the North and the South, has recently been cited.

Unfortunately, while this right has long been recognized as relevant to governmental obligations under the ICESCR, its implications for health and health-related issues are only just beginning to be recognized. The human right to health should be understood, in the first instance, with reference to the description of health set forth in the preamble of the WHO Constitution and repeated in many subsequent documents.

Health is a 'state of complete physical, mental, and social well-being, and not merely the absence of disease or infirmity'. This definition has important conceptual and practical implications, and it illustrates the indivisibility and interdependence of rights as they relate to health. Rights relating to discrimination, autonomy, information, education, and participation are an integral and indivisible part of the achievement of the highest attainable standard of health, just as the enjoyment of health is inseparable from that of other rights, whether categorized as civil and political, economic, social, or cultural.

While the right to health has been set out in a number of international legal instruments, government obligations under this right are quite narrowly defined. As first elaborated in the ICESCR, the right is set forth only as 'the right to the highest attainable standard of physical and mental health', with obligations understood to encompass both the underlying preconditions necessary for health and the provision of medical care. It is worth noting that the apparent tension between the broad definition of health proposed by the WHO, which includes the notion of social well being, and the more restrictive definition set out in the ICESCR reflects the very different purposes of these two documents.

The WHO definition projects a vision of the ideal state of health as an eternal and universal goal to strive constantly towards, and has as its main purpose defining directions for the work of the Organization and its member states. The ICESCR definition differentiates the two attributes of health-physical and mental well being-and is specifi-cally concerned with assigning particular responsibilities to the governmental health sector; it assigns obligations relevant to social well being to the same governments under other articles of the treaty.

The right to health as stated in the ICESCR is the principal framework for understanding governmental obligations under the right to health. Governments are responsible not only for not directly violating rights, but also for ensuring the conditions which enable individuals to realize their rights as fully as possible. This is understood as an obligation to respect, protect, and fulfil rights, and governments are legally responsible for complying with this range of obligations for every right in every human rights document they have ratified.

Governmental obligations towards ensuring that every individual enjoys the right to health are summarized below as an illustration of the range of issues relevant to respecting, protecting, and fulfilling all human rights.

1. Respecting the right means that a state cannot violate the right directly. A government violates its responsibility to respect the right to health when it is immediately responsible for providing medical care to certain populations, such as prisoners or the military, and it arbitrarily decides to withhold that care.

2. Protecting the right means that a state has to prevent violations of rights by non-state actors and offer some sort of redress that people know about and can access if a violation occurs. This means that the state would be responsible for making it illegal to deny insurance

or health care automatically to people on the basis of a health condition, and that they would be responsible for ensuring some system of redress that people know about and can access if a violation does occur.

3. Fulfilling the right means that a state has to take all appropriate measures-including but not limited to legislative, administrative, budgetary, and judicial-towards fulfilment of the right, including the obligation to promote the right in question. A state could be found to be in violation of the right to health if it failed to allocate sufficient resources incrementally to meet the public health needs of the communities within its borders.

In all countries, resource and other constraints can make it impossible for a government to fulfil all rights immediately and completely. The human rights machinery recognizes this and acknowledges that, in practical terms, a commitment to the right to health requires more than just passing a law. It will require financial resources, trained personnel, facilities, and, more than anything else, a sustainable infrastructure.

Therefore, realization of rights is generally understood to be a matter of progressive realization of making steady progress towards a goal. The principle of 'progressive realization' is fundamental to the achievement of human rights. This is critical for resource-poor countries that are responsible for striving towards human rights goals to the maximum extent possible. It is also of relevance to wealthier countries in that they are responsible for respecting, protecting, and fulfilling human rights not only within their own borders, but through their engagement in international assistance and co-operation.

Limitations on Human Rights

In spite of the importance attached to human rights, there are situations where it is considered legitimate to restrict rights in order to achieve a broader public good. As described in the International Covenant on Civil and Political Rights, the public good can take precedence to 'secure due recognition and respect for the rights and freedoms of others; meet the just requirements of morality, public order, and the general welfare; and in times of emergency, when there are threats to the vital interests of the nation'.

Public health is one such recognized public good. Traditional public health measures have generally focused on curbing the spread of disease by imposing restrictions on the rights of those already infected or thought to be most vulnerable to becoming infected. In fact, coercion, compulsion, and restriction have historically been significant components of public health measures.

Although the restrictions on rights that have occurred in the context of public health have generally had as their first concern protection of the public's health, it is also true that the measures taken have often been excessive. Interference with freedom of movement when instituting quarantine or isolation for a serious communicable disease-for example, Ebola fever, syphilis, typhoid, or untreated tuberculosis-is an example of a restriction on rights that may be necessary for the public good and therefore could be considered legitimate under international human rights law.

Conversely, arbitrary measures taken by public health authorities that fail to consider other valid alternatives may be found to be abusive of both human rights principles and public health 'best practice'. In recent times, measures taken around the world in response to HIV/AIDS provides examples of this type of abuse. Certain rights are absolute, which means that restrictions may never be placed on them, even if justified as necessary for the public good.

These include such rights as the right to be free from torture, slavery, or servitude, the right to a fair trial, and the right to freedom of thought. Paradoxically, the right to life, which might at first glance appear to be inalienable, is not absolute; what is forbidden is the arbitrary deprivation of life. Interference with most rights can be legitimately justified as necessary under narrowly defined circumstances in many situations relevant to public health.

Limitations on rights, however, are considered a serious issue under international human rights law, regardless of the apparent importance of the public good involved. When a government limits the exercise or enjoyment of a right, this action must be taken only as a last resort and will only be considered legitimate if the following criteria are met.

1. The restriction is provided for and carried out in accordance with the law.
2. The restriction is in the interest of a legitimate objective of general interest.
3. The restriction is strictly necessary in a democratic society to achieve the objective.
4. There are no less intrusive and restrictive means available to reach the same goal.
5. The restriction is not imposed arbitrarily, i.e. in an unreasonable or otherwise discriminatory manner.

Whereas this approach, often called the Siracusa Principles because they were conceptualized at a meeting in Siracusa, Italy, has long been recognized by those concerned with human rights monitoring and implementation as relevant to analysing a government's actions, it has also recently begun to be considered a useful tool in a number of places by those responsible within government for health-related policies and programmes. This framework, although still rudimentary, may be helpful in identifying public health actions that are abusive, whether intentionally or unintentionally.

The degree of governmental compliance with the obligations to respect, protect, and fulfil human rights are of direct relevance to the people affected, but they are also of interest to the international community. The accountability of governments for their legal commitments is monitored at the international level through the reporting process and, in many places, at the national level by governments themselves through the creation of commissions and ombudspersons, as well as by non-governmental organizations.

Once a government has ratified a human rights treaty, it is obliged to report every several years to the specific body responsible for monitoring government action under that treaty. Governments are responsible for showing the ways that they are and are not in compliance with the treaty provisions, and must show constant improvement in their efforts to respect, protect, and fulfil the rights in question.

Health-oriented United Nations institutions, such as the WHO, UNAIDS, or UNICEF, are invited to provide the treaty bodies with information on the state of health and the performance of health systems in the country under review. Non-governmental organizations can also submit informal reports providing additional information, as well as stating their views on the situations and issues at stake.

All of the human rights treaty bodies have expressed a commitment to exploring the implications of health broadly defined, as well as the specific issues raised by both HIV/AIDS and reproductive health concerns, for governmental obligations under the treaties. While several of the treaties contain specific health-related provisions, the added impetus to pay attention to health in the context of monitoring work can largely be attributed to the interest generated from international conferences and the political commitments made there about governmental responsibility for ensuring the human rights of individuals in relation to health.

For each of the human rights treaties, general guidelines for reporting provide guidance to governments as to how to present the information about their compliance with their obligations to the treaty bodies. The information requested by the treaty bodies concerning health-related issues explains what governments are doing with respect to both the underlying preconditions for health and the ways in which health policies, programmes, and services are designed and implemented.

From a health perspective, however, the actual information requested under current requirements is largely insufficient to get at this range of issues. The increasing links among the work of the treaty bodies, the United Nations specialized agencies, and non-governmental organizations are useful to the treaty monitoring process, but they are also beginning to contribute directly to the enhancement of the implementation of human rights at the country level by governments as well as other actors.

The role of the technical and specialized agencies, funds, and programmes of the United Nations in the treaty monitoring process is growing, with respect to both provision of information and interactions with the treaty bodies and governments in question. This includes primarily UNICEF, UNAIDS, and the WHO but also, increasingly, the International Labour Organization, the United Nations Development Programme, and the United Nations Population Fund.

These agencies and programmes have increasingly been providing the treaty bodies with statistical information and other data collected as part of their routine work concerning the country in question to assist the treaty bodies in their review of government compliance. They have also been providing treaty bodies with guidelines and other examples of 'best practice' they have produced, which can assist the treaty bodies in their analysis of the information provided by the government and in the drafting of their concluding comments and observations. To date, however, the input of these agencies has been somewhat uncoordinated, even within the same institution, often resulting in heavy servicing of some treaty bodies in some specific ways while virtually ignoring others.

UNICEF has been involved in the treaty monitoring process in other ways as well. For example, it has expended considerable resources on helping governments to prepare their reports as well as increasingly framing technical assistance to countries according to the provisions of the Convention on the Rights of the Child. This approach to the work of United Nations agencies and programmes at the country level has increasingly been considered of interest by the other technical agencies of the United Nations, especially UNAIDS and the WHO, and may help to frame some of their future work.

Non-governmental organizations have a critical role to play in monitoring government compliance with treaty provisions. Within countries, non-governmental organizations are increasingly using government obligations under the human rights treaties, as well as the concluding comments and observations of the treaty bodies, in their advocacy efforts.

The input of non-governmental organizations is also crucial at the international level in that they are able to provide treaty monitoring bodies with the necessary additional outside information on the action (or inaction) of the government in question, which can then be used by the treaty body in its dialogue with that government.

Although non-governmental organizations are sometimes present during the formal dialogue, this information is most often presented in shadow reports. There is no formal mechanism, however, for ensuring that non-governmental organization information reaches the treaty bodies, and, unfortunately, non-governmental organizations generally do not co-ordinate with each other on the information they provide. At times, the same information about a particular situation has been presented to a treaty body from numerous sources, while other potentially critical information of a more general nature is never provided.

In addition, many local non-governmental organizations are unaware of or lack access to the treaty monitoring process, resulting in a number of problems. Firstly, only the most publicized cases come to the attention of the monitoring body. Secondly, the lack of functioning non-governmental organizations in a majority of countries results in both a dearth of information from countries with some of the worst human rights records and a privileging of the information provided by well-established international human rights non-governmental organizations such as Amnesty International and Human Rights Watch, which have more contacts and closer relationships with the treaty body members than other organizations do.

This last point is of particular concern in relation to health-related human rights issues, as these issues often fall outside the purview of mainstream human rights organizations, and therefore little alternative information on health-related issues reaches the relevant bodies. As a result, while the utility of the involvement of non-governmental organizations to this process is at this point undisputed, mechanisms for ensuring their involvement in a comprehensive way, particularly with respect to health-related information, still remain to be worked out.

In the past 5 years, there have been increasing efforts to draft authoritative interpretations of the right to health in order to ensure state responsibility and accountability with respect to health in a structured way. These authoritative interpretations have taken the form of general comments or general recommendations, which are drafted and endorsed by the treaty monitoring body in question and which form the basis of the treaty body's formal understanding of the content of a particular right or issue.

For example, the right to health as formulated in international treaties contains no mention of primary health care. This is mainly because the concept of primary health care had not yet been internationally recognized at the time that the ICESCR was drafted. While the guidelines for reporting contain substantive mention of primary health care, the relationship between a primary health care approach and government obligations under the treaty are not detailed.

Thus, in the absence of a general comment or recommendation emphasizing a primary health care approach, it is difficult to judge a country that pays little or no attention to primary health care not to be in compliance with its health-related obligations. Until very recently, no general comments or recommendations had been issued by any of the treaty bodies specifically related to health. In 1999, the United Nations Committee on the Elimination of Discrimination Against Women (UNCEDAW), which monitors governmental compliance under the Women's Convention, issued a General Recommendation on Health, and in 2000 the Committee on Economic, Social and Cultural Rights, the body responsible for monitoring the ICESCR, issued a General Comment on the Right to Health.

The ICESCR General Comment on the Right to the Highest Attainable Standard of Health, which was adopted in 2000, may help to provide some useful guidelines. In parallel, as described below, the WHO is developing a new set of tools and recommendations aimed at redirecting the attention given to monitoring global health indicators from diseasespecific morbidity and mortality trends towards others that are more reflective of the degree to which health and human rights principles are respected, protected, and fulfilled.

How and to what extent these instruments will be put to use and how effective they will be in advancing the health and human rights agenda has yet to be seen, but there are several factors that, even at this early stage, allow for guarded optimism. Firstly, the treaty bodies and international organizations concerned with health are doing this work based on open dialogue and a degree of collaboration that greatly exceeds the level and quality of interagency collaboration traditionally observed within the United Nations machinery.

This is exemplified by the sharing of goals and the collective technical co-operation that has prevailed in the current processes of defining obligations and monitoring methods and standards relevant to health and human rights in the process of operationalizing both the international treaties and the recommendations promulgated at the international conferences. Potentially, this work will help not only to monitor what governments are doing, but also to build their capacity to incorporate health and human rights principles into their policies and programmes.

In several countries, including Brazil, Thailand, and South Africa, human rights principles relevant to health have recently found their way into national legislation and new constitutions, thereby ensuring citizens the right to seek fulfilment of their right to care, for example, through national juridical means. As the methods and tools for monitoring and accountability of health-related issues mature, it is likely that cases of human rights violations related to health will increasingly be heard both within countries and at the regional and international level.

A focus on monitoring and redress of violations of the right to health is but one means of ensuring action using the human rights documents. Equally important are the steps being taken to build national and international capacity to develop and reform public policy and laws in line with international human rights norms and standards as they apply to health. Governments, the WHO and other intergovernmental agencies should strive to create the conditions favourable to health, even in situations where the base of public finance threatens to collapse'.

The process of 'mainstreaming human rights', currently well underway in the United Nations system, is specifically aimed toward this goal. Mainstreaming human rights is 'the process of assessing the human rights implications of any planned action, including legislation, policies or programmes, in all areas and at all levels. It is a strategy for making human rights an integral dimension of the design, implementation, monitoring and evaluation of policies and programmes in political, economic and social spheres'.

Two examples illustrate how this is done. In the 1990s, UNICEF adopted the Convention on the Rights of the Child (CRC), thereby ensuring that their policy and programmatic work would be guided by the principles and standards established by the CRC, as well as the Convention on the Elimination of All Forms of Discrimination Against Women. The 1996 Mission Statement says explicitly that pursuit of the rights of children and women is a fundamental purpose of the organization.

These efforts have led to a restructuring of UNICEF and a rights-based approach to all programming efforts at all levels of its work. In the WHO, a similar process began in 1999 with the aim of defining the goals of human rights mainstreaming for their national and international health work. The process was begun following the 1998 World Health Assembly Resolution that set out the need to 'promote and support the rights and principles, actions and responsibilities enunciated in the through concerted action, full participation and partnership, calling on all peoples and institutions to share the vision of health for all in the twenty-first century, and to endeavour in common to realize it'.

In 2000, work began towards a strategy document which would incorporate health and human rights into the policy and programme work of the WHO. Towards this aim, health and human rights are considered relevant to each of the WHO's four strategic directions: reducing excess mortality, morbidity, and disability, especially in poor and marginalized populations promoting healthy lifestyles and reducing risk factors to human health that arise from environmental, economic, social, and behavioural causes developing health systems that equitably improve health outcomes, respond to people's legitimate demands, and are financially fair developing an enabling policy and institutional environment in the health sector and promoting an effective health dimension to social, economic, environmental, and development policy.

The WHO is proposing to contribute to the building of skills and knowledge within the WHO and within countries. Over 50 years ago, the Constitution of the WHO projected a vision of health as a state of complete physical, mental, and social well being-a definition of health that is more relevant today than ever. It recognized that the enjoyment of the highest attainable standard of health was one of the fundamental rights of every human being and that governments have a responsibility for the health of their peoples, which can be fulfilled only through the provision of adequate health and social measures.

The 1978 Alma-Ata Declaration called on nations to ensure the availability of the essentials of primary health care, including: education concerning health problems and the methods for preventing and controlling them promotion of food supply and proper nutrition an adequate supply of safe water and basic sanitation maternal and child health care, including family planning immunization against major infectious diseases prevention and control of locally endemic diseases appropriate treatment of common disease and injuries provision of essential drugs.

In 1998, the World Health Assembly reaffirmed the commitment of nations to strive towards these goals in a World Health Declaration that stressed the 'will to promote health by addressing the basic determinants and prerequisites for health' and the urgent priority 'to pay the greatest attention to those most in need, burdened by ill health, receiving inadequate services for health or affected by poverty'. These ambitious objectives of health development must be examined from the perspective of the role of governments in ensuring equal and equitable access to medical care and health promotion while striving to create the underlying conditions necessary for health.

Health will then be placed in the broader context of human development in order to underscore the relevance of a broad array of governmental obligations, well beyond the health sector, that may impact on health. Health as it connects to human rights analysis and implementation concerns two related but different disciplines: medicine and public health. Historically the territorial boundaries of medicine and public health reflected not only professional interest and skill, but also the environments within which these skills were practised: homes, clinics, hospitals, and clinical laboratories on the one hand; institutes, public health laboratories, offices, and field projects on the other.

Recently, the apparent differences between the two professions -the first primarily understood to focus on the health of individuals, the second on the health of populations-have profoundly impacted the ways in which the relationship between health and human rights has been understood by different actors. From a rights perspective, this ancient division resulted in the assumption that, of the two, medicine was more concerned with the health and rights of the individual, while the primary focus of public health was the protection of collective interests, even at the cost of arbitrarily restricting individual rights.

For example, coercion and restrictions of rights had been critical to traditional smallpox eradication efforts. Yet as the human rights approach has made increasingly clear, this stark differentiation between medicine and public health is no longer fully relevant either to human rights or to health. Although they apply different methods of work, both medicine and public health seek to ensure every person's right to achieve the highest attainable standard of health, and both have a strong focus on the individual.

Medicine is more concerned with analysing, diagnosing, and treating disease, as well as preventing ill health in individuals through such methods as immunization, appropriate diet, or prophylactic therapies. Public health seeks to address health and ill health by focusing on individual and collective determinants, be they behavioural, social, economic, or other contextual factors. Three sets of factors have contributed to blurring traditional boundaries between medicine and public health.

Firstly, the transitions in health status through which many populations have been recently evolving have called for a closer understanding of the links between individual health, public health, and the environment. Current thinking about optimal strategies for disease control have evolved, as efforts to confront the most serious global health threats (including cancer, mental disorders, cardiovascular and other chronic diseases, reproductive and sexual health, infectious diseases, and violence) have increasingly emphasized the role of personal behaviour within a broad social context.

The transition of the global disease burden from communicable to non-communicable diseases (which are heavily dependent on lifestyle), has evoked a medical need to care for patients in their own social contexts. There has been increasing understanding that behaviours and their social, economic, and cultural contexts are inextricably linked with the biology of health and disease, and are therefore relevant to individual care.

Secondly, the tools and technologies of each field have been found to be of increasing utility to the other. For example, new technologies developed through biomedical research in such fields as immunology, molecular biology, and genetics are of increasing relevance to public health. Scientific discoveries in molecular virology have provided tools that are as useful to individual diagnosis and care as they are to epidemiology, vaccine development, and public health programmes.

Likewise, traditional public health tools, drawn from epidemiology, ecology, and social and behavioural sciences, have demonstrated their usefulness in deciphering powerful determinants of health and of disease outcomes, thus creating stronger bridges between biomedical care and public health interventions.

Thirdly, the human rights framework has shown that the state's human rights responsibilities to respect, protect, and fulfil rights relating to health include obligations concerning both medicine and public health. In the context of a health and human rights analysis, a challenge to the now artificial dichotomy between medicine and public health is not merely rhetorical or of analytical interest; it also brings into play the range of obligations of the state towards every individual.

The health and human rights paradigm is relevant to clinical practice, community health, large-scale health programme development, implementation, and policy. The synergistic health and human rights perspective aims to guarantee that every individual can achieve the highest attainable standard of physical, mental, and social well being. Human rights are progressively being understood to offer an approach for considering the broader societal dimensions and contexts of the well being of individuals and populations, and therefore to be of utility to all those concerned with health.

The definition of health enshrined in the WHO Constitution was an important step in helping to move health thinking beyond a limited biomedical- and pathology based perspective towards the more positive domain of well being, understood to include recognition of individuals and their need to realize aspirations, to satisfy needs, and to change or cope with their environments. The societal dimensions of this effort were emphasized in both the Alma-Ata Declaration and the Ottawa Charter for Health Promotion.

The Alma-Ata Declaration describes health as a social goal whose realization requires the action of many social and economic sectors in addition to the health sector. The

Ottawa Charter proposes that the fundamental conditions and resources for health are peace, shelter, education, food, income, a stable ecosystem, sustainable resources, social justice, and equity. When the WHO was created to improve health 50 years ago, there were hopes that antibiotics and the progress achieved in vaccines and biomedical technology would provide the tools sufficient to enable individuals worldwide to reach the highest attainable standard of physical, mental, and social well being.

However, decades later, as reflected in both the Alma-Ata Declaration and the Ottawa Charter, it is clear that, regardless of the effectiveness of technologies, the underlying civil, cultural, economic, political, and social conditions at both a global and local level have to be addressed as well. The major determinants of better health are increasingly understood to lie outside the health system and to include better education and information, as well as fulfilment of an array of rights which are relevant to, but not intrinsically connected with, the right to health.

Thus health requires attention to the increasingly complex relationship of people to their environment and an understanding of respecting, protecting, and fulfilling human rights as a necessary prerequisite for the health of individuals and populations. Globalization and the direct and indirect impacts of intensifying global flows of money, trade, information, culture, and people on health and related aspects of human development, have brought out a new set of human rights issues. These issues need particular attention, as they have largely been ignored.

The process of globalization has proceeded at a much faster pace than the development of policies aimed at maximizing its benefits to human development and preventing or mitigating its harmful effects. Globalization, and the privatization of the means of production and services that inherently accompanies it, can contribute to the advancement of health through the sharing of information, technologies, and resources, as well as through the competition it generates to provide more effective, more widely available, and higher-quality services.

Globalization can create new employment opportunities in some populations or sectors of the economy, but at times may do so to the detriment of others. It can also stimulate the spread of health hazards and disease as a result of intensified population mobility, or through the worldwide marketing of harmful substances, such as tobacco and alcohol. If poorly conceived and monitored, globalization can contribute to the widening of inequalities by increasing the autonomy and well being of some sectors of the population while producing negative consequences for others without access to safety nets to support the fulfilment of essential needs.

In the wake of globalization and privatization, increasing attention must be paid to the role of non-state actors because they are now influencing the health and well being of people to an unprecedented extent, comparable even to the influence of governments. The role of the state is to ensure that all human beings are guaranteed their basic human rights, including the right to the highest attainable standard of health, whether this obligation is fulfilled directly through government-run services or through private intermediaries.

Governmental roles and responsibilities are increasingly being delegated to non-state actors (for example, biomedical research institutions, health insurance companies, care providers, health management organizations, and the pharmaceutical industry) whose accountability for what they do, do not do, or should do about people's health is poorly defined and inadequately monitored. There is a universal need to reinforce the commitment and capacity of governments to ensure that actions taken by the private sector and other actors in civil society relevant to health and other aspects of human development, both within and outside the boundaries of nation-states, are informed by and comply with human rights principles.

Current structures are generally insufficient for non-governmental organizations or governments to monitor effectively and hold corporations operating on a national scale accountable. This problem is compounded when these companies are multinational. Attention to health reveals that multinationals are more than agents of economic change whose decisions are increasingly affecting the distribution of wealth, the fabric of society, and the creation of conditions favourable to advancing health; they are also increasingly the institutions called upon by political and social forces to create and operate alternative mechanisms to extend health and social services and to make available new and affordable vaccines and drugs.

Yet because they are multinational, they largely escape the realm of legal accountability within states, and, while they may choose to adopt ethical guidelines and codes of conduct, there is no international human rights law that directly applies to them or to their actions. The fora where world issues are debated have expanded from assemblies of governments-for example, under the United

Nations umbrella-to gatherings and congresses such as the Davos forum that give a prominent role to these non-state actors, demonstrating that the state and non-state actors leading the world economy have become inseparable partners.

From a health and human rights perspective, the desirable forms and extent of responsibility for multinational actors within the international legal system have yet to be defined in ways that help to shape international trade agreements effectively and to ensure their accountability. This is the next and most important challenge in the world of human rights, and it will have far-reaching health consequences. Human rights can help to provide an approach for redefining the ways in which governments and the international community as a whole are accountable for what is done and not done about the health of people.

This requires an understanding of the content of the health issues most relevant to the health and well being of individuals and populations, as well as of those actions which ought to be taken at the national level to move towards health development. As the approaches set out by the WHO are relevant to all its member states, this discussion will be framed around the strategic framework laid out by the WHO in its 1999 corporate strategy.

From a strategic perspective, the issues relevant to health development can be understood to lie along four converging axes: (a) reducing excess mortality, morbidity, and disability; (b) promoting healthy lifestyles and reducing risk factors to human health that arise from environmental, economic, social, and behavioural causes; (c) developing health systems that equitably improve health outcomes, respond to people's legitimate demands, and are financially fair; (d) developing an enabling policy and institutional environment in the health sector while promoting an effective health dimension to social, economic, environmental, and development policy.

Recent WHO information reveals that six preventable or curable diseases cause 90 per cent of infectious disease deaths worldwide, as well as half of all premature deaths, most of which occur in children and young adults living in developing countries. Reduction of excess mortality, morbidity, and disability calls for a combination of sound health interventions-some of a clinical nature, such as diagnosis and treatment of communicable and non-communicable diseases, and others building on large-scale programmes to inform, immunize, or apply population-based prophylactic therapies.

From a health and human rights perspective, it is worth recognizing that the growing health disparity between the North and the South creates compelling needs both for every country to develop effective disease prevention and control programmes targeted to their specific needs, and for global sharing of technology and resources in order to enable poorer countries to accelerate progress in health development. Therefore, priority must be given both locally and globally to poor and marginalized communities.

Promoting healthy lifestyles and reducing risk factors to human health that arise from environmental, economic, social, and behavioural causes. Modern public health recognizes the influence of external factors on the ability of individuals to adopt healthy behaviours or to access care when ill health has set in. Health promotion is the process of enabling people to increase control over and improve their health. To do so, individuals or groups must be informed and able to identify and realize aspirations, satisfy needs, and change or cope with their environment.

The concept of interventions aimed at reducing risk is familiar to those working on such health issues as HIV/ AIDS and other sexually transmitted diseases, tobacco, and other types of substance use or occupational hazards. Risk reduction interventions can also bring attention to the inadequacy of public services to address such issues as reproductive health, access to safe blood transfusion, or access to clean water. All of these paradigms recognize the importance of integrating morbidity, mortality, and disability reduction programmes with interventions to mitigate or address the factors underlying the occurrence of these events.

Reducing susceptibility or vulnerability requires understanding of who is affected and how and to what extent these people are exposed to and able to cope with the factors that impact on their health, and then designing interventions that can enable them to cope effectively. From a health and human rights perspective, this process is linked to the need to create conditions conducive to health through information, education, and the development or strengthening of health systems and social support programmes that promote healthy behaviours, impact on risk-taking behaviours, and increase individual and collective commitment and capacity to engage in these processes.

The WHO World Health Report 2000 has proposed measures that reflect responsibility and create the grounds for accountability within health systems with regard to three dimensions of health: health outcome, fairness, and responsiveness. The responsibilities of health systems in relation to health outcomes largely determines the type of services, interventions, and technologies they offer.

If analysed on the basis of health outcomes, the accountability demanded of health systems must take into consideration the capacity of these systems to recognize and respond to health issues, as well as such factors as personal behaviours or unforeseen social, economic, or environmental situations or events. From an accountability perspective, it is worth recognizing that some of these latter factors may impact on health outcomes but are beyond the responsibilities assigned to health systems.

They must be taken into account in other ways-for example, in relation to governmental accountability for education, employment, freedom of movement or association, or in relation to other rights that impact on health. Underlying this attention to the responsibility and accountability of health systems is the concept of equality, which implies that health systems are capable of defining and recognizing the characteristics and specific needs of populations within a nation who experience a disproportionate level of mortality, morbidity, and disability.

This, in turn, requires that health data be collected and analysed with a degree of sensitivity and specificity sufficient to determine who is likely to require additional attention; what behaviours and practices have to be supported, induced, or changed; what service provisions have to be enhanced and in what ways; and what financial mechanisms are necessary to provide the safety nets necessary to ensure that those who need more actually receive more.

Therefore, it follows that the information used to develop, monitor, and evaluate policies and programmes must accurately reflect characteristics that may be associated with discrimination and inequality, including sex, age, rural/urban location, and other relevant behavioural, social, or economic factors.

The WHO World Health Report 2000 proposes that 'the way health care is financed is perfectly fair when the burden that health spending represents on the household, or its relative health financial contribution is identical for all households, independent of their income, their health status or their use of the health system'. Although the principle of fairness is not articulated as such in human rights treaties, it builds on an array of rights, such as nondiscrimination, equality, and participation, that, together with obligations directly related to health, can be used to consider the responsibilities of governments for health systems.

The financing of health systems must be considered from the perspective of competing human development priorities within a nation, as well as that of the intrinsic priorities within health systems themselves. No global benchmark can therefore be proposed to establish the minimum national spending for health systems, whether from public or private sources, and the debate must remain open as to the extent to which and the ways in which governments will invest in the health of their populations.

Within health systems, the decisions concerning allocation of public funds for specific health initiatives can draw from epidemiological, economic, or political considerations and can use a variety of methods and processes, including cost-effectiveness analysis, as well as human rights considerations. The concept of financial fairness implies that these systems should enable all individuals to seek and receive services that are commensurate to their needs and economically affordable.

Finally, the concept of responsiveness imposes on health systems a requirement that they be sensitive to people's aspirations, needs, and demands with full respect for human rights, and that they offer support and services. The principles of non-discrimination, protection of confidentiality (privacy), and respect for people's dignity are central to both the design of health systems and to the attitude and practices of health providers.

From a health and human rights perspective, each of the components considered necessary for health systems to improve health outcomes equitably raises additional issues to be considered from the perspective of governmental responsibility and accountability. Developing an enabling policy and institutional environment in the health sector while promoting an effective health dimension to social, economic, environmental, and development policy.

If it is clear that policies and practices within health systems may impact positively or negatively on health, it is also clear that policies and practices concerned with the broad spectrum of human development may also impact significantly on health status and health-seeking behaviours. A large-scale industrial project may, for example, create selective migratory movements that may result in accentuated health hazards, whether these are linked to inadequate working conditions, housing, or social or cultural uprooting.

The association between enhanced vulnerability to HIV/AIDS among migrant labourers and economically motivated mobility in Africa and Asia provides one example. Similarly, factors such as the amount of pollution that industries have generated, or the impact that the use of pesticides in agriculture has had on the health of some populations, imply that health impacts must be considered at all stages of human development programmes.

From a health and human rights perspective, this requires attention to health impacts in the design of human development programmes; this would include preventing or counterbalancing their potential negative health effects, as well as ensuring that health indicators are built into the monitoring of human development initiatives. While the above categorization of strategic directions for health is useful because it reflects the approach being taken by the WHO and is guiding the current global health agenda, a perspective of governmental human rights obligations towards health development emerges more clearly if these strategies are divided into the following three domains.

1. The highest attainable standard of health. This is measured by morbidity, mortality, and disability, by positive health measures of growth and development in children, and by demographic variables, reproductive health, healthy lifestyles, behaviours, and practices in adults. The focus here is on health outcomes affecting individuals and populations.

2. Access to health systems which provide affordable and goodquality preventive, curative, and palliative care services and related social support. The focus here is on health systems.

3. A societal and physical environment conducive to health promotion and protection, including access to education, information, and other positive expressions of rights necessary for health as well as protection from violence, environmental and occupational hazards, harmful traditional practices, and other factors that may impact directly and

negatively on health. The focus here is on the societal and environmental preconditions for health.

The development and application of governmental policies transcends all three of these domains of health development and is equally relevant to governmental responsibilities both to promote and protect health and to respect, protect, and fulfil human rights. A systematic analysis of the responsibilities of governments for health, considered with respect to their obligations under international human rights law, begins to lead us towards the practice of health and human rights.

There are two approaches to analysing the relationship between health and human rights that help not only to illustrate their connection, but also to provide a framework for considering the implications of the health and human rights relationship for government responsibility and accountability. The first focuses consideration on the ways in which health policies, programmes, and practices can promote or violate rights in the ways they are designed or implemented.

Health policies, programmes, and practices in and of themselves can promote and protect or, conversely, restrict and violate human rights, whether by design, neglect, or ignorance. The second approach examines how violations or lack of attention to human rights can have serious health consequences. The promotion, protection, restriction, or violation of human rights all can be seen to have direct and indirect impacts on health and well being. Looking at health through a human rights lens means recognizing not only the technical and operational aspects of health interventions but also the civil, political, economic, social, and cultural factors that surround them.

These factors may include, for example, gender relations, religious beliefs, homophobia, or racism, which individually and in synergy influence the extent to which individuals are able to access services or to make and effect free and informed decisions about their lives-and, therefore, the extent of their vulnerability to ill health. Thus, health and human rights interact in numerous ways, both direct and indirect.

Public health and human rights each recognize the ultimate responsibility of governments to create the enabling conditions necessary for people to make choices, cope with changing patterns of vulnerability, and keep themselves and their families healthy. Using human rights concepts, one can look at the extent to which governments are respecting, protecting, and fulfilling their obligations for all rights-civil political, economic, social, and cultural- and how these government actions influence both the patterns of mortality, morbidity, and disability within a population and what is done about them.

Health Policies, Programmes, and Practices on Human Rights

A human rights framework can help to identify potential burdens on the lives of individuals and populations that are created by health policies, programmes, and practices. An obvious example, as was recognized in the International Conference on Population Development Programme of Action, is demographic goal-driven family planning programmes, which may by their very nature violate basic human rights.

More subtle human rights issues may arise from health programmes that fail to provide services to certain populations or are not appropriately tailored to meet the needs of marginalized groups. Responsibilities for public health are largely carried out through policies and programmes promulgated, implemented, and, at the very least, supported by the state.

Therefore, a human rights approach to public health requires analysis of every stage of the design, implementation, and evaluation of health policies and programmes. This section teases out some of the issues that a human rights analysis can raise at various stages of policy and programme design and implementation. HIV/AIDS, sexual health, and reproductive health will serve as primary examples in this section because, in recent years, these issues have been especially important in illuminating the impact that health policies and programmes can have on human rights.

Human rights considerations arise at the initial formulation of health policies and programmes. Relevant issues would be raised, for example, if a state decides to approach a health issue in a particular way but refuses to disclose the scientific basis of its decisions or permit any debate on its merits, or if a government wilfully or neglectfully fails to consult with members of affected communities in reaching its decisions, or in any number of ways refuses to inform or involve the public in policy or programme development.

Human rights issues may also interact with the development of health policies and programmes when prioritization of certain health issues is based less on actual need than on existing discrimination against certain population groups. This can occur when, for example, minor health issues that predominantly impact the dominant group are systematically given higher priority in research, resource allocation, and policy and programme development than other more major health problems.

Restrictive laws and policies that deliberately focus on certain population groups without sufficient data, epidemiological and otherwise, to support their approach may raise an additional host of human rights concerns. Two examples might be policies concerning the involuntary sterilization of women from certain population groups that are justified as necessary for their health and well being, and sodomy statutes criminalizing same-sex sexual behaviour that are justified as necessary to prevent the spread of HIV/AIDS.

Human rights also need to be considered when choosing which data are collected to determine the type and extent of health problems affecting a population, as this choice has a direct impact on the policies and programmes that are designed and implemented. The choice of issues to be assessed and the way in which a population is defined in these assessments are of primary relevance. Likewise, the scarcity or absence of HIV-related services in a number of places can well be understood to have resulted in a disproportionate burden of health consequences that could have been prevented or alleviated through simple and affordable prevention messages and methods of early diagnosis and treatment.

Once a decision is made that a particular health problem will be dealt with, human rights issues can come into play in both the articulation and the implementation of the health policy or programme. An example is programmes that provide contraception to young boys but deny access to young girls, with the stated rationale that access might prompt girls to be sexually active. From a human rights perspective, this distinction can be understood to be treating young girls unfairly and unjustly on the basis of their sex. The prohibition of discrimination in the human rights documents does not mean that differences should not be acknowledged, but rather that different treatment must be based on reasonable and objective criteria.

Therefore, applying different approaches to girls and boys in policy and programme development must be based on a valid recognition of gender-related differentials in risk and vulnerability with respect to the particular health issue and with an attempt to minimize the influence of prescribed gender roles and cultural norms in making this determination. The severity of the devastating tuberculosis epidemic in developing countries, and in marginalized communities in affluent nations, draws attention to the relevance of a human rights analysis for the implementation of a health policy and programme.

While the directly observed therapy strategy (DOTS) is widely recognized for its efficacy in controlling tuberculosis, the issues raised by the very different ways this strategy is administered in different countries, and to different population groups, demonstrates how discrimination may be relevant to the ways in which health programmes are implemented. Many health practitioners argue that the speed with which tuberculosis is spreading and the potential impact of individual non-compliance to treatment are likely to aggravate both the spread of the disease and the currently observed prevalence of multiple-drug resistance.

The DOTS strategy aims to combat this by enrolling patients diagnosed with active tuberculosis in a programme where drugs are administered under the direct observation of a care provider, rather than self-administered by the patient. The strategy requires frequent visits by patients to the site where drugs are administered, which can potentially involve work absenteeism and in some cases out-of-pocket travel expenses. In small communities, the strategy may also lead to breaches of the right to privacy, as frequent visits to a treatment point may be associated with the stigma commonly attached to the disease.

In cases of non-compliance to regular treatment administered in this way, measures up to and including mandatory hospital admission may be taken to motivate defaulting patients to comply. There is ample evidence to suggest, however, that in a number of places the level of coercion exercised by health practitioners in the decision to apply DOTS, as well as in the application of mandatory institutionalization, is directly associated with the levels of discrimination against particular population groups within the society in question.

Attention must also be given to whether health and social services take into account logistic, financial, and sociocultural barriers to access and enjoyment, as a failure to do so can result in discrimination in practice, if not in law. This includes attention to the factors that may impact on service utilization, such as hours of service and accessibility via public transportation. Issues are also raised by decisions concerning the location of prevention and treatment services for certain health issues.

An extreme example relates to the location of sexually transmitted disease diagnosis, prevention, and care services, which may be integrated into the reproductive health services generally available to women or offered only in centres dedicated to sexually transmitted disease prevention and treatment. Evidence suggests that individuals, and women in particular, are less likely to take advantage of sexually transmitted disease services that operate under this latter designation for fear of stigma and discrimination within the community if they are seen at the facility.

Laws and policies that may seem neutral but neglect to detail sufficiently the steps necessary for their implementation may raise additional human rights issues. Illustrative of such a situation are laws and policies that mandate the reporting of HIV infection but fail to spell out the actors responsible for doing so, or fail to take into account a lack of infrastructure to ensure that privacy can be respected and that mechanisms for redress exist if breaches of confidentiality occur.

Indeed, collecting personal information from individuals about their health status (for example, HIV infection, cancer, or genetic disorders), or behaviours (for example, sexual orientation or the use of alcohol or other substances) has the potential for misuse by the state, whether directly or because this information is intentionally or inadvertently made available to others. In recent times the most explicit examples of the impact of misuse or neglect of privacy protections are found in the context of HIV/AIDS.

Misuse of personal information related to HIV status has led to restrictions on the right to marry and found a family, and the right to work and education, as well as, in extreme cases, limitations on freedom of movement, arbitrary detention, or exile, and even cruel, inhuman, and degrading treatment. The release of information concerning a person's HIV status to others has, in many places, led to loss of employment and housing, as well as harassment and verbal and physical attacks.

In countries where the HIV/AIDS pandemic has matured, some 15- to 16-year-old girls attending antenatal clinics for their first pregnancy are already infected with HIV, and no information is available as to the cause of this infection (that is, whether it involved sex or another mode of transmission). The degree to which gender factors influence the relative risk of becoming infected through various routes of transmission during childhood, and how they may influence patterns of access to care and the quality of care provided to boys and girls once HIV infection has set in, remains unknown.

There has been very little attention to the general failure to differentiate by sex in the collection and analysis of epidemiological information on 'children' younger than 15. This raises a host of human rights concerns and may result in neglect of the very real differences between female and male adolescents in the prevention and care programmes that do exist. Violations of the right to information in the context of health policies and programmes must be mentioned specifically, as these can have substantial health impacts.

Examples include decisions by governments to withhold or block access to valid scientific information that would enable people to participate in the improvement of their health, avoid disease, or claim and seek better care. Such is the case for young women who become unwillingly pregnant or acquire sexually transmitted diseases because they are denied information considered too sexually explicit for them-even though they became pregnant or infected because they were sexually active.

The health and human rights approach determines whether health policies, programmes, and practices are valid from both a public health and a human rights perspective. When health is understood to include physical, mental, and social well being, it seems reasonable to conclude that the violation or neglect of any human right will impact adversely on health.

While this is certainly true with respect to specific rights, such as non-discrimination or education, the impact of neglect or violation of rights is also compounded by the number of rights brought into question by any particular situation. The health impacts of certain severe human rights violations, such as torture, imprisonment under inhumane conditions, summary executions, and disappearances have long been understood. Much work has been done in this field, and efforts in this regard continue to expand. Such efforts include exhumations of mass graves to ascertain how people have died, the coding and matching of genetic information to reunite families separated during war and massive political repression, examination of torture victims to bring perpetrators to justice and to assist with asylum claims, and entry into prisons and other state-run institutions, such as detention centres, to assess health conditions and the health status of confined populations.

The impacts on health of these human rights violations can be both obvious and subtle. For example, torture is a violation that causes immediate and direct harm to health. Yet only recently has the full impact of torture begun to be recognized, including the lifelong injury to the victim, the effects on the health of families and of entire communities, and the transgenerational damage.

There is increasing recognition of the need to assess the duration and extent of the health impacts of such human rights violations, including the direct and immediate impact of being subjected to torture oneself, but also its severe and lifelong effects on survivors and the trauma associated with being forced to witness summary executions, rape, and other forms of torture and trauma perpetrated on others.

Health practitioners can-and in most cases do-have a strong positive influence on the promotion and protection of human rights within the populations they serve. Yet violations of human rights perpetrated by health professionals regularly occur. These include not only such egregious examples as doctor participation in torture and other severe violations of human rights, but also actions in the provision of treatment and care, for example when care providers make decisions concerning patient access to available prevention services, or when children with a chronic fatal disease or disability are denied immunization against measles and other preventable childhood infections.

In many countries, rich and poor, patients with diabetes, carcinoma, chronic renal syndrome, mental disability, haemophilia, or other severe health conditions may receive a lower standard of care than others not only with respect to the health issue in question but in general because their possibility of cure is regarded as limited. A less obvious impact of neglect of human rights on health concerns the many children from poor or marginalized communities, where poor nutrition and ill health prevail, that have a below-average school enrolment and attendance rate and, as a result, below-average educational attainment.

The deprivation of these children from access to basic health services, coupled with the imposition of school fees, leads to a limitation of their ability to exercise their right to education, producing lifelong effects on their health and well being. In addition to the impact of egregious violations of rights on health, the more subtle effects of neglect or violations of rights on health can also be considered. These would include exposures to ill health resulting from violations of such rights as work, free movement, association, and participation.

The impact of neglect or violation of factors considered to form the underlying preconditions for health must also be considered. In addition to medical services, these have been understood to include such factors as adequate housing, education, food, safe drinking water, sanitation, access to information, and protection against discrimination. Understood in human rights terms, neglect of these rights, particularly in combination, can have serious negative consequences on health. No community is fully protected from neglect or violation of rights and its detrimental consequences to individual and public health.

In particular, gender-based discrimination poses a pervasive threat to health. Girls and women who are denied access to education, information, and various forms of economic, social, and political participation are particularly vulnerable to the impact of discrimination on their health. This is true when discrimination is recognized, tolerated, acknowledged, or even condoned by governments, but also when it remains insidiously hidden or deliberately ignored behind an accepted *status quo*.

One example, drawn from the world of reproductive health, dramatically illustrates this point. There is now general acknowledgement that violations of human rights, including systematic gender discrimination, create an environment of increased risk in relation to women's health. Access to information, education, and quality services is critical, as are services adequately targeted to respond to the needs of women of different ages and from different communities. Underlying all this is the impact that gender roles and gender discrimination have on both health status and service delivery.

The relevance of human rights to this analysis becomes clear when considering the gaps and inequalities in services and structures in relation to the social roles that construct male and female identity. Equally important is how these factors play out at the policy and programme level in terms of reproductive health research, policy, financing, and service delivery. Traditional public health focused on the need for information, education, contraception, counselling, and access to quality services.

These elements of health practice were, and still are, central to improving women's reproductive health. However, even if these services are available, an individual woman has to be able to decide when and how she is going to access these services. This implies that she has to have the ability to control and make decisions about her life. In this example, considering the impact that violation or neglect of human rights has on health highlights the societal context that would hinder or empower an individual woman's ability to make and act on the free and informed choices necessary for her reproductive health.

From a broader policy and programme perspective, this insight reveals that linking the human rights framework to health implies recognizing that individual health is largely influenced by one's environment. This means that the integration of human rights in the design, implementation, and evaluation of health policies and programmes is necessary not only because of a government's human rights obligations, but also in purely pragmatic public health terms.

Thus, attention to the civil, political, economic, social, and cultural factors that are relevant to a person's life, such as gender relations, racism, or homophobia, and the ways this combination of factors projects itself into who becomes ill and what is done about it, is central to sound health and human rights practice. The process of documenting evidence on the health impacts resulting from violations or neglect of human rights must be thorough and thoughtful because of the multifarious effects on health of human rights neglect or violations.

The involvement of communities that are disproportionately affected by human rights violations in the development, implementation, and monitoring of decisions affecting them is crucial to mitigating these impacts. Affected individuals working together in defence or advocacy groups-be they concerned with breast cancer, diabetes, renal syndromes, haemophilia, chronic disabilities, or other health issues-have been effective in bringing to light some of the more subtle mechanisms that come into play in linking health status with the human rights violations to which people are subjected.

A crucial step in optimizing the relationship between health and human rights is to conduct a systematic review of how and to what extent governmental policies and programmes are respectful of human rights and of benefit to public health. The importance of the human rights framework to policies and programmes is that it can provide a method of analysis and a framework for action, which can then be used to help shape specific interventions aimed at reducing the impact of health conditions on the lives of individuals and populations.

This approach requires work with the international human rights documents to determine the specific rights applicable to a given situation, and then considering how and to what extent morbidity, mortality, disability, risk behaviours, and vulnerability to ill health are caused or exacerbated by insufficient realization of human rights. This analysis will be most effective if done in partnership with people with substantive knowledge of human rights.

Another dimension of developing the health and human rights relationship is the application of mechanisms, methods, and tools to monitor progress and shortcomings in implementation of health and human rights at the national and international level. In order to improve the knowledge and understanding of health status and trends, and to relate these trends to health system performance, the WHO has developed the following five global indicators.

1. *Healthy life expectancy*: a composite indicator incorporating mortality, morbidity, and disability in a disability-adjusted life years measure. This indicator will reflect time spent in a state of less than full health.
2. *Health inequalities*: the degree of disparity in healthy life expectancy within the population.
3. *Responsiveness of health systems*: a composite indicator reflecting the protection of dignity and confidentiality in and by health systems, and people's autonomy (that is, their individual capacity to effect informed choice in health matters).
4. *Responsiveness inequality*: the disparity in responsiveness within health systems, bringing out issues of low efficiency, neglect, and discrimination.

5. *Fairness in financing*: measured by the level of health financing contribution of households.

4

Human Rights Law and Freedom of Association

In 1948, in the nascent field of international human rights law, there were two striking developments. The first in time was the adoption by the ILO of the Freedom of Association and Protection of the Right to Organise Convention; the second was the adoption by the United Nations of the Universal Declaration of Human Rights a few months later. The close relation between some aspects of the two at the time has been maintained through the ILO's supervisory process ever since. The Universal Declaration is, of course, of great importance to the ILO in its work for the promotion and defence of human rights.

As the ILO's Committee of Experts on the Application of Conventions and Recommendations stated in the report of its 1997 Session:

> The Universal Declaration ... is generally accepted as a point of reference for human rights throughout the world, and as the basis for most of the standard

> setting that has been carried out in the United Nations and in many other organizations since then. ... The ILO's standards and practical activities on human rights are closely related to the universal values laid down in the Declaration, ... [T]he ILO's standards on human rights along with the instruments adopted in the UN and in other international organizations give practical application to the general expressions of human aspirations made in the Universal Declaration, and have translated into binding terms the principles of that noble document.

It is of particular interest to the ILO that the Universal Declaration of Human Rights proclaims in its Article 23, paragraph 4, that: "Everyone has the right to form and to join trade unions for the protection of his interests." This is a more specific manifestation of the right laid down in article 20 of the Universal Declaration to "the right of freedom of peaceful assembly and association".

The inclusion of this principle in the Universal Declaration had been preceded by its inclusion in three important ILO instruments. The first of these is the ILO's Constitution, which in its original version as Part XIII of the Treaty of Versailles proclaimed that the High Contracting Parties considered that the right of association "for all lawful purposes" is of "special and urgent importance", both for workers and employers.The Preamble to the Constitution explicitly cites trade union rights among the measures that could improve working conditions and thus assure peace.

When in 1944 the ILO adopted the Declaration of Philadelphia, the second of these fundamental texts, and in 1946 incorporated it into the Constitution, it reaffirmed freedom of association as one of the fundamental principles on which the Organization was based, and characterized it as "essential to sustained progress". It also referred to "the effective recognition of the right of collective bargaining, the co-operation of management and labour in the continuous improvement of productive efficiency, and the collaboration of workers and employers in the preparation and application of social and economic measures".

The third of these fundamental texts was the Freedom of Association and Protection of the Right to Organise Convention, 1948. The adoption of a specific Convention on this subject in the ILO was not easy, as is outlined in Harold Dunning's article in this issue of the International Labour Review. It was put off many times as being too difficult to agree on, and its lack began to be felt early. In 1921, the ILO adopted the Right of Association (Agriculture) Convention (No. 11), which recognized in very general terms that workers in agriculture have the same rights of association as workers in industry - but at the time the ILO had not yet defined the freedom of association rights of industrial workers.

When the time did come, events moved fairly quickly. In the ILO itself, the 1944 Declaration of Philadelphia contained the provision mentioned above. In addition, the Third Conference of American States Members of the ILO adopted in 1946 a resolution on freedom of association that spelt out the basic principles which would be included in Convention No. 87. In 1947, the International Labour Conference adopted the Right of Association Convention, which refers not only to the right of employers and workers to associate for any legal purpose, but also to collective agreements, consultations and the solution of labour conflicts.

Though ratified by only four countries, this Convention had an important effect on the development of international law on the subject. The same year, the Economic and Social Council of the United Nations (ECOSOC) examined reports on freedom of association from the World Federation of Trade Unions (WFTU)and the American Federation of Labor (AFL), and decided to ask the ILO to include these subjects on the agenda of its Conference.

The ILO did so in 1947, and adopted a resolution which prepared the ground for the adoption of Convention No. 87 in 1948, before the adoption of the Universal Declaration, and of Convention No. 98 shortly thereafter, in 1949. The adoption of international human rights law in a "legislative" process in international Conventions adopted by the ILO and the United Nations - really began only in 1948, with that of Convention No. 87 and the Universal Declaration. Before the ILO was established, there had been some early attempts to adopt international agreements on workers' rights by negotiation between States, but they had not been terribly successful.

At the end of the First World War, in 1919, the League of Nations and the International Labour Organization were established, and the ILO set about adopting international Conventions on conditions of work. The only instruments which really amounted to what are called "human rights" treaties today were the Slavery Convention adopted by the League of Nations in 1926, and the Forced Labour Convention adopted by the ILO in 1930 to develop the coverage of labour aspects of slavery. But no other human rights instruments were adopted until after the Second World War.

Since 1948, the ILO and the United Nations have developed along parallel lines as far as freedom of association issues are concerned - and other human rights questions as well - and regional organizations have also developed both standards and supervisory capacity. But consideration will first be given to how the United Nations and other organizations developed the concepts, and then to the development of these principles by the ILO through its Conventions and supervisory process.

Article 23(4) of the Universal Declaration on Human Rights, quoted above, is couched in language deriving directly from Convention No. 87, and is a general statement of the same philosophy. Article 2 of Convention No. 87 reads: Workers and employers, without distinction whatsoever, shall have the right to establish and, subject only to the rules of the organisation concerned, to join organisations of their own choosing without any previous authorisation.

The main difference between this text and that of the Universal Declaration is that the latter omits any reference to employers. Also, of course, it stops at the general expression of the principle, as is its vocation. In 1966, the United Nations codified the principles laid down in the Declaration in two seminal texts: the International Covenant on Civil and Political Rights, and the International Covenant on Economic, Social and Cultural Rights. Both Covenants came into force ten years later once they had received a sufficient number of ratifications; they are the most influential international human rights instruments of broad coverage. They also followed the earlier ILO provisions on freedom of association.

Article 22 of the International Covenant on Civil and Political Rights is its only detailed article on freedom of association. The first paragraph of that Article is an almost exact restatement of Article 23(4) of the Universal Declaration. The second paragraph states that no restrictions may be placed on the exercise of this right "other than those which are prescribed by law and which are necessary in a democratic society" and allows "lawful restrictions on members of the armed forces and of the police in their exercise of this right", as does Convention No. 87. The third paragraph reads as follows:

> Nothing in this article shall authorise the States Parties to the International Labour Organisation Convention of 1948 concerning Freedom of Association and Protection of the Right to Organise to take legislative measures which would prejudice, or apply the law in such a manner as to prejudice the guarantees provided for in that Convention.

Entire legislative conformity is guaranteed with Convention No. 87 in this remarkable provision, which was incorporated in the other Covenant as well.

The International Covenant on Economic, Social and Cultural Rights contains a more detailed treatment of the same subject, in Article 8:

1. The States Parties to the present Covenant undertake to ensure:

   (a) The right of everyone to form trade unions and join the trade union of his choice, subject only to the rules of the organisation concerned, for the promotion and protection of his economic and social interests. No restriction may be placed on the exercise of this right other than those prescribed by law and which are necessary in a democratic society in the interests of national security or public order or for the protection of the rights and freedoms of others;

(b) The right of trade unions to establish national federations or confederations and the right of the latter to form or join international trade-union organisations;

(c) The right of trade unions to function freely subject to no limitations other than those prescribed by law and which are necessary in a democratic society in the interests of national security or public order or for the protection of the rights and freedoms of others;

(d) The right to strike, provided that it is exercised in conformity with the laws of a particular country.

2. This article shall not prevent the imposition of lawful restrictions on the exercise of these rights by members of the armed forces or of the police or of the administration of the State.

3. Nothing in this article shall authorise the States Parties to the International Labour Organisation Convention of 1948 concerning Freedom of Association and Protection of the Right to Organise to take legislative measures which would prejudice, or apply the law in such a manner as to prejudice the guarantees provided for in that Convention.

In comparing this provision with ILO standards, Valticos and von Potobsky point out the relative merits of the two approaches: This provision is not as detailed as Convention No. 87. Moreover, the restrictions which it authorizes might reduce considerably the extent of the protection which it affords. This applies to the limitations which, contrary to Convention No. 87, are permitted as regards the members of the administration of the State. This is also the case as regards the limitations "which are necessary in a democratic society in the interests of national security or public order or for the protection of the rights and freedoms of others", for which there is no equivalent in Convention No. 87.

However, the obligations arising from that Convention are expressly reserved by the saving clause contained in Article 8, para. 3, of the Covenant. On the other hand, this Article recognizes the right to strike, but it leaves the conditions of its exercise to the discretion of national legislations.Thus, while there are some differences, the ILO and United Nations texts are almost completely consistent one with the other; certainly they have not been developed by the supervisory bodies of the two organizations in a way which gives rise to any difficulties.

Protection on the regional level is most thorough in Europe, where it is contained in two instruments. The European Convention on Human Rights (1950) provides for freedom of association and protection of the right to organize in terms adopted later (1966) in the International Covenant on Economic, Social and Cultural Rights, in its Article 11. The European Social Charter (1961) takes an approach much more similar to that of the ILO standards, in its Articles 5 (the right to organize) and 6 (the right to bargain collectively). Article 6, para. 4, of the Charter contains the first express authorization in an international instrument of the right to strike.

Article 31 (1) of the Charter, in turn, provides that:

> The rights and principles set forth ... and their effective exercise ... shall not be subject to any restrictions or limitations not specified ... except such as are prescribed by law and are necessary in a

> democratic society for the protection of the rights and freedoms of others or for the protection of public interest, national security, public health, or morals.

Article 8, which closely resembles the provisions of the International Covenant on Economic, Social and Cultural Rights. It contains one provision not found in any of the other standards examined here, affirming that no one may be compelled to belong to a trade union. This makes trade union security clauses or practices contrary to the Protocol. In Africa, the African Charter on Human and Peoples' Rights contains no provision directly on freedom of association for employers or workers. It does contain, at Article 10, a general assertion for everyone of the "right to free association provided that he abides by the law"; and, at Article 11, the right to freedom of assembly.

International law is thus fairly clear and remarkably consistent on the question of freedom of association and protection of the right to organize and to bargain collectively. It is also clear that all these provisions emerge more or less directly from Convention No. 87 and the closely related text of the Universal Declaration.

Before examining how the supervisory bodies have perceived the obligations under the ILO's Constitution and standards, it may be helpful to review the kinds of supervision that operate. All ratified ILO Conventions are dealt with by the ILO's Committee of Experts on the Application of Conventions and Recommendations. Governments report at regular intervals, and the Committee of Experts makes any comments that may be called for.

In more difficult cases, the situation is referred to the tripartite Conference Committee on the Application of Standards in the annual session of the International Labour

Conference, where the government concerned may be invited to come and discuss its situation in a public forum, as with other ILO Conventions. It is also possible to invoke the constitutional complaints procedures for freedom of association Conventions, as for all other Conventions.

Representations under article 24 of the Constitution are generally referred to the Committee on Freedom of Association. Complaints under article 26 of the Constitution may also be filed, and are examined by a Commission of Inquiry convened by the Governing Body. The arrangements described above apply to all ratified Conventions. In the case of freedom of association and the right to collective bargaining, however, the ILO has made additional provisions.

The Governing Body decided in January 1950 to create the Fact-Finding and Conciliation Commission on Freedom of Association,following discussions with ECOSOC. In November 1951, the Governing Body created a special committee from among its own members to carry out prior examination of the cases submitted to that Commission; this was the Committee on Freedom of Association. The Fact-Finding and Conciliation Commission on Freedom of Association may examine cases only if the government against which a complaint was filed agrees to the examination. The first governments against which the procedure was invoked refused this consent, and the Commission was thus blocked from any action until 1964.

Because of this blockage, the Committee on Freedom of Association, which required no such agreement, evolved from a body whose role was originally conceived as a filtering mechanism for the Commission into an independent body which was able to examine complaints;

to date it has examined nearly 2,000 such complaints. The Committee is composed of nine titular and nine substitute members, drawn on a tripartite basis from the ILO Governing Body; it meets three times a year.

Complaints may be submitted by governments or by employers' or workers' organizations, alleging that the right of freedom of association has been infringed. The distinguishing characteristic of the Commission and of the Committee is that they may examine complaints whether or not the country concerned has ratified any ILO Convention on the subject - their authority derives directly from the Constitution, and complaints may thus be filed against any member State of the ILO.

If the government concerned has not ratified the relevant ILO Conventions, the Committee on Freedom of Association itself follows up the effect given to complaints; if it has, the Committee of Experts on the Application of Conventions and Recommendations is charged with the follow-up. The principles contained in the Conventions and in the Constitution have thus been subject to intense scrutiny over the past 50 years. With 122 ratifications of Convention No. 87, and reports from ratifying States at twoyearly intervals or less, the Committee of Experts has continuously had to evaluate whether given situations were in compliance with the Convention.

And the Committee on Freedom of Association has been employed in a similarly intense manner deciding on the 2,000 cases arising from complaints. There are two principal sources for examining the opinions of the ILO supervisory bodies. The primary source for the Committee of Experts is its own comments on individual country situations. Each year the Committee of Experts also carries out a General Survey on one or more ILO Convention(s) and Recommendation(s) reviewing the situation around the world as regards ratification and difficulties encountered in their application by governments.

Freedom of association and civil liberties as developed by the ILO supervisory bodies. This subject is of overarching importance in the field of freedom of association, and bears a special relationship to the principles laid down in the Universal Declaration of Human Rights. There is a general consensus that respect for civil and political rights is necessary for the exercise of trade union rights. The Committee on Freedom of Association in particular has stated that a "genuinely free and independent trade union movement can only develop where fundamental human rights are respected".

The Committee considers that the guarantees set out in the international labour Conventions, in particular those relating to freedom of association, can only be effective if the civil and political rights enshrined in the Universal Declaration of Human Rights and other international instruments, notably the International Covenant on Civil and Political Rights, are genuinely recognized and protected. These intangible and universal principles, the importance of which the Committee wishes to emphasize particularly on the occasion of the 75th anniversary of the creation of the ILO and the 50th anniversary of the Declaration of Philadelphia, should constitute the common ideal to which all peoples and all nations aspire.

According to a Resolution concerning trade union rights and their relation to civil liberties, adopted by the Conference in 1970, the civil liberties essential for the normal exercise of trade union rights include: "(a) the right to freedom and security of person and freedom from arbitrary arrest and detention; (b) freedom of opinion and expression and in particular freedom to hold opinions without interference and to seek, receive and impart information and ideas through any media and regardless of frontiers; (c) freedom of assembly; (d) the right to a fair trial by an independent and impartial tribunal; (e) the right to protection of the property of trade union organizations."

Right to Personal Security

There are several aspects to this principle. As regards physical integrity, the complaints received by the Committee on Freedom of Association refer principally to loss of life, injury, torture or other ill treatment, and "disappearance" of trade unionists. The Committee has placed special emphasis on the importance of setting up an independent judicial inquiry in such cases.As regards torture, cruelty and ill-treatment in particular, the Committee has pointed out that during their detention trade unionists, like all other individuals, should enjoy the safeguards provided by the Universal Declaration of Human Rights and the International Covenant on Civil and Political Rights.

The Committee frequently invokes the right to be tried promptly under normal judicial procedures. During a state of emergency the same safeguards of a speedy trial of trade unionists, with the guarantees of a regular judicial procedure, must be applied.The Committee has often stated that the forced exile of trade unionists is not only contrary to human rights, but also particularly serious since it deprives them of the possibility of working in their countries and separates them from their families. It also constitutes a violation of freedom of association, since it weakens trade union organizations by depriving them of their leaders and key activists.

Freedom of Opinion and Expression

The Committee on Freedom of Association considers that the full exercise of trade union rights calls for a free flow of information, opinions and ideas, and that workers, employers and their organizations should enjoy freedom of opinion and expression at their meetings, in their publications, and in the course of their other activities.A question of particular interest for the ILO is the freedom of speech of delegates to the International Labour Conference.

The functioning of the Conference would be considerably hampered and the freedom of speech of the workers' and employers' delegates paralysed, if they were to be threatened with prosecution based, directly or indirectly, on the contents of their speeches at the Conference. Article 40 of the ILO Constitution provides that delegates to the Conference shall enjoy "such privileges and immunities as are necessary for the independent exercise of their functions in connection with the Organization".

The arrest and sentencing of a delegate as a result of his or her speech to the Conference, or by reason of information given on the debates thereof, jeopardize freedom of speech for delegates as well as the immunities that they should enjoy in this regard.

Freedom of Assembly

The Committee has pointed out many times that freedom

of assembly constitutes a fundamental aspect of trade union rights. The authorities should refrain from any interference which would restrict this right or impede its lawful exercise, provided that the exercise of these rights does not cause a serious and imminent threat to public order.

Protection of Trade Union Premises

The Committee has often stated that trade union premises are inviolable. They should only be searched when a warrant has been issued by the regular judicial authority, when that authority has good reason to believe that evidence for criminal proceedings under the ordinary law will be found on the premises, and on condition that the search is restricted to the purpose for which the warrant was issued.

Special situation during states of emergency

The Committee of Experts has noted that a state of emergency is frequently invoked to justify exemptions from the obligations arising under the Conventions on freedom of association, but that such a pretext cannot be used to justify restrictions on the civil liberties that are essential to the proper exercise of trade union rights, except in cases of extreme gravity.

Any such restrictions must be limited in scope and duration to what is strictly necessary to deal with the situation in question. While it is conceivable that the exercise of some civil liberties, such as the right to public assembly or the right to hold street demonstrations, might be limited, suspended and even prohibited, it is not permissible that the guarantees relating to the security of the person should be limited, suspended or abolished.

Article 2 of Convention No. 87 provides that "Workers and employers, without distinction whatsoever, shall have the right to establish and ... to join organizations of their own choosing". Only the members of the armed forces and of the police may be excluded, and the Convention covers both wage-earners and other workers. In adopting the term "without distinction whatsoever", the Conference emphasized that the right to organize should be guaranteed without distinction or discrimination of any kind as to occupation, sex, colour, race, creed, nationality or political opinion.

Public employees are covered along with other workers.

The Committee of Experts has emphasized this means that "all public servants and officials should have the right to establish occupational organizations, irrespective of whether they are engaged in the state administration at the central, regional or local level, are officials of bodies which provide important public services or are employed in state-owned economic undertakings". As concerns nationality, in principle ILO standards apply to all workers. The Discrimination (Employment and Occupation) Convention, 1958 (No. 111) does not list nationality among prohibited grounds of discrimination, but various ILO instruments provide that equal treatment should be given to migrant workers, and some provide specifically for this to be the case for freedom of association.

There are special problems concerning the coverage of agricultural workers, and the fact that these workers have special difficulties has also been recognized by the adoption of the Rural Workers' Organisations Convention and Recommendation, 1975, which recognize their special status. Nevertheless, they continue to benefit from the guarantees provided for in other freedom of association Conventions, in particular Conventions Nos. 87 and 98.

Political opinion, including political activities, should not be a basis for discrimination concerning the right to join a trade union. Furthermore, conviction for a political offence should in no case constitute a valid ground for withdrawal of the right to trade union membership.Employers should enjoy the same right to organize as workers. This principle applies in particular to countries in which private enterprise does not exist or where it has only a marginal importance under the existing political system - a decreasing number of countries now, but until recently there was a significant number of them.

The Committee of Experts has emphasized that employers, including managerial staff and executive staff in state-run enterprises, are covered by Convention No. 87 and that their right to organize should be fully protected.There is only one category of exception allowed by Convention No. 87, in Article 9 (1): "The extent to which the guarantees provided for in this Convention shall apply to the armed forces and the police shall be determined by national laws or regulations."

This provision permits either the total exclusion of this category of workers from the coverage of the Convention, or the recognition of some limited rights of freedom of association. The Committee on Freedom of Association, in particular, has made it clear that "this is a matter which has been left to the discretion of the States Members of the ILO".

Article 2 of the Convention lays down the right of workers and employers to establish their organizations "without previous authorization". This principle often comes into play when occupational organizations request "legal personality", as required by the legislation of some countries. The Convention refers explicitly to this question in Article 7, providing that "[t]he acquisition of legal personality by workers' and employers' organizations, federations and confederations shall not be made subject to conditions of such a character as to restrict the application" of the various guarantees provided in the Convention.

The supervisory bodies have repeatedly spoken against provisions that allow excessive discretionary powers to the national authorities. The Committee on Freedom of Association has stated, for example, that where the authority competent to register a union has the discretionary power to refuse registration this is not very different from cases in which prior authorization is required.The Committee of Experts considers that genuinely discretionary power to grant or reject a registration request is tantamount to a requirement for prior authorization, which is not compatible with Article 2 of the Convention.In addition, the possibility of appealing to the courts against an administrative decision rejecting registration has been considered an especially important safeguard.

Right to establish and join organizations of their own choosing

The requirement of Article 2 that workers and employers "shall have the right to establish and ... to join organizations of their own choosing" is one of the most important aspects of the ILO's concept of freedom of association, and has been vigorously defended by the supervisory bodies. The questions of trade union pluralism and unity are examined on the basis of this provision, as are other questions relating to the structure and composition of occupational organizations.

For instance, the supervisory bodies have stated that a requirement for a minimum number of workers or of a certain proportion of workers for the creation of a trade union may be incompatible with the Convention. The Committee of Experts has therefore said that this number or proportion should be kept at a reasonable level so as not to constitute an obstacle to the creation of organizations.

The Committee on Freedom of Association has been more concrete, saying that a requirement for 50 founding members of a trade union is "obviously too high a figure", while a legal requirement that there be a "minimum number of 20 members to form a union does not seem excessive". Limitation of the geographical region within which a trade union can be established has also been found by the supervisory bodies to be contrary to Article 2, and restriction of the right to organize to workers in the same occupation or branch of activity can also cause a problem, both in the private and in the public sectors.

When trade union unity is imposed by law, this kind of unity does not correspond to the principle of free choice which is laid down in Article 2 of the Convention. This does not, however, prevent a voluntary decision by workers or employers to choose to have a single organization to represent them, to avoid the problem of having parallel organizations at the general, sectoral or enterprise levels. Article 2 of the Convention favours neither unity or diversity for trade unions. Nor does it make trade union diversity an obligation, but it does require that at the very least diversity should always remain possible.

Both the Committee of Experts and the Committee on Freedom of Association consider that there is a fundamental difference between cases in which a trade union monopoly is imposed or maintained by law, and situations in some countries in which the workers or their unions voluntarily combine into one organization, independently of legislation. In the latter case, the laws should not institutionalize a factual monopoly; even in a situation where at some point all workers have preferred to unify the trade union movement, they should still remain free to choose to set up unions outside the established structures should they so wish.

Examples of cases which the supervisory bodies have considered contrary to Article 2 of the Convention are the legal registration of only one first-level organization for all the workers in an undertaking, or by occupation or branch of activity;the requirement that at least 50 per cent of the workers join in order to establish or register an organization;and the power to impose an obligation on all workers in the category to pay contributions to the single national trade union, the establishment of which is permitted by branch of industry and by region, as this represents a consecration and strengthening of a trade union monopoly.

Both the Committee on Freedom of Association and the Committee of Experts have insisted that the principle of free choice should allow the continued existence of minority organizations as an alternative in the future to the union which presently is recognized for the exclusive exercise of certain rights of representation. This does not imply equal representation for all the organizations that may coexist, but it does require that some of these rights remain in force.

The definition of "organization" in Article 10 of the Convention is important here: "any organization of workers or of employers for furthering and defending the interests of workers or of employers". If a law allows the existence of a minority trade union organization, but deprives it of trade union functions to the point that it no longer corresponds to this definition, the implicit result is the prohibition of the existence of another union than the majority, "recognized" one, and this would be contrary to Article 2 of the Convention.

In practical terms, the Committee of Experts considers that laws which distinguish between the most representative trade union and others are not in themselves contrary to the principle of freedom of association, so long as the distinction is limited to recognizing certain rights (particularly for such purposes as collective bargaining, consultation by the authorities or the designation of delegates to international organizations) for the most representative union, determined under objective and previously established criteria.

Freedom to refrain from joining and union security clauses (the "closed shop") are a distinct issue. The Conventions on freedom of association, the right to organize and collective bargaining protect the positive right to organize, and do not deal with the right not to join an occupational organization.

While Article 2 of Convention No. 87 thus recognizes only the positive right to associate, the Committee of

Experts has found that Article 2 of that Convention leaves it to the practice and regulations of each State to decide whether it is appropriate to guarantee the right of workers not to join an occupational organization or, on the other hand, to authorize and, where necessary, to regulate the use of union security clauses in practice.In other words, under Convention No. 87 it is acceptable either to adopt the prohibition of trade union security clauses in order to guarantee the right not to associate, or to authorize and regulate practices which restrict or cancel this negative right.

The first two Articles of Convention No. 87 deal with the individual's right to join an organization and the rights deriving from its exercise, especially as concerns the formalities of constitution of organizations, their composition and structure, and the problems of trade union unity or pluralism. Article 3 of that Convention introduces the collective rights of organizations of employers and of workers, beginning with their internal autonomy and their "right to draw up their constitutions and rules, to elect their representatives in full freedom, to organize their administration".

It continues with their right to organize their "activities and to formulate their programmes", thus protecting the exercise of the socio-economic functions of these organizations. The Article reaffirms the general principle of the autonomy of these organizations by stipulating that: "The public authorities shall refrain from any interference which would restrict this right or impede the lawful exercise thereof."

The Committee on Freedom of Association hás not accepted provisions which appear to imply subordination of trade unions to the economic policy of the government, which minutely regulate the internal election procedures of a trade union, or which provide for the maximum number of votes for each organization within a federation. This kind of question must be freely decided upon by each organization. On the other hand, the Committee has accepted that the law may require that the majority of the members of a trade union must decide on certain questions which affect the very existence or structure of a union (adoption and amendment of the constitution, dissolution, etc.), if this is intended to guarantee the members' right to participate democratically in the organization.

The free election of representatives of employers' and workers' organizations can be seen from different points of view, and this has given rise to problems concerning the principles laid down in the Convention. This con- cerns in particular the procedures for trade union elections, eligibility conditions, re-election, and dismissal of leaders.The autonomy of organizations can be assured only if the organizations themselves regulate these questions in their constitutions. The supervisory bodies have repeatedly ruled against close control over elections by the authorities. This may constitute interference that violates the Convention, and carries the risk of arbitrary interference.

If supervision is deemed necessary, it should be exercised by a judicial authority in order to guarantee an impartial procedure.The access of trade union leaders to the workplace has also been subject to comment. The Committee of Experts considers that the rights arising from Articles 2 and 3 of the Convention imply that the leaders of a trade union must be able to remain in contact with the members of the union, and vice versa.

When the union is organized on a wider basis than the undertaking, the leaders should be able to have access to the workplaces if necessary, as an essential condition for the promotion and defence of the interests of their members. This question is also covered in the Workers' Representatives Recommendation, 1971 (No. 143), and, for rural workers, in the Rural Workers' Organisations Convention (No. 141) and Recommendation (No. 149), 1975.

Concerning financial administration, the Committee on Freedom of Association has stated that, in accordance with the principle of trade union autonomy, provisions which give the authorities the right to restrict the freedom of a trade union to administer and use its funds as it wishes for normal and lawful trade union purposes, are incompatible with the principles of freedom of association, which presuppose financial independence. Workers' organizations should not be financed in such a way as to allow the public authorities to enjoy discretionary powers over them.

On financial control over internal activities, the Committee on Freedom of Association has stated repeatedly that the rights laid down in Article 3 of the Convention do not prevent the supervision of the internal activities of a trade union if those activities violate legal provisions or rules. Nevertheless, it is important that such control and the power to take measures for the suspension or dissolution of the union should be exercised by the judicial authorities, to avoid the risk that measures taken by the administrative authorities should appear to be arbitrary.

The Committee of Experts considers that there is no infringement of the right of organizations to organize their administrations if, for example, the supervision is limited to the obligation to submit periodic financial reports or if there are serious grounds for believing that the actions of an organization are contrary to its rules or to the law (which should not violate the principles of freedom of association).

Similarly, there is no violation of the Convention if such verification is limited to exceptional cases, for example in order to investigate a complaint, or if there have been allegations of embezzlement. Both the substance and the procedure of such verifications should always be the subject of review by the competent judicial authority, affording every guarantee of impartiality and objectivity. The question of political activities ranks among the problems most frequently raised under Article 3 of the Convention.

The difficulty here lies in defining the scope of trade union action "for furthering and defending the interests of workers", which is the purpose of a workers' organization according to Article 10 of the Convention. This function of these organizations cannot be pursued strictly within the limits of worker-employer relations. Their activities naturally extend into the wider area of economic and social policy because of the repercussions of these policies on the situation and the interests of workers.

The Committee of Experts considers that legislative provisions which establish a close relationship between trade union organizations and political parties, as well as those which prohibit all political activities for trade unions, give rise to serious difficulties with regard to the principles of the Convention. At the same time, it is only in so far as trade unions do not allow their occupational demands to assume a clearly political aspect that they can legitimately claim that there should be no interference in their activities. In recent years the Committee of Experts has noted a significant change in this respect.

Until recently, legislation in several countries had established a close relationship between trade union organizations and the single authorized political party. Although this type of subordination still exists in some countries, the Committee has noted with satisfaction in recent years - and in particular since the fall of the Berlin Wall in 1989 - a clear trend towards its abolition. The right to strike51 Although the right to strike is expressly recognized in instruments such as the International Covenant on Economic, Social and Cultural Rights, the Inter-American Charter of Social Guarantees and the European Social Charter, it is not provided for in any ILO Convention or Recommendation.

Nevertheless, the ILO's supervisory bodies have had to deal with this question more often than any other subject in labour relations, and it is through this supervisory process that the ILO's principles have developed. The general principle is that "the right to strike is an intrinsic corollary of the right of association protected by Convention No. 87", and strike action therefore cannot be seen in isolation from industrial relations as a whole. The provisions of Convention No. 87 which give a legal basis for this principle are Articles 3, 8 and 10.

The general principle was recognized very early by the ILO' s supervisory bodies, in spite of the absence of an explicit provision in the Convention. As early as its second meeting in 1952, the Committee on Freedom of Association affirmed the principle of the right to strike, stating that it is one of the "essential elements of trade union rights";and stressed shortly afterwards that "in most countries strikes are recognised as a legitimate weapon of trade unions in furtherance of their members' interests".

The Committee of Experts stated in 1959 that the prohibition of strikes by workers other than public officials acting in the name of the public powers "may sometimes constitute a considerable restriction of the potential activities of trade unions ... [T]here is a possibility that this prohibition may run counter to Article 8, paragraph 2 of Convention No. 87". In its 1973 General Survey, it further stated that a "general prohibition of strikes constitutes a considerable restriction of the opportunities open to trade unions for furthering and defending the interest of their members and of the right of trade unions to organize their activities" (Article 3).

The supervisory bodies also consider that the right to strike is not an absolute right, and can be exercised only under certain conditions. Nevertheless, the juridical basis of recognition of the right rests fundamentally on Articles 3 and 10 of the Convention, which refer to the rights and objectives of workers' organizations. In any case, the Committee on Freedom of Association has accepted that under Convention No. 87 the right to call a strike is the sole preserve of trade union organizations.

The general prohibition of the right to strike is normally not acceptable. It may be justified in a situation of acute national crisis, but only for a limited period and to the extent necessary to meet the requirements of the situation. This means genuine crisis situations, such as those arising as a result of serious conflict, insurrection or natural disaster in which the normal conditions for the functioning of the society are absent.

It is acceptable to prohibit strikes for certain categories of workers, that is for certain public officials and for workers in essential services. For the former, the origin of the exception is found in the preparatory work for the Convention. The supervisory bodies have interpreted public service and essential services in a restrictive way as concerns strikes. The prohibition should be limited to officials exercising authority in the name of the State, and essential services are "those the interruption of which would endanger the life, personal safety or health of the whole or part of the population".

The Committee of Experts has stated that it would not be desirable - or even possible - to attempt to draw up a complete and fixed list of services which have been considered as essential. However, the Committee on Freedom of Association has accepted as essential services the hospital sector, the furnishing of water and electricity, and the telephone service and air traffic control; but it has not accepted governments' claims that banks, ports, petroleum, agricultural activities, teaching, or transport in general are essential services in the strict sense of the term.

Nevertheless, there are sometimes special circumstances under which non-essential services might become essential if a strike affecting them exceeds a certain duration or extent so that the life, personal safety or health of the population are endangered.As a condition for accepting the restriction or prohibition of strikes in these cases, compensatory guarantees should be provided to workers who are deprived of this essential means of defending their socio-economic and occupational interests.

These guarantees include conciliation and mediation procedures leading, in the event of deadlock, to arbitration machinery perceived to be reliable by the parties concerned. The workers should be able to participate in determining and implementing the procedure, which should provide sufficient guarantees of impartiality and rapidity; arbitration awards should be binding on both parties and, once issued, should be implemented rapidly and completely.

It is essential that all the members of the bodies entrusted with mediation and arbitration should not only be strictly impartial, but should also appear to be impartial both to the employers and to the workers concerned, in order to gain the confidence of both sides.Subject to the guarantees mentioned above, the prohibition of strikes in State undertakings is accepted by the Committee on Freedom of Association only when the undertaking is an essential service; it is not acceptable in others, to which the general principles on the right to strike apply.These principles on prohibition of strikes in essential services apply to both public-sector and private-sector undertakings.

In many cases the applicable legislation requires that certain conditions must be met before being able to declare a strike. These may include, for example, the exhaustion of conciliation or mediation procedures, a waiting period and advance notice; compliance with a collective agreement; or prior approval by a certain percentage of workers in a secret strike ballot. The Committee on Freedom of Association considers these requirements to be compatible with freedom of association.

However, the conditions laid down should be reasonable and in any event not such as to place a substantial limitation on the means of action open to trade unions. This could be the case when an absolute majority is required for the calling of a strike, or a quorum of two-thirds of the members, in particular where unions have a large number of members covering a large area.

As concerns the objectives of a strike, the supervisory bodies have said that the right to strike should not be limited to conflicts arising from collective bargaining. Although strikes that are purely political in character do not fall within the scope of freedom of association, trade unions should be able to have recourse to (peaceful) protest strikes, in particular to criticize the economic and social policy of the government.

The Committee of Experts pointed out in its 1994 General Survey that sympathy strikes, which are recognized as lawful in some countries, are becoming increasingly frequent because of the move towards the concentration of enterprises, the globalization of the economy and the delocalization of work centres. It considers that a general prohibition of sympathy strikes could lead to abuse and that workers should be able to take such action, provided the initial strike they are supporting is itself lawful.

The supervisory bodies have accepted that various forms of strike action are valid, and have said that limitations imposed by governments on such actions as a slow-down in work (go-slow strike), work rules being applied to the letter (work-to-rule), and occupation of the work place, would only be justified if the strike ceased to be peaceful. Special problems are created by the requisition or mobilization of workers who are on strike, and by the establishment of minimum services.

The supervisory bodies have said that requisitioning may be justified by the need to ensure the operation of essential services in the strict sense of the term, in circumstances of the utmost gravity during an acute national emergency.The imposition of minimum service may be justified in the event of a strike the extent and duration of which might result in an acute national crisis endangering the normal living conditions of the population.

This kind of service should meet two conditions: it must be limited to the operations which are strictly necessary to meet the basic needs of the population in terms of life, safety and health; and workers' organizations should be able to participate in defining such a service, along with employers and the public authorities. A system of minimum service may also be appropriate in strikes in essential services, as an alternative to a total prohibition of a strike.

The supervisory bodies consider that picketing is acceptable so long as it is in accordance with the law, remains peaceful and does not disturb public order. Finally, as concerns sanctions for strike action, the ILO supervisory bodies take into account their effect on labour relations, which may be endangered if the authorities apply severe sanctions in an inflexible way, especially penal sanctions. Arrests and dismissals of strikers on a large scale involve serious risks of abuse, and place freedom of association in grave jeopardy; and generally, the authorities should not have recourse to imprisonment for the mere fact of organizing or participating in a peaceful strike.

Article 4 of Convention No. 87 states that: "Workers' and employers' organisations shall not be liable to be dissolved or suspended by administrative authority." In other words, if it is necessary for the authorities to take such an extreme measure, it should be done by a judicial proceeding which provides all legal guarantees to the organization concerned. Other measures which would have similar effects to the suspension or dissolution of an organization would also violate the Convention if they are the kinds of measure covered by Article 4.

These might include cancellation of the registration of the organization or annulment or suspension of its legal personality, resulting in the loss of advantages essential to carrying out its activities. For Article 4 to be correctly applied, the right to appeal to the courts against an administrative decision is not sufficient; it is also necessary that the decision should not take effect until a final decision is handed down. In addition, the supervisory bodies have considered that the right of recourse to the courts does not always constitute a sufficient guarantee, since if the authorities have a discretionary right to take a decision, the judges may only ensure that the legislation has been correctly applied.

The judges should therefore be able also to deal with the substance of the case. The supervis-ory bodies hold the same position in relation to registration of organizations in order that they may acquire legal existence. Recourse to the courts has also been upheld by the Committee on Freedom of Association regarding the suspension or dissolution of organizations in situations when a state of national emergency has been declared.

Federations, confederations and international affiliation

Article 5 of the Convention provides that: "Workers' and employers' organisations shall have the right to establish and join federations and confederations". Article 6 goes on to stipulate that "[t]he provisions of Articles 2, 3 and 4 [of the Convention] apply to federations and confederations". In other words, the rights concerning the establishment of organizations, their administration and their activities, as well as concerning their suspension and dissolution, apply to bodies operating at a higher level as well as to firstlevel organizations.

Article 5 also provides that any "organisation, federation or confederation shall have the right to affiliate with international organisations of workers and employers". This lays down the legal basis for international solidarity of occupational organizations, and is very important for the functioning of the ILO because of the consultative status held by the major organizations of employers and workers.

The problems encountered in practice concerning federations and confederations are related principally to the constitution and activities of these organizations. The supervisory bodies have stated that the following constitute a violation of Article 5: prohibition on establishing federations or confederations; authorization to establish only one such organization for an occupation or region, or for the whole country; requirement of an excessively large minimum number of member organizations; prohibition on grouping organizations from different branches of activity or occupations; prohibition on establishing federations of organizations in different regions of the country; and more generally, any excessive conditions or requirement for prior authorization concerning their establishment.

The general principle is that under Article 2 of the Convention, to which Article 6 refers, first-level organizations have the right to establish and join, without prior authorization, the federations and confederations of their own choosing, subject only to their own statutes. In application of this principle, it would also be incompatible with Article 5 to prohibit the creation of a national confederation which would group organizations representing different economic sectors or regions of a country.

More specifically, the supervisory bodies have said that public-sector organizations should have the right to join federations and confederations which include organizations from the private sector, so long as this does not include an obligation to join strikes. As concerns unions of agricultural workers, a government's refusal to allow them to affiliate with a national centre of workers' organizations including industrial unions is incompatible with Article 5 of the Convention.Any restriction on the activities of federations and confederations concerning their rights to strike or to bargain collectively, also violate Article 5.

The Convention is violated if affiliation is made subject to prior authorization by the government, as this is not compatible with the principle of free and voluntary affiliation with such organizations.This principle also implies the right of national trade unions to receive assistance as a result of affiliation, including financial assistance and subsidies, remaining in contact and exchanging trade union publications, and sending representatives to meetings.

In 1948, when the Conference adopted Convention No. 87, it again examined the problem on the basis of a formula included in the preamble of the draft Convention prepared by the Office, under which workers, employers and their organisations, like any other person or body, were required to respect the law in the exercise of their rights. The workers, with the support of a number of government members, would not accept a formula which made the international right of freedom of association subject to national legislation.

Under Article 10 of the Convention provides: "In this Convention, the term 'organisation' means any organisation of workers or of employers for furthering and defending the interests of workers or of employers." The promotion and defence of the interests of its members are what distinguish and characterize an organization of workers or of employers, whatever it may be called.

In some cases the supervisory bodies have based themselves on this definition in formulating their conclusions. As already seen, in dealing with the question of the most representative organizations, a minority organization which by law does not have certain representation rights which are given preferentially or exclusively to the majority organization should still be able to exercise some functions in order to remain covered by this definition. The supervisory bodies have considered that a general prohibition on strikes considerably limits the functions of a trade union as recognized in this definition, and is incompatible with freedom of association.

5

Connecting Mental Health and Human Rights

The health and social services authorities have responsibility for providing assistance, care and treatment for people with mental health problems in accordance with their statutory duties and prevailing mental health law. Traditionally the provision of care and treatment has been broadly premised upon a principle of individual autonomy: the principle's underlying concept being the preservation of a person's right to decide whether to accept proposed care and/or treatment, assuming that person is deemed to have sufficient mental health and capacity to do so.

Most difficulties and complexities in mental health law, policy and practice, generally arise in three types of situation:

(1) Where a person is not mentally competent to make a relevant decision;

(2) Where a mentally competent person is unwilling to consent to proposed care and/or treatment; and/or

(3) Where a person with mental health problems presents a risk of harm to self and/or others.

Where health and social services professionals conclude that a person requires care and/or treatment, but that person is unable or unwilling to give consent, the law should facilitate the adoption of an appropriate course in the circumstances. Involuntary intervention in whatever form causes considerable controversy in the field of mental health, and raises a plethora of human rights concerns.

For example, pursuant to the prevailing mental health legislation in Northern Ireland, persons involuntarily detained may be treated against their will, even if mentally capable. The legislation permits the use of electro-convulsive therapy (ECT), a potentially irreversible treatment, in the treatment of competent persons. Such non-consensual intervention arguably constitutes one of the most invasive provisions in Northern Ireland law.

The law should provide a framework for the care and treatment of people with mental health problems that is specifically designed to facilitate only that degree of intervention which is appropriate in the given circumstances, whilst seeking to protect the rights and interests of the particular person. Consequently, it is imperative that Northern Ireland mental health law, policy and practice complies with applicable human rights law, and takes appropriate account of relevant human rights standards, to ensure that due regard is afforded to the rights, interests and dignity of persons with mental health problems.

The enactment of the Human Rights Act 1998 (which incorporates the European Convention into domestic law) and the establishment of the Northern Ireland Human Rights Commission have contributed to momentum for a critical evaluation of the mental health law, policy and practices applicable in this jurisdiction. The Commission has funded this research project specifically for the purpose of analysing Northern Ireland mental health law, policy and practice from a human rights perspective.

An initial consideration is the principles upon which mental health legislation should be based and whether these should be included in legislation and/or the Code of Practice. The principles on which the Mental Health (NI) Order 1986 should be currently interpreted are contained in the Code of Practice. These are that people with mental health problems should:

— "be treated and cared for in such a way as to maintain their dignity;

— receive respect for and consideration of their individual qualities and background -social, cultural, and religious;

— have their needs taken fully into account notwithstanding the fact that within available resources it may not always be practical to meet them;

— receive any necessary treatment or care with the least degree of control and segregation consistent with their safety and the safety of others;

— be discharged from any form of constraint or control to which they are subject under the Order immediately this is no longer necessary;

— be treated or cared for in such a way as to promote their self-determination and encourage personal responsibility to the greatest possible degree consistent with their needs, wishes and abilities".

The European Convention on Human Rights, its case law and the Council of Europe'sWhite Paper on mental health and human rights have focused more on the protection of negative rights than establishing general principles relating to people with a mental disorder, but as discussed later some more positive rights to services may be argued. The United Nations' 25 Mental Illness (MI) Principles were "the first step in providing a global set of minimum standards for protecting persons with mental illness and improving mental health care",and so are very useful but necessarily general.

The principles include that "all persons have the right to the best available mental health care, which shall be part of the health and social care system"; that "every person with a mental illness shall have the right to live and work, as far as possible, in the community"; and that "every patient shall have the right to be treated in the least restrictive environment and with the least restrictive or intrusive treatment appropriate to the patient's health needs and the need to protect the physical safety of others".

The Richardson Committee which reviewed the mental health law for England and Wales recommended that the new legislation should include statements of principle covering "informal care, the provision of the least restrictive alternative compatible with the delivery of safe and effective care, consensual care, reciprocity, respect of diversity and the recognition of the role of carers".

It also defined reciprocity as meaning "if society is to impose a duty to comply with care and treatment on some of those who suffer from mental disorder it must impose a parallel duty on health and social care authorities to provide an appropriate standard of care and treatment for those subject to compulsion".

Part One of the Draft Bill does refer to some of these principles but states they should be detailed in the Code of Practice rather than the Bill itself which perhaps lessens their impact. The Law Society has suggested that the principle of reciprocity should be included in the Mental Health Bill. In Scotland, the Millan Committeeproposed a very comprehensive list of principles to be included in the Act and Code of Practice: non discrimination, equality, respect for diversity, reciprocity, informal care, participation, respect for carers, least restrictive alternative, benefit and child welfare.

Some of these principles have been included in the Mental Health Act 2003. Establishing the underpinning principles and deciding which should be explicitly included in legislation would appear to be an important foundation for mental health law.

The main possibilities appear to be patient, client, service user, customer, consumer, survivor, people with mental disorder, people with mental health problems, people with mental health needs and people with learning disabilities. 'Patient' has been criticised for implying a passive, dependent role with the professional as expert and 'client' has sometimes been used as an alternative to move away from the medical model.

A recent survey,however, found most people preferred 'patient' to 'client'. 'Service user', 'consumer' and 'customer' all suggest choice but perhaps do not acknowledge that sometimes people do not have a range of options and are sometimes not using services voluntarily. The Acheson Report on inequalities in health found that:

— Mental health varies markedly by social class.

— The use of psychiatric, especially in-patient hospital services is positively correlated with high levels of deprivation and unemployment.

— Suicide is more common in men than in women, and in lower socio-economic groups.

— Caring for young children in disadvantaged circumstances, particularly as a lone mother, carries with it an increased risk of poor mental health.

— Race was identified as a significant factor, a finding reinforced in the National Service Framework for Mental Healthwhich stated that, at present, services are not meeting the needs of black and ethnic minority communities.

There is particular concern about the over-representation of young, black men sectioned under the Mental Health Act 1983 in England. These concerns have also recently been expressed locally by the Northern Ireland Council for Ethnic Minorities.Other equality issues have also been identified as important:

— Age has been highlighted as older people are less likely to be referred for counselling, are more likely to experience certain forms of mental health problems and suicide rates increase with age.The mental health needs of children and young people have also been dramatically under-estimated and there remain substantial gaps in service provision.This has lead to the unacceptable situation where young people are detained and treated on adult psychiatric wards.

— The impact of 'the Troubles' and sectarianism on mental health is a further local consideration.

— Researchhas also identified the discrimination and prejudice that lesbians, gay men and bisexual men and women face within mental health services, and the impact of oppression from wider society. Particularly alarming is the finding that lesbian and gay young people are up to six times more likely to attempt suicide than heterosexual young people.

— Finally, the combined impact of the many different forms of discrimination should be considered as it appears rare for one form of oppression to be experienced in isolation.

Inequalities in mental health arise, not only through broad social factors such as poverty, discrimination, isolation and poor housing, but also through the delivery of mental health services which may incorporate the discrimination of wider society and create, either actively or passively, inequalities of access to care. Access goes beyond the basics of physical and geographical access to how people find out about and perceive the services and how they are enabled to use them effectively.

Assessment and Civil Detention of People With Mental Health Problems

The area of the assessment and civil detention of people with mental health problems. The following issues arise in relation to this area and potentially cause interference with human rights:

— The definition of mental disorder;

— The process of assessment and civil detention;

— The rights of voluntary patients;

— The role of the nearest relative;

— Access to information and representation; and

— The potential extension of compulsory powers to the community.

Each of these issues separately and examines:

— The relevant international standards;

— Law, policy and practice in Northern Ireland;

— The potential human rights violations or concerns arising;

— The experience of other jurisdictions: in particular England, Wales and Scotland including the proposals for mental health law reform in those jurisdictions; and

—Makes recommendations in relation to addressing the human rights issues identified in Northern Ireland.

International Standards European Convention on Human Rights

Article 5.1 of the European Convention on Human Rights (ECHR) states: "Everyone has the right to liberty and security of person. No one shall be deprived of his liberty save in the following cases and in accordance with a procedure prescribed by law..." part (E) then allows "the lawful detention of persons for the prevention of the spread of infectious disease, of persons of unsound mind, alcoholics or drug addicts, or vagrants". The Convention therefore requires a finding of unsoundness of mind to justify detention but does not define the term.

The Council of Europehas suggested "an alternative proposal to the use of mental disorder is to use the concept of mental incapacity whereby decisions are based on the ability of the individual, as determined by medical and other professional staff, to understand the nature of treatment or admissions, weigh up the benefits of such, make a choice and communicate that choice".

The UN Principles

The United Nations'"Principles for the Protection of Persons with Mental Illness and for the Improvement of Mental Health Care" (the MI Principles) do not specifically define 'mental disorder' but Principle 4 states that "a determination that a person has a mental illness shall be made in accordance with internationally accepted medical standards". It is debatable whether this Principle entails that this determination should be made by a specialist, a psychiatrist, or whether any medical practitioner is qualified to do so. However, given the potential implications of this determination, a specialist assessment would appear more appropriate.

World Health Organisation

More recently the World Health Organisation has discussed the concept of mental health: "mental health has been defined variously by scholars from different cultures. Concepts of mental health include subjective well-being, perceived self-efficacy, autonomy, competence, intergenerational dependence and self-actualisation of one's intellectual and emotional potential, among others. From a cross-cultural perspective, it is nearly impossible to define mental health comprehensively. It is however, generally agreed that mental health is broader than a lack of mental disorder".

'Mental disorder' is defined in Article 3.1 of the Mental Health (Northern Ireland) Order 1986 as "mental illness, mental handicap and any other disorder or disability of mind". Article 3.2 specifically excludes detention "by reason only of personality disorder, promiscuity or other immoral conduct, sexual deviancy or dependence on alcohol or drugs".

Potential Human Rights Violations

The main human rights concern associated with the definition of 'mental disorder' is that if the definition is too broad and does not have specific exclusions it could allow the detention of people on the basis of moral, social, political or cultural judgements rather than mental health and safety necessity. As has been mentioned, because understanding of mental health is still developing it is difficult to define 'mental disorder' very precisely, however, it does not seem to be an adequate safeguard to defer entirely to medical opinion at the time of assessment.

There is currently no lower age limit which means that children can be detained using the Order and are sometimes placed in adult psychiatric wards which are inappropriate environments. Concerns have been raised that, at present, the diagnosis of personality disorder may be used to inappropriately restrict people's access to services.

The Richardson Committee in the Report of the Review of the Mental Health Act, 1983, recommended keeping the term 'mental disorder' and including a very broad definition within the new act with more specific definition in the Code of Practice. It also suggested, however, that learning disability should be removed when not coexisting with another 'mental disorder' as it is better viewed from a welfare, rather than a treatment, perspective.

A broad definition was indeed included in the Draft Mental Health Bill for England and Wales.It defined 'mental disorder' as "any disability of mind or brain which results in an impairment or disturbance of mental functioning" leaving further definition to the Code and not specifying any exclusions. The earlier controversial proposals involving the preventative detention of people diagnosed as having dangerous severe personality disorder have not been explicitly included in the Draft Bill but the lack of definition of 'mental disorder' and the extraordinarily wide meaning of 'treatment' do still allow for this form of detention.

A central issue of concern is that a system of indeterminate detention is premised on a concept that is ill-defined and controversial .The Joint Committee on Human Rights has responded that "the proposed definition of 'mental disorder' appears to us to be over-inclusive, potentially covering a number of conditions which would not normally be characterised as mental disorders and allowing health professionals to act as guardians of morality as well as health". The Law Societyhas suggested that further ways of qualifying these criteria would be to include: "(i) a capacity criterion and (ii) a 'health benefit' to replace the 'treatability' test".

Under the new Scottish Act 'mental disorder' is defined as 'any mental illness; personality disorder; or learning disability, however caused or manifested; and cognate expressions shall be construed accordingly'. The new Act also states that "a person is not mentally disordered by reason only of any of the following - sexual orientation; sexual deviancy; transexualism; transvestism; dependence on, or use of, alcohol or drugs; behaviour that causes, or is likely to cause, harassment, alarm or distress to any other person; acting as no prudent person would act". In the Republic of Ireland the Mental Health Act, 2001, defines 'mental disorder' as "mental illness, severe dementia or significant intellectual disability".

International Standards European Convention on Human Rights

In addition to Article 5.1(e) the minimum criteria for detention to be lawful under the European Convention on Human Rights (ECHR) were specified in Winterwerp v The Netherlands: "except in emergency cases, the individual concerned should not be deprived of his liberty unless he has been reliably shown to be of 'unsound mind'. The very nature of what has to be established before the competent national authority - that is, a true mental disorder - calls for objective medical expertise.

Further, the mental disorder must be of a kind or degree warranting compulsory confinement. What is more, the validity of continued confinement depends upon the persistence of such a disorder" .So, what is needed is a 'true mental disorder', established by medical expertise, of a kind or degree warranting compulsory confinement which is dependent on the persistence of the 'disorder'.

Although the Mental Health Review Tribunal system will be dealt with in more detail in a later Chapter these articles suggest a hearing should be speedy and perhaps automatic rather than dependent on a request. It seems obvious that a person with mental disorder may not be sufficiently able to make such a request, by reason of their mental disorder. A request dependent safeguard, where the person who has been detained has to apply for a hearing, in many circumstances amounts to no safeguard at all.

UN Convention on the Rights of the Child

For those under the age of 18, the UN Convention on the Rights of the Child sets international standards for the protection of children's rights. Article 23 states that a child with a mental disability should enjoy a full and decent life in conditions which ensure dignity, promote self-reliance and facilitate the child's active participation in the community. Article 24 provides for the right of the child to the enjoyment of the highest attainable standard of health and to facilities for the treatment of illness and rehabilitation of health.

States are under a positive obligation to ensure that no child is deprived of the right to access such health care services. If a child is deprived of his or her liberty then it is necessary to treat the child in a manner which takes into account his or her age. Article 37 states in particular that children should be separated from adults in detention unless it is considered in the child's best interests not to do so. The UK has entered a reservation to this aspect of the Convention.

The Mental Health (NI) Order 1986 sets out the conditions under which a person not involved in criminal proceedings may be compulsorily detained in hospital. Article 4(2) states: "An application for assessment may be made in respect of a patient on the grounds that (a) He is suffering from mental disorder of a nature or degree which warrants his detention in a hospital for assessment; and

(b) Failure to so detain him would create a substantial likelihood of serious physical harm to himself or to other persons".

Article 12 states that to be detained for treatment a doctor, who has been appointed by the Mental Health Commission for this purpose, usually the person's consultant psychiatrist, must state: "(a) that, in his opinion, the patient is suffering from mental illness or severe mental impairment of a nature or degree which warrants his detention in hospital for medical treatment; and (b) that, in his opinion, failure to so detain the patient would create a substantial likelihood of serious physical harm to himself or to other persons".

Under Article 10 if a person is only admitted for the assessment period and not further detained under Article 12 then, presumably to protect the person from discrimination, this period can be disregarded for certain purposes, although not in judicial proceedings. It is not clear, however, how far this protection extends. If, for example, an occupational health questionnaire asked the person if they had ever had any contact with mental health services, rather than had they ever been detained, could the person still legally deny this contact?

Children are detained within adult psychiatric units in Northern Ireland usually as a result of there being insufficient age-appropriate facilities available. This raises particular concerns as an adult ward is an inappropriate environment to care for children. Although the procedure for detention is prescribed by law, in accordance with Article 5.1 of the ECHR, it does not appear to offer the automatic, speedy involvement of a court or independent and impartial tribunal to determine the lawfulness of detention as required by Articles 5.4 and 6.1.

The persistence in detention alongside adults is contrary to Article 37 of the Convention on the Rights of the Child and was highlighted by the Committee on the Rights of the Child in its 2002 report. The current gaps in services for young peopleare creating huge difficulties for young people and mental health services as well as for parents, teachers and society in general.

The draft Mental Health Bill for England and Wales proposes to introduce a three stage process of examination, assessment and Tribunal, and similar proposals have been included in Scotland. The main proposed changes are that, except for offenders, a Mental Health Tribunal will consider all detention beyond 28 days and community based compulsory orders may be used.

The Mental Health Commission

In order to promote and protect the rights of people with mental health problems it is necessary to have a body that has clear responsibility for monitoring the implementation of mental health legislation and ensuring law, policy and practice is compatible with the agreed human rights standards. "Whatever the rights, 'the language of rights does not guarantee their realisation', risking accusations of them being a mere 'hollow mantra'.

Rights can only protect if society legally endorses and enforces them".In Northern Ireland the body charged with reviewing the care and treatment of people with mental health problems and monitoring the implementation of the Order is the Mental Health Commission (the Commission).

Mental Health and the Criminal Justice System

The law, policy and practice relevant to the human rights of people with mental health problems in contact with the criminal justice system. A number of issues will be considered including:

— The definition of this group;

— The concepts of responsibility and diversion;

— The relevant international standards;

— The current law, policy and services in Northern Ireland;

— The human rights implications of inappropriate and inadequate services.

There is no generally agreed operational definition of this grouphowever in this Chapter a broad definition will be used to include people who have not been convicted of an offence but may have committed an offence or are at a high risk of offending. A concise definition was used by the Social Services Inspectoratewho used 'mentally disordered offenders' to refer to "the full range of people with a mental disorder...who come into contact with the criminal justice system or are at risk of offending".

The four main groups in this area are:

— The people who have committed offences, some of which may not have been detected, or formally recorded, or reported, for example, non-reported assaults on staff in residential settings, as well as those referred for police investigation, or the subject of prosecution;

— People with mental health problems who are in custody, under probation or have been diverted away from the criminal justice system;

— People in the mental health services whose offences are ignored; and

— Those in special hospitals, regional secure unitsand under probation orders with a condition of psychiatric treatment.

The concept of responsibility is central to consideration of the human rights of people with mental health problems. It is a general principle of law "that the person liable to be punished should at the time of his crime have had the capacity to understand what he is required by law to do, and to control his conduct in the light of such decisions. Normal adults are generally assumed to have these capacities, but they may be lacking where there is mental disorder or immaturity, and the possession of these normal capacities is very often signified by the expression 'responsible for his action".

If someone is not responsible for his/her actions then it is argued they should not be punished for them and instead diverted to the appropriate services. The courts, therefore, have to consider a number of factors when deciding on the appropriate 'disposal'. These include "the safety of the public, retribution for the offence, the general deterrent effect of the sentence on the offender and on others, and...the interests of the offender...In general...there is a presumption against prosecuting a person who was mentally disordered at the time of the offence unless over-ridden by public interest as in serious cases".

It has also been suggested, however, that "excusing offending may not always be in the patients' interests [this quote refers specifically to in-patients]. The formal legal process can be a valuable exercise in reality testing. The patient can measure his or her own perceptions of his or her own behaviour against those of society. This can be useful preparation for life outside hospital. The knowledge that prosecution is routine rather than exceptional may deter further assaults and help aggressive patients to accept responsibility for their behaviour.

Sometimes encouraging such patients to accept responsibility can be clinically beneficial".It has also been highlighted that "diversion is an inherently offender-orientated process, its primary focus being his or her needs, and that there is therefore a danger that other principles within the criminal justice system, such as respect for public safety and the rights of victims may be jeopardised".The potential tension between the human rights of the person with mental health problems and the rights of others is a recurring theme in this area.

A number of cases under the European Convention of Human Rights have implications for the law, policy and practice affecting the human rights of this group.

In Northern Ireland the Mental Health (NI) Order 1986 provides a range of powers for the courts to seek more information about a person's mental health and, if appropriate, divert or transfer them from prison to hospital. The most frequently used power is a Hospital Order (under Article 44) which enables the Court to detain a person who has been convicted of an offence in hospital or (rarely) place them under guardianship rather than sending them to prison. The specific powers available to the Courts are:

— Remand to hospital for a report on the accused's mental condition (Article 42).

— Remand to hospital for treatment (Article 43).

— Order hospital admission or guardianship for people who have been convicted (Article 44) or impose an interim hospital order (Article 45).

— Restrict discharge from hospital (Article 47).

People may also be treated by mental health services as a condition of probation. The current policy context for this group was set out in the Regional Strategy for 1997-2002 which stated that "By 2002 a medium secure unit should be established in Northern Ireland and comprehensive arrangements should be in place so that, where appropriate, people with mental illness can be diverted from the criminal justice system".

The new Scottish Parliament then passed the Mental Health (Public Safety and Appeals) (Scotland) Act 1999 which allowed detention on the basis of treatment being likely to prevent deterioration. Anderson at al argued this breached Article 5.1(e) but this was rejected first by the Court of Session in 2000 and then at appeal by the Judicial Committee of the Privy Council in 2001 who agreed with the previous ruling that restricted patients could remain detained in the interests of public safety even if their condition was not susceptible to treatment.

Protection of Rights

People who have the capacity to make decisions about their everyday life should be encouraged to make these decisions. This is consistent with the right to respect for private life, the right to freedom of expression and association and the right to marry and found a family. Those who do not have capacity also have these rights but may require assistance in exercising them and in order to prevent abuse, there is an obligation on public authorities to provide appropriate protection.

In Northern Ireland at present there is a vacuum in law as regards decision-making for people with incapacity. There is no protection of their autonomy, a lack of clarity for those seeking to make decisions and a lack of access to justice when disputes arise. A particular area of concern is decision-making about sexual relationships. There is also a potential gap in practice as regards protection by the criminal justice system for those with learning disabilities due to presumptions being made about their capacity and a failure to make appropriate adjustments.

Everyone has the right to respect for his or her private life, which includes their sexual activity, as protected by Article 8 of the ECHR. Article 14 prohibits discrimination on the basis of disability in the protection of rights without reasonable and objective justification. Other relevant rights include the right to freedom of association (Article 11), the right to freedom of expression (Article 10) and the right to marry and found a family (Article 12). This can be interpreted as the need for states to ensure that people are appropriately protected from physical and sexual abuse.

This extends to ensuring that everyone can vindicate their right to respect for private life through the courts on an equal basis.The right not to be subjected to degrading treatment contained in Article 3 also imposes a positive duty on the state to arrange protection where necessary. Articles 8, 10, 11 and 12 can also be regarded as amounting to an obligation on states not to interfere with decisions made about sexual activity. If the approach of the state towards those with less capacity is different then that practice must be justified in accordance with Article 14.

Article 23 provides that a child with mental health difficulties should enjoy a full and decent life, in conditions which ensure dignity, promote self-reliance and facilitate the child's active participation in the community.

At present the common law is the basis for non-financial decision-making on behalf of most people with mental incapacity. There is no legislation dealing with decisionmaking in relation to people with incapacity. Disputes which arise can be settled in the High Court by way of a declaration as to what is the best decision in terms of common law, or by judicial review. The person with incapacity may be represented by the Official Solicitor. This is an expensive and cumbersome way to resolve disputes and can in reality only be accessed by those who are able to claim legal aid or those with sufficient independent means.

As regards protection from crime of those with mental disabilities, there is a general obligation to report arrestable offences to the police.Victims with learning disabilities are often reliant on care workers to help them report an offence to the police.The Mental Health Order provides that sexual intercourse with a woman with a severe mental handicap is an offence. The Department of the Director of Public Prosecutions for Northern Ireland sought to take account of the needs of vulnerable witnesses.

There is a fair hearing issue as regards the decision not to proceed with prosecution on the basis of the lack of competence of a victim or witness to give evidence. At present this decision may be made by a lawyer with no need for expert advice or representations from the person or his or her representative. The requirement on a person leading a vulnerable witness to prove that he or she is competent to give evidence is contrary to the common law presumption of competence, with the burden being on the person seeking to show incompetence to do so.

This makes it more difficult for a victim or a witness to participate in the justice system and can leave them in the vulnerable position of trying to overcome prejudice to prove that they are competent. The treatment of victims or witnesses with learning disabilities or mental health difficulties may be in contravention of section 75 of the Northern Ireland Act 1998 as there is not due regard paid in current procedures to their equality of opportunity with those who do not have a disability.

6

Human Rights and Conflict

During 2002-2003 much of the world's attention was on the military action in Iraq. Across the globe, however, armed conflicts continued to endanger and disrupt the lives of millions. Few of today's conflicts involve standing armies and pitched battles. They are mostly the consequence of ethnic, religious, resource or territorial disputes within a single state.

They may last for years and it can be difficult to distinguish between the various warring parties and to understand their goals and their motivation. This means that these conflicts often do not have a high profile in the outside world. Tragically, this does not reduce the effect of the conflict on those whom it touches. The worst violations of human rights often occur in internal conflicts, where the distinction between combatant and non-combatant is blurred.

The on-going conflicts in the Democratic Republic of Congo (DRC), Nepal and Chechnya are examples of this. Conflict creates an environment in which respect for human rights is often forgotten. Armed groups often think that they can murder, rape and loot with impunity. People in the conflict zones are forced to flee their homes and their land, becoming internally displaced or refugees abroad. And conflict has a serious negative effect on the enjoyment of economic, social and cultural rights including through disruption of hospitals, transport, policing, welfare systems and the economy.

During conflict many schools are forced to close and children lose their right to an education. In many countries children's rights are further jeopardised when they are forcibly recruited as soldiers. The wider effects of drawn out conflicts can destabilise entire regions. This is vividly illustrated in the Great Lakes region of Africa where conflict has engulfed Rwanda, Burundi and the DRC in the past decade. The on-going violence in Israel and the Occupied Territories has a serious effect on the stability and development of the whole of the Middle East. The abuse of human rights is not only a consequence of conflict but often also a warning sign of conflict to come.

An increase in attacks on minority groups, in the use of hate speech or in discriminatory laws not only indicates that a state may be on the edge of violence but can also directly contribute to conflict. The UK addresses these wider issues in its work to prevent conflict around the world. In particular, the FCO works strategically with the MOD and DFID to identify and act on areas of potential conflict. The Global Conflict Prevention Pool focuses resources on practical projects to diffuse tension including through building respect for human rights.

This year there have been further attempts to secure peace in Sri Lanka, Sudan and Burundi. There has been no fresh outbreak of violence in Angola or between Ethiopia and Eritrea. Strengthening the culture of human rights in all these countries will be vital in maintaining the peace. Last year, the UK worked in post-conflict situations around the world on projects that included building free and independent media in Afghanistan, training for human rights trainers for the districts of Rwanda and a radio series and regional training programme to help sustain the peace process in Burundi.

Conflict Prevention

The FCO, the Department for International Development (DFID) and the Ministry of Defence (MOD) set up two funds in 2001-the Africa Conflict Prevention Pool and the Global Conflict Prevention Pool. The pools have now been operating for two financial years with the joint Public Service Agreement (PSA) target: "to improve the effectiveness of the UK contribution to conflict prevention, leading to a reduction in the number of people whose lives are affected by violent conflict and a reduction in potential sources of future conflict, where the UK can make a difference ".

DFID chairs the Africa Conflict Prevention Pool, which has £50 million for programmes in sub-Saharan Africa in 2003 -2004. The FCO chairs the Global Conflict Prevention Pool with a budget of £74 million for 2003 - 2004 for programmes in a wide range of countries outside Africa, and for thematic strategies such as security sector reform which aim to improve the understanding of what types of intervention are successful and spread best practice.

The pools primarily address the medium and long-term causes of conflict and tension, although there are also some short-term interventions. These include aspects of social exclusion and human rights abuses that are related to conflict. The joined-up approach to conflict prevention is now becoming embedded within the three departments, bringing better focus and cohesion to the UK Government's response to hanging situations around the world.

In the global pool there are now 14 strategies covering conflict or potential conflict in Afghanistan, the Balkans, Belize/Guatemala, Central and Eastern Europe, the former Soviet Union, India and Pakistan, Indonesia/East Timor, the Middle East and North Africa, Nepal and Sri Lanka.

There are thematic strategies dealing with security sector reform, small arms and light weapons, the UN's capacity to manage conflict and its peacekeeping operations and the OSCE's activities. Most of the programmes include human rights and governance projects, where these relate to the underlying cause of a particular conflict: improving these areas is vital in preventing or managing conflict and in post-conflict reconstruction.

For example, Balkans Conflict Prevention Strategy provides funds to GONG, a local NGO in Croatia ,which encourages people to play an active part in the democratic process. GONG monitors elections and educates people about election laws and processes. It also runs a range of ongoing programmes, including the Open Parliament project, which gives citizens access to parliamentary sessions, and the Citizens 'Hour project, which encourages regular communication between constituents and their elected representatives.

The Nepal Conflict Prevention Strategy helps fund work by the Nepali NGO the Centre for the Victims of

Torture (CVICT), which trains medical professionals to recognise, record and treat victims of torture. CVICT has set up mobile clinics and a women-only treatment centre in Kathmandu, and is training lawyers to provide legal support to victims. The pool also funds the development of a community mediation programme in 11 districts across Nepal, and a series of small projects to help human rights organisations raise human rights awareness and increase accountability.

These projects include capacity-building work for the National Human Rights Commission and support for the UN OHCHR to establish a presence in Nepal. The Global Conflict Prevention Pool will publish a report later this year on its operation so far. The report describes the global pool strategies and the programmes they fund. A responsible and independent media, free from manipulation, is an essential part of democratisation. An independent media is vital for a nation to resolve conflict, to enable people to participate in politics, and for long-term peace and stability.

But in the past two decades in Afghanistan ,many journalists fled the country or were killed. Those who survived within the country did so by strictly censoring their own work. New media ventures are emerging quickly in Afghanistan, but the basic principles of responsible reporting are still largely unknown. Institute for War and Peace Reporting (IWPR) work is therefore helping to develop a free and democratic media in Afghanistan.

African leaders and institutions have taken a greater role in resolving conflict in the past 18 months. There has been solid progress in tackling some of Africa's big conflicts. In Angola, the civil war ended with the defeat of UNITA in 2002. Credible peace processes moved forward in Burundi and Sudan. Sierra Leone continued to onsolidate peace. However, the African political environment has remained fragile and prone to conflict, as demonstrated in the outbreak of civil war in Côte d 'Ivoire in September 2002, the continued violence in the DRC and the turmoil in Liberia.

The UK is concerned about all conflicts in Africa. The problem of conflicts in Africa and to galvanise international and African efforts to tackle the problem effectively through the UN, the EU, the G8 Africa Action Plan and through the bilateral dealings with African and non-African partners.

At the G8 Evian Summit in June 2003, G8 leaders endorsed a Joint G8-Africa Plan to Enhance African Capabilities to Undertake Peace Support Operations. This plan aims to mobilise technical and financial assistance so that, by 2010, African countries are able to engage more effectively to prevent and resolve violent conflict on the continent and undertake peace support operations in accordance with the United Nations Charter.

The plan identifies a number of building blocks that will help channel existing resources in support of the developing African vision and institutional framework for peace and security on the continent. Early building blocks, to be achieved by 2010, include: the establishment, equipping and training of coherent, multinational, multi-disciplinary standby brigade capabilities at the African Union (AU) and regional level that would be available for UN-endorsed missions; the development of capacities to provide humanitarian, security and reconstruction support for complex peace support operations; and the development of continental and sub-regional institutional capacities to prevent conflict.

Bilaterally, military training teams in South Africa, Ghana and Kenya to enhance regional peacekeeping capacity. Through the UK's Africa Conflict Prevention Pool, continued to fund the Conflict Management Centre at the African Union's Directorate of Peace and Security in Ethiopia. The Africa Conflict Prevention Pool is now in its third year of operation. The pool is chaired by the Secretary of State for International Development Baroness Amos and drives UK policy on conflict prevention and resolution in Africa.

It draws on diplomatic, military and developmental expertise and tools from across the FCO, the MOD and DFID. In the Great Lakes, low-level conflict and serious human rights violations have continued in the DRC, particularly in the east of the country.

The Africa Conflict Prevention Pool has also supported disarming, demobilising and repatriating Rwandan rebels fighting in eastern DRC. This is a central part of the peace process and an important priority. In West Africa, the Economic Community of West African States (ECOWAS) and France have been working on resolving the conflict in Côte d 'Ivoire . In Ghana ,the Africa Conflict Prevention Pool is funding the Kofi Annan International Peacekeeping Training Centre, which will become a regional centre of excellence for training in conflict management.

The Africa Conflict Pool continued to support peacekeeping training at the Ghana armed forces and staff college in Accra. In southern Africa , a good working relationship with South Africa to prevent and resolve conflict in the rest of the continent have developed. Diamonds underpin the economies of many developing countries. In India ,800,000 people are employed in the diamond industry. Botswana ,whose economy thrives in comparison with some of its neighbours, would be far lessprosperous without its diamonds. But diamonds and the wealth they provide can sometimes be more of a curse than a blessing: in Sierra Leone and Angola ,rebel forces have relied on illegal diamond mining to fund their activities and support conflict.

In the past two years there has been a huge international effort to hoke off the flow of these so-called 'conflict diamonds', not only to protect the lives of those in areas affected by civil wars, but also to protect those employed in the legitimate diamond industry worldwide from the very real threat of a consumer boycott of all diamonds.

On 5 November 2002 at Interlaken in Switzerland, the governments of 52 diamond producing and trading nations endorsed the final Kimberley Process document, which constituted the blueprint for an international certification scheme to close the world's markets to conflict diamonds. The Interlaken Declaration is the culmination of two years of co-operation between governments, industry and civil society. It set a deadline of 1 January 2003 for governments and industry to implement the certification scheme.

EU member states and the European Commission began preparing the legislation to implement the certification scheme in the European Community. The FCO set up a new unit to operate the scheme in the UK. The Government Diamond Office is responsible for verifying that diamonds for export are conflict-free and for issuing export certificates. It has recruited a team of diamond experts who will carry out inspections of export consignments with FCO officials.

In the same vein of tripartite co-operation upon which the original Kimberley Process negotiations were based, industry and civil society representatives attended workshops organised by the FCO. The workshops developed working procedures that would place as light an administrative burden as possible on the industry, while maintaining the integrity of the scheme.

Drug Trafficking

The cultivation, production and trafficking of illicit drugs fuels disorder and instability in many parts of the world. In Afghanistan, where much of the world's heroin originates, the drugs trade has been a major factor in sustaining conflict. In Colombia, which produces around 80 per cent of the world's supply of cocaine, the drugs industry has intensified the internal conflict. Illegal armed groups fighting over lucrative trafficking routes have abused people's human rights and caused large numbers of people to flee the fighting, and thus become internally displaced.

The consumption of drugs brings human suffering and social exclusion for addicts and their families both in the West and along trafficking routes in countries such as Iran, Pakistan and Turkey. In Jamaica, which is often used by traffickers as a transit route, levels of violence have increased. Drugs money and the proceeds of other international crime distort economies and threaten financial systems.

The UK tackles international drugs issues bilaterally and through multilateral fora such as the UN, EU and G8. In December 2002 the UK Government published its Updated Drug Strategy 2002 .This builds upon progress and lessons learned since the launch in 1998 of the ten-year strategy Tackling Drugs to Build a Better Britain .The strategy has four main strands: young people, communities, treatment and availability. The FCO focuses its activity on achieving the targets addressing the availability of drugs.

Around 90 per cent of the heroin in the UK originates in Afghanistan .In addition, opiate addiction rates are rising in Afghanistan and neighbouring countries. The fall of the Taliban provided with a unique opportunity to target the drugs trade in one of its main strongholds. The UK is spending £25 million in 2003 to assist the Afghan government to implement its national drug control strategy. This includes supporting law enforcement,reducing demand, helping people find alternative livelihoods and building judicial capacity.

The FCO Drugs and Crime Fund has supported counter-narcotics initiatives, such as counter-narcotics training courses for the Afghan police. Funded by the FCO, and provided by HM Customs and Excise, the training covers basic investigation and intelligence techniques, drugs recognition, evidence gathering, legislation and human rights. The Drugs and Crime Fund supported UN projects to develop local capacity in controlling drugs and helping people find alternative livelihoods, and another UN project in Iran to raise drug awareness among Afghan refugees returning to Afghanistan.

The programme presents information on the risks and consequences of cultivating drugs, processing, trafficking and abuse through radio, video and pamphlets. Activities to address the source of opiates in Afghanistan are complemented by bilateral assistance to neighbouring states that are affected by trafficking into Europe. FCO funding has allowed Pakistani NGOs to expand their activities to regional centres where addicts are rehabilitated and trained to take on sustainable livelihoods.

Refugees

A refugee is a person who "owing to a well-founded fear of being persecuted for reasons of race, religion, nationality, membership of a particular group, or political opinion, is outside the country of his nationality, and is unable to or, owing to such fear, is unwilling to avail himself of the protection of that country.

The UN High Commissioner for Refugees (UNHCR) currently cares for nearly 20 million uprooted and vulnerable people. Eighty per cent of the world's refugees are women and children. Flows of refugees and people who are displaced within their own countries are very often the result of conflicts and human rights abuses.

The UNHCR was set up in 1951 with a limited three-year mandate to help resettle the people in Europe who were unable to return to their homes after the Second World War. Today, the UNHCR protects refugees in several ways and its work is closely connected to broader progress in human rights.

Using the 1951 Geneva Refugee Convention as its major tool, it ensures the basic human rights of vulnerable people and ascertains that refugees will not be returned involuntarily to a country where they face persecution. In the longer-term, the UNHCR helps civilians repatriate to their homeland, integrate in countries of asylum or resettle in third countries. It also seeks to provide at least a minimum of shelter, food, water and medical care in the immediate aftermath of any refugee exodus.

However, many economic migrants misuse asylum laws in order to enter and work in developed countries. The widespread misuse of asylum systems is threatening to undermine the 1951 Geneva Convention, designed to protect people who are fleeing persecution for their beliefs or identity. Refugees in need of international protection and economic migrants, who are not entitled to legal asylum. When a person who has not been subject to persecution claims asylum, expensive procedures, designed to establish if a person is a refugee, are called into play.

The resources used to process that claim could have helped a person who does have a genuine fear of persecution, such as those who have spoken out against a repressive regime in their home country. Economic migrants normally leave their country voluntarily to seek a better life. The UNHCR is strengthening the 1951 Refugee Convention with new proposals in Convention Plus. These proposals will make sure that the international protection regime protects those who are forced to flee conflict for their own well-being and challenges the ways some people are using the Refugee Convention for economic migration.

The UK was active in UNHCR's Global Consultations and the Agenda for Protection. An international agreement setting out the roles and responsibilities of countries of origin, transit and destination would be a significant step forward in discouraging secondary movement.

In an important step towards finding long-term solutions, the UK set out its commitments to durable solutions such as voluntary return, integration and resettlement in the Nationality Immigration and Asylum Act 2002, and is establishing a UK refugee resettlement scheme later in 2003. "The European Union must develop a unified internal approach along with new global strategies if it is to effectively address the politically charged issues of asylum and migration." The UK believes that the current system of protection for refugees is failing on several levels.

Support for refugees is badly distributed and is failing to help the people who need it most. The asylum system usually requires people fleeing persecution to enter the West illegally, often by paying criminal organisations huge sums of money; and up to 70 per cent of those claiming asylum in Europe do not meet the criteria of full refugees. It is essential to develop new international approaches to refugee protection. The UK has put forward proposals to set up 'zones of protection ',which would aim to manage better the asylum process globally, reduce unfounded applications and provide more equitable protection for genuine refugees.

More than 90 per cent of the world's refugees remain in developing countries. It cannot be right that only a tiny minority -not necessarily the most persecuted or the most vulnerable -benefit from the effective protection that developed states an provide. The remainder languish in often appalling conditions without any prospect of a durable solution to their plight. Zones of protection complement the EU approach to asylum called for at a Summit of EU leaders at Tampere, Finland, in 1999;and also the work initiated at a meeting of EU leaders in Seville in June 2002 to tackle illegal immigration.

The UK's proposals for 'zones 'draw on the UNHCR's plans for modernising the international protection system in Convention Plus. This requires an international approach. Working with EU partners and the countries of the developing world, will need to use diplomatic, economic and if necessary military resources to tackle the underdevelopment and conflict that blight so many lives.

In principle, better regional protection should discourage flows of irregular migrants into Europe. Within these zones, they would receive the protection and humanitarian support they are seeking until conditions were suitable for their return. The UK will develop these proposals in line with its international obligations and in close collaboration with organisations such as UNHCR. For the Zones of Protection to become credible and workable solutions, they must start from the premise of international co-operation and partnership between origin, transit and destination countries.

NGOs also have important roles to play. These proposals are not about shifting the responsibility of refugee protection onto the already stretched resources of developing countries; rather they seek to make the international protection regime sustainable in the modern world. The internal conflicts in Burma and the safety and welfare of refugees and internally displaced people who are fleeing fighting and persecution. Many of them go to Thailand ,where the Thai authorities have a long record of providing a safe haven. The border areas of Burma are too unstable to allow refugees to return home.

DFID funds the work of the UNHCR, the International Committee of the Red Cross (ICRC) and the Burmese Border Consortium (BBC) on the Thai-Burma border. The BBC is a consortium of humanitarian agencies that provides basic food and relief supplies and, since 1984, BBC has taken the lead role in providing relief assistance to the registered refugees in Thailand. DFID is one of many agencies supporting the consortium's work. DFID funded UNHCR's work in 2002 -2003 to promote the protection, safety and well-being of Burmese refugees in Thailand until the conditions are met for their safe, voluntary repatriation.

In Cambodia ,the plight and resettlement of 900 Vietnamese refugees came to a head in the wake of a US decision in 2002 to offer all of them resettlement in the US. The resettlement programme is underway, but a small group of fewer than 30 remains in Cambodia. The Cambodian government has indicated by its actions that it will no longer accept refugees crossing into Cambodia and has said that new arrivals will be considered as illegal migrants and will be deported.

In 2001, over 200,000 refugees from Sierra Leone and Liberia were living in camps in southern Guinea .The refugee crisis worsened in early 2003 following intensified fighting in Liberia and the rebellion in Côte d 'Ivoire. Many of the new arrivals spent long periods of time in the bush, walking long distances to arrive at the camps in a weakened state. The N 'Zérékoré region of southern Guinea is now home to some 64,000 registered refugees. Many others live in surrounding towns and villages.

The UNHCR runs the main camps with support from Mèdicin Sans Frontières (MSF), the European Commission Humanitarian Aid Office (ECHO) and other NGOs in the region. UNHCR began a repatriation programme for Sierra Leoneans in 2002. The arduous 10-day drive through Guinea was shortened when UNHCR constructed a more direct road from the camps to Sierra Leone, cutting the journey time down to three days.

This has allowed the successful repatriation of most Sierra Leoneans, freeing space in camps to allow other refugees to be moved away from dangerous border areas. However, the environmental impact in Guinea is considerable. Camps require large amounts of resources, especially firewood, water and, with World Food Programme assistance, food for up to 30,000 people. Often the conditions inside camps are better than in surrounding villages, creating tensions between the local population and refugees.

The influx of people to the region has led to increased crime and the highest HIV/AIDS rates in the country. The extra drain on scarce resources has forced prices up in surrounding towns. UNHCR has worked hard to improve conditions in the camps: working to prevent sexual violence, instigating rubbish collection, and using local people to work on building projects within the camp to aid integration and ensure some of the money generated goes into the community. Sensitisation programmes educate refugees to their situation and options for the future and on their responsibilities.

The UK continues to co-operate with other countries and international organisations to fight the exploitation of migrants by people smugglers who put lives at risk by using ships that are overcrowded and not seaworthy to transport them across the seas. The UK Government is committed to fulfilling its obligations under the 1951 United Nations Convention relating to the Status of Refugees. It is right that those who are fleeing persecution should be given the protection they need. Each application for asylum is considered on its individual merits to determine whether the applicant has demonstrated a well-founded fear of persecution in his or her country of nationality for one of the reasons set out in the convention. These are reasons of race, religion, nationality, membership of a particular social group or political opinion.

However, the convention has increasingly been misused and exploited, and major receiving states spend billions operating elaborate processes to deal with asylum claims, many of which are not well-founded. On 7 November the Nationality Immigration and Asylum (NIA) Act 2002 received Royal Assent. A central aim of this legislation was to deter unfounded asylum claims and to discourage economic migrants who apply for asylum in the hope of spending months or years in the UK before being removed.

Speeding up the process will not only deter unfounded claims but also enable those with genuine claims to be granted asylum more quickly. The non-suspensive appeal (NSA) process is a key element of the UK Government's strategy to reduce unfounded asylum claims. The NIA Act provides for UK immigration caseworkers to certify as clearly unfounded any asylum or human rights claim from a designated list of countries, unless they are satisfied that the claim is not clearly unfounded. The NIA Act further provides that once caseworkers have issued an applicant with a certified refusal we can remove them from the UK without them having a right to appeal in this country. They can, however, lodge an appeal from the country to which they have been removed.

The Act initially listed 10 EU accession states as designated countries: Cyprus, the Czech Republic, Estonia, Hungary, Latvia, Lithuania, Malta, Poland, Slovakia and Slovenia. It provides a mechanism for the UK Government to add to the list of designated countries by affirmative order procedure (an order which must be approved by both Houses of Parliament).

To add a country to the list the Home Secretary must be satisfied that there is, in general, no serious risk of persecution in that country and removal of a person to that country would not, in general, be a breach of the UK's obligations under the European Convention on Human Rights. In April, a further seven countries were added to the NSA list: Albania, Bulgaria, Jamaica, Macedonia, Moldova, Romania and Serbia and Montenegro. In July seven more countries were added:

Bangladesh, Bolivia, Brazil, Ecuador, South Africa, Sri Lanka and Ukraine. A designated country is not assumed to be entirely safe for every national of that country. But such a country is safe formost of its people. The majority of NSA cases are processed at Oakington. The applicant resides at Oakington while their claim is decided, usually for a period of 7-10 days.

The conflict in Chechnya has now entered its fourth year. The UK has always recognised Russia's territorial integrity and its right to defend its citizens from terrorism. Russian and international human rights organisations believe that Russian forces are responsible for the majority of these disappearances. Chechen groups, particularly extremist elements associated with Al Qa 'ida, have carried out terrorist attacks within Chechnya and elsewhere in Russia, including last year's theatre siege in Moscow and a wave of suicide bombings in Moscow, Chechnya and North Ossetia. The majority of those killed or injured in these attacks have been civilians.

Chechen militants have also murdered members of the civil administration, have maltreated and killed Russian prisoners and continue to use landmines indiscriminately. President Putin made a series of commitments to the Chechen people shortly before the referendum vote. He promised a broad degree of autonomy for Chechnya within the Russian Federation, presidential and parliamentary elections before the end of the year, amnesty for militants who had not committed serious offences, compensation payments for people whose homes had been destroyed in the fighting, and a reduction in the number of troops whose subsequent role would be to support the local Chechen police force.

Continued human rights violations remain a significant obstacle to a lasting political settlement. The failure to curb these abuses and to prosecute those responsible risks creating a climate of impunity in the republic, which in turn could bolster support for extremists such as those responsible for the recent wave of suicide attacks in Chechnya. For the fourth year in succession, the UK supported an EU-sponsored Resolution on Chechnya at this year's session of the UN Commission on Human Rights. The UK worked hard in Geneva and in capitals to secure the resolution's adoption but unfortunately the resolution was defeated by 21 votes to 15, with 17 abstentions.

In May 2002, Chechnya and the neighbouring Republic of Ingushetia agreed a 20-point plan to close down camps for internally displaced persons (IDP) in Ingushetia and to repatriate the residents to temporary shelters in Chechnya. However, many residents did not want to return to Chechnya, primarily because of the security situation in the republic and because the temporary shelters in Chechnya were inadequate.

The Ingush government withdrew food, water and energy supplies to a number of camps in late summer and early autumn, presenting the residents with little choice but to move. Sustained international pressure, in which the UK played a leading role within the EU, reminded the Russian government of their obligations under the 1951 UN Convention on Refugees and stressed that any movement by displaced persons must be strictly voluntary.

In mid-December, President Putin publicly criticised the closure programme and ordered it to stop, until more suitable arrangements for handling IDPs could be found. The UK also remains a major contributor to humanitarian aid programmes for Chechen IDPs. The conflict between Armenia and Azerbaijan over Nagorno Karabakh has remained frozen since Russia brokered a ceasefire in 1994. The two countries have been involved in negotiations to resolve the conflict under the auspices of the OSCE Minsk Group, first established in 1992.

Through the Global Conflict Prevention Pool (GCPP), the FCO, DFID and the MOD are financing a project to underpin the Nagorno Karabakh conflict resolution process. Under this project, a consultant will designand implement a range of separate, but linked, activities to improve long-term social and economic development possibilities in the two countries and thereby improve the prospects for a permanent settlement of the Nagorno Karabakh conflict.

The GCPP continues to fund the South Caucasus Parliamentary Initiative, a project facilitated by the UK NGO LINKS that brings together parliamentarians from Georgia, Armenia and Azerbaijan to discuss regional co-operation. Militant violence in Kashmir is often indiscriminate, killing and injuring civilians. The militants must renounce violence and pursue their objectives through peaceful, democratic means. The Kashmir problem can only be resolved through dialogue between India and Pakistan that takes account of the wishes of the Kashmiri people.

The Maoist insurgency in Nepal continues to affect the country's stability. The Maoists, who have been operating an armed struggle since 1996, now effectively control half of Nepal. The conflict has pushed the economy deeper into trouble and efforts towards a peace process had, until recently, been further complicated by the suspension of the normal democratic institutions, including parliament.

The Nepalese government and the Maoists declared a ceasefire on 29 January 2003. It is too early to speculate on how this will develop, but it is the first real opportunity to kick-start a peace process since the last round of negotiations failed in November 1994. The signing of a ceasefire Code of Conduct on 13 March 2003 further boosted efforts towards a substantive peace process. The UK has urged all sides to observe and respect the Code of Conduct, and to understand that any violence, abduction, intimidation or extortion is not only a breach of the Code of Conduct, but also a violation of democratic standards and human rights.

Despite the ceasefire, the Nepalese people continue to face a human rights crisis and there are reports of human rights violations by both the Nepalese security forces and the Maoists. There is now undeniable proof that both sides committed numerous human rights abuses against civilians and combatants during the conflict. The Maoists were guilty of widespread torture and execution.

The security forces were responsible for extensive and systematic illegal detentions, torture and summary executions. Reports of new cases have decreased since the ceasefire, but human rights violations continue and the halt in the conflict has brought to light previously unreported cases.

An inactive judiciary and civil society has compounded Nepal's human rights problems. Civil society's failure to monitor the situation effectively makes it difficult to assess the overall human rights picture and fear and intimidation puts pressure on the legal system. Lawyers continue to be wary of representing those who have been arrested on charges related to insurgency, for fear of being arrested themselves.

The UK continues to lead initiatives on co-ordinating the international community's response to the conflict. On 24 February 2003 Sir Jeffrey James as the UK Special Representative for Nepal. Sir Jeffrey impressed on the Nepalese authorities, through regular contact with senior Nepalese government and military officials, the need to address its human rights record and that failure to do so risks undermining the developing peace process.

A British army team of human rights and legal experts visited representatives of the Royal Nepalese Army (RNA) to raise awareness of the operational aspects of human rights and to investigate strengthening the recently formed RNA human rights cell and increase accountability. In September 2002, DFID-Nepal began a programme of police reform that has a strong human rights element. The programme will establish an independent police commission and support community policing. The UK has provided £11,000 for the National Human Rights Commission and will provide an additional £30,000 this year.

The Nepalese government signed a headquarters agreement with the International Committee of the Red Cross (ICRC) and gave the ICRC access to all detention facilities. DFID funds ICRC Nepal operations with £1.5 million annually. The UK supported Advocacy Forum, a key human rights NGO, with £30,000 for its monitoring activities. These NGOs will identify a coalition of Nepalese NGO partners for longer-term work in civil society capacity-building. DFID is currently funding the Centre for Victims of Torture (CVICT) over three years to establish community mediation fora, including groups to advocate for human rights and justice. DFID is also planning to extend the scope of an important conflict resolution programme, which includes a component for victims of torture. In February 2002 the Sri Lankan government and the Liberation Tigers of Tamil Eelam (LTTE) signed a formal agreement to cease hostilities and begin peace talks to end the tragic internal conflict that has caused suffering in Sri Lanka for over 20 years.

Five rounds of peace talks were held and at the third round of talks in December 2002 the parties agreed to explore a solution founded on the principle of self-determination for the Tamil people, based on a federal structure within a united Sri Lanka. The LTTE suspended participation in the peace talks on 21 April 2003 and did not attend a Donors Conference in Tokyo in June, citing poor implementation of development projects. However, the ceasefire remains in operation.

The government has submitted proposals to the LTTE for an interim administration in which the LTTE will have a majority role within the region, with powers overadministration and development. The LTTE is considering the proposals and is expected to respond by September. UK Ministers have had regular contact with the two Sri Lankan ministers leading the peace process and the Sri Lankan prime minister met Prime Minister Tony Blair when he visited the UK in June 2003.

The UK is the second largest bilateral donor to Sri Lanka. At the Tokyo conference the UK pledged £43 million over a three-year period. In the wake of the Bindunuwewa rehabilitation camp massacre of 25 October 2000,the international community and human rights organisations criticised the Sri Lankan government for not providing adequate security to the detainees.

A special presidential commission was set up to inquire into the incident while a prosecution also progressed separately under normal Sri Lankan law. The commission made recommendations to the president on how to prevent such incidents in the future and also identified the shortcomings on the part of the police which had failed to prevent the massacre. Following preliminary inquiries, the Sri Lankan attorney-general recommended that the case be taken up as a trial-at-bar (trial without jury, heard by three judges of the high court).

Initially, 41 suspects -10 of whom were police officers and the rest of whom were villagers -were harged on 83 counts in relation to the attack on the 41 inmates of the camp. The charges included the murder of 27 inmates and the attempted murder of the other 14 as well as unlawful assembly. Twenty-three of those charged were released due to lack of evidence. The trial proceeded against the remaining 18 defendants. The trial lasted for nearly 16 months ending at the beginning of July 2003. Out of the 18 defendants, were cleared of all charges, and five, including two police officers, were sentenced to death. The five are expected to appeal.

On election day in December 2001 in Udathalawinna, supporters of General Anuruddha Ratwatte,a former deputy defence minister, allegedly killed 10 Muslim youths. The general, his two sons and 11 others were arrested and the case was committed for a trial-at-bar. The accused made several unsuccessful applications for bail. However, on 11 July 2003 the supreme court decided to grant the accused bail but directed them not to leave the country. The trial hearings continue.

During earlier rounds of peace talks, the LTTE made commitments to the Sri Lankan government and the international community to stop child recruitment: since the ceasefire, some 350 children have been returned to their families. The LTTE has developed an action plan with UNICEF on children affected by war in the north and east and as part of this, a rehabilitation centre has recently opened. However, reports of child recruitment continue.

Reports of extortion by the LTTE continue. There have also been a number of assassinations of Tamil politicians opposed to the LTTE. The strategy UK Support for Peace building and Reconciliation in Sri Lanka. On the security sector, the UK funds a human security project in the east (to develop an early warning mechanism to mitigate and prevent conflict), and an audit of existing peace work (to encourage co-operation and avoid overlap).

Social issues including human rights and education have also been identified as a main area for support under the High Commissioner's Small Grants Scheme for Sri Lanka, in addition to conflict management, consolidating peace building efforts, health, nutrition, water and sanitation. At least 100,000 civilians have died in the decade of insurgency by Islamic armed groups in Algeria . Despite a limited amnesty offered by the Algerian government which was in force up to 13 January 2000, two armed groups in particular are still active: the Groupe Salafiste pour la Predication et le Combat (GSPC) and the Groupe Islamique Armee (GIA).

As a result the conflict continues to claim around 100 lives a month and armed groups continue to commit horrific crimes against civilians. As well as the terrorist violence committed by the Islamic armed groups, there are numerous documented cases of human rights abuses by the security forces and state-armed militias, including the enforced disappearances of at least 4,000 people, torture and extrajudicial killings. Although the overall level of human rights abuses has fallen over the last few years, it remains high.

Amnesty International visited Algeria in February 2003. This was the first time in two years that the Algerian government had allowed an Amnesty International delegation into the country .Following the visit, Amnesty International "expressed concern that civilians continue to be killed, albeit at lower levels than in previous years "and highlighted "prevalent and systematic "torture and impunity. The delegation, despite its concerns, noted in its concluding press conference that there was more open space for public debate and engagement with human rights issues in the country.

Amnesty International also issued a press release stating that the delegation was informed by the Algerian government that, "reforms were being gradually implemented ...at many levels with the aim of moving towards greater transparency and the rule of law." The UN Mission for the Referendum in Western Sahara (MINURSO) continues to work in the region monitoring the continuing ceasefire (among its various activities), but so far a solution has not been found.

Within the UN Security Council fully supported the efforts of the UN Secretary-General and his Personal Envoy James Baker to help resolve the situation in Western

Sahara. The last substantive UN Security Council Resolution on Western Sahara, passed in July 2002, stressed the council's determination to secure a just, lasting and mutually acceptable political solution to the dispute, which provides for the self-determination of the people of Western Sahara.

The human rights record in Burundi is poor with abuses occurring on both sides. FAB (Burundi military) have killed armed rebels and unarmed civilians, including women, children and the elderly. In the past, rebel attacks on the military were often followed by FAB reprisals against civilians suspected of co-operating with the insurgents. Despite signing the ceasefire, the FDD continues to commit serious abuses against civilians, including killings, rapes, theft and forced labour. The FNL (Rwasa) also carries out serious abuses.

The issue of impunity for those who commit serious human rights violations, and the lack of accountability of those who committed past abuses, remain key factors in the country's continuing instability. There are other issues that urgently need addressing: prison conditions remain dire; the justice system lacks independence and resources and suffers from systemic corruption and administrative disruption; and the indigenous Twa (Pygmy) people remain marginalised economically, socially and politically.

A DFID grant of nearly £100,000 enabled International Alert's project Human Rights Promotion in Burundi to increase respect for human rights by improving the ways Burundians promote human rights. The project team produced and disseminated human rights materials relevant to the Burundian context, in Kirundi and with clear illustrations - this was vital given the population's high illiteracy rate. In each province, the project identified human right promoters from a range of civil society groups. These people participated in workshops organised by the Burundi-based Centre for Human Rights and Prevention of Genocide (CPDHPG) to learn how to make the best use of human rights materials.

Burundi is Africa's second most densely populated country, with a population of 6,054,714 in an area of only 27,830 square kilometres. The Hutu tribe (Bantu) makes up the majority of the population (85 per cent) followed by the Tutsi Hamitic; 14 per cent and the Twa (Pygmy;one per cent). There has been conflict in Burundi since 1993 due to the same Hutu-Tutsi tensions that led to the genocide in 1994 Rwanda.

Thousands of people have died in the civil war and thousands more have been internally displaced. After protracted efforts by different governments and the international community the Arusha Peace Accord, facilitated former South African President Nelson Mandela, was signed the Burundi government and most of the rebel groups in August 2000.

The human rights record in Burundi is poor with abuses occurring on both sides. FAB (Burundi military) have killed armed rebels and unarmed civilians, including women, children and the elderly. In the past, rebel attacks on the military were often followed by FAB reprisals against civilians suspected of co-operating with the insurgents. Despite signing the ceasefire, the FDD continues to commit serious abuses against civilians, including killings, rapes, theft and forced labour.

The FNL (Rwasa) also carries out serious abuses. The issue of impunity for those who commit serious human rights violations, and the lack of accountability of those who committed past abuses, remain key factors in the country's continuing instability. There are other issues that urgently need addressing: prison conditions remain dire; the justice system lacks independence and resources and suffers from systemic corruption and administrative disruption; and the indigenous Twa (Pygmy) people remain marginalised economically, socially and politically.

A DFID grant of nearly £100,000 enabled International Alert's project Human Rights Promotion in Burundi to increase respect for human rights by improving the ways Burundians promote human rights. The project team produced and disseminated human rights materials relevant to the Burundian context, in Kirundi and with clear illustrations - this was vital given the population's high illiteracy rate. In each province, the project identified human right promoters from a range of civil society groups.

These people participated in workshops organised by the Burundi-based Centre for Human Rights and Prevention of Genocide (CPDHPG) to learn how to make the best use of human rights materials. The materials included 10,000 posters in 10 different designs, illustrating key principles from the Universal Declaration of Human Rights; 30,000 cartoon books in Kirundi for children; and 10,000 illustrated booklets in Kirundi for adults.

Liberia's internal conflict has endured for almost a quarter of a century. For over a decade, the country has been at the heart of instability in the Mano River Union, which comprises Guinea, Liberia and Sierra Leone. President Taylor's regime backed the brutal Revolutionary United Front (RUF) rebels in Sierra Leone, exploited instability in Côte d 'Ivoire, and has resulted in hundreds of thousands of refugees, particularly into Guinea. Since March 2003 fighting intensified between the government and the Liberians United for Reconciliation and Democracy (LURD) rebels.

In April, a new rebel group emerged in the south of Liberia: the Movement for Democracy in Liberia (MODEL). LURD made several concerted attacks on the capital Monrovia and MODEL took the port city of Buchanan. These attacks displaced large numbers of civilians and brought panic to Monrovia, causing the international community to evacuate its nationals. Food, water and power are in short supply and outbreaks of cholera have been reported. Since March 2003, the UK has provided £2.75 million of emergency aid to the NGOs working in Liberia.

The rebel advances increased military pressure on the regime and, coupled with the renewal and extension of UN sanctions, forced all sides to negotiate under the auspices of the Economic Community of West African States (ECOWAS) at peace talks in Ghana in June 2003. The talks focused on negotiating a ceasefire and forming a transitional government.

On 4 June 2003, the Special Court for Sierra Leone announced its indictment of Taylor as one of those bearing the greatest responsibility for those war crimes, crimes against humanity and other serious violations of international humanitarian law that had occurred in Sierra Leone since 1996. President Taylor left Liberia on 11 August in return for political asylum in Nigeria. The international community accepted that the immediate need was for Taylor to leave Liberia in order for the peace process to have a chance. However, the UK does not support impunity. It remains to be seen whether Taylor will try to play a continuing role in Liberia.

The UN Security Council adopted Resolution 1478 on 6 May renewing and amending targeted sanctions against Liberia. These include a full arms embargo, applying to all groups within Liberia, a diamond embargo and a travel ban against senior members of the Liberian government, their immediate families and those in violation of the arms embargo, including members of the rebel groups. The resolution also imposed a ban on the import of all round logs and timber products originating in Liberia.

Sanctions target the funding sources for arms and those who break the arms embargo. In addition the UK has lobbied Liberia's neighbours to improve border security, stop arms flows to either side and to stay out of the conflict. On 1 August 2003 the UN Security Council passed UN Resolution 1497 authorising a multinational force for Liberia. The force has a mandate to provide security and to reate an environment which will permit the delivery of humanitarian assistance.

The resolution mandated the UN Mission in Sierra Leone (UNAMSIL), to provide logistical support for the force and allows for the creation of a UN stabilisation force. On 4 August Nigerian troops deployed as part of the vanguard of the multinational force. The UK has already committed £1 million to the peacekeeping operation in Liberia.

Finally, in June 2002, war-weariness and international pressure brought the government of Sudan and the Sudan People's Liberation Movement (SPLM) back to the negotiating table. Despite some difficulties ,including outbreaks of fighting, the peace talks continue to make progress. On 15 October 2002 the parties signed a Memorandum of Understanding (MoU) on a cessation of hostilities and unimpeded humanitarian access.

Foreign Secretary Jack Straw and the then Secretary of State for International Development Clare Short welcomed this MoU, which has helped reduce the number of human rights abuses related to the conflict. The MoU and its Addendum, signed on 4 February 2003, was extended until the end of June 2003 and then again until the end of September. In February 2002 the Foreign Secretary announced the appointment of UK Special Representative for Sudan, Alan Goulty.

A boundary dispute in 1998 triggered a violent conflict between Ethiopia and Eritrea .The two governments signed a peace agreement in Algiers in December 2000 which mandated a boundary commission to decide the position of the border. They continued to express their commitment to the peace process throughout 2002. In April 2002 they accepted the boundary commission decision on the position of the border between the two countries and committed to releasing all their prisoners of war.

The UN Mission to Ethiopia and Eritrea (UNMEE) deploys a 4,000-strong peacekeeping force in the temporary security zone between the two countries, led by British Force Commander Major General Gordon. Under the peace agreement, UNMEE will remain in place until the delimitation and demarcation of the border has been completed.

The UN Security Council adopted Resolution 1466 on 14 March. This resolution extended UNMEE's mandate until 15 September 2003 and demarcation is due to begin before November 2003. Both sides submitted their comments to the boundary commission on certain aspects of the commission's decision, particularly in the central and western sectors. Ethiopia continues to raise its concerns with the boundary commission.

The international community has increased its efforts to keep the peace process on track. The US and EU have carried out démarches in Asmara and Addis Ababa, the capitals of Eritrea and Ethiopia, and Resolution 1466 calls for parties to co-operate fully and promptly with the boundary commission.

Prime Minister Tony Blair raised the commission's decision when the Ethiopian Prime Minister Meles Zenawi visited the UK in February and July 2003. The UN Secretary-General also has a crucial role, as a bridge between the parties and also to the boundary commission.

7

Economic Social and Cultural Rights

After the UN adopted the Universal Declaration of Human Rights (UDHR) in 1948, the intention was to draw up a single treaty covering all the human rights set out in the UDHR. But there soon emerged an ideological debate about the relative importance of civil and political rights on the one hand, and economic, social and cultural rights on the other. This situation resulted in the drawing up of two separate treaties: the International Covenants dealing with Civil and Political Rights (ICCPR) and Economic, Social and Cultural Rights (ICESCR) both of which were adopted in 1966.

Throughout the Cold War the communist bloc emphasised and argued for the international prioritisation of the realisation of economic and social rights, which it saw as better suited to the communist vision of social organisation than more individualist civil and political rights. Many western states argued the opposite. With the end of the Cold War it became more possible to establish a more neutral and considered international consensus. In 1993 at the Vienna World Conference on Human Rights, the international community reasserted that all human rights were "universal, indivisible, interdependent and interrelated ".

Since then, however, as international attention has rightly begun to focus more on the problems of poverty and underdevelopment in many parts of the world, some states have argued that development requires the prioritisation of economic and social rights over civil and political ones. Many developing states perceive developed countries as emphasising individual civil and political rights at the expense of economic development, which they see as dependent on the realisation of economic and social rights. Some states claim that underdevelopment is in itself a cause of human rights violations.

They argue that being poor, they are not responsible for human rights violations in their countries, since they have insufficient capacity to address these without international assistance. A few states often those with very bad human rights records have even argued that active suppression of civil and political rights may be necessary to allow economic development. This forms the backdrop to much of the current debate in multilateral fora such as the UN Commission on Human Rights.

The UK has never subscribed to these positions. As Bill Rammell told the UN Commission on Human Rights in March 2003, the choice between economic, social and cultural rights and civil and political rights is a false one. It is clear to us that realisation of the rights set out in one treaty is the best guarantee of fulfilling the rights enshrined in the other. A country where the dignity of the individual, the rule of law and the right to freedom of opinion and expression are respected, is a country in which a society can reach its full economic and cultural potential.

Conversely, unless people have adequate access to food, shelter and health care they will never be able to enjoy fully the full range of civil and political rights. International assistance is an important factor in helping to achieve development, and the UK is both a major aid donor and a leading advocate of more and better international co-operation in the field of development and debt relief. But underdevelopment cannot be used as an excuse for human rights violations.

Human rights are at the heart of the UK Government's development work. The UK Government operates a rights-based approach to development that sees development as an outcome best achieved through the realisation of all human rights. Development, to be sustainable, must be locally owned: the beneficiaries must be involved in the decisions and processes that affect their lives.

The promotion of human rights is an essential part of raising standards of development because human rights provide a means of empowering all people -including the poorest -to make effective decisions about their own lives. Some of the differences in attitude towards economic, social and cultural rights stem from the way in which the rights are expressed.

When the International Covenant on Economic, Social and Cultural Rights was drafted, it was recognised that states would not all be able immediately to guarantee all economic and social rights to the fullest extent in the same way that certain civil and political rights could be fulfilled. This reflected the fact that civil and political rights often applied negative obligations upon states, namely that the state should refrain from a certain activity.

For example, to respect freedom from torture, the obligation is that states do not torture individuals, or allow others to do so. Positive obligations also stem from civil and political rights -for example the state must take affirmative action to ensure mechanisms are in place to protect people from torture. However, economic and social rights tend to require more widespread positive action by the state to protect, respect and fulfil them. They therefore carry very substantial budgetary implications.

Such rights include the right to education, the right to the highest attainable standard of physical and mental health, and the right to an adequate standard of living - including the right to adequate food, housing and clothing. In recognition of the extensive demand on governments ' budgets, the Covenant therefore requires each state to "take steps ...to the maximum availability of resources, with a view to achieving progressively the full realisation of the rights recognised in the present Covenant by all appropriate means, including particularly the adoption of legislative measures." (Article 2 of the Covenant).

In practice, this progressive approach means that states are expected to improve enjoyment of these rights on a continuous basis. But it also recognises that they are starting from very different positions of national wealth and capacity. So, it allows states to comply with their legal obligations in a way that is commensurate with their resource capacity and in line with the social, economic and cultural character of their societies. Against this background, retrogression by the state in meeting these obligations could be seen as a violation of the Covenant.

And certain elements of the Covenant, for example that states guarantee the rights will be exercised without discrimination, can be implemented immediately. The

Covenant does not require that it be incorporated directly into domestic law, or that all the rights be given direct legal effect. However, some NGOs argue that all the rights should be incorporated directly into UK law in the same way as the Human Rights Act has incorporated the civil and political rights guaranteed under the European Convention on Human Rights into domestic law.

The UK Government disagrees with this view. It believes that the way in which economic and social rights are expressed in the Covenant does not lend itself easily to justiciable decision-making, meaning decisions with direct legal enforceability in UK courts. There are several reasons, which include:

— the obligation on states is to take steps to improve the realisation of these rights, which are to be applied progressively. It is not clear how courts could judge whether there had been an absence of general progress in a particular case where an individual claimed that they had not fully enjoyed, for example, the right to education;

— since the progressive realisation of these rights is achieved within the constraints of finite budgetary resources, a judicial decision to the effect that greater progress should have been made in one area such as health would amount to a judgement against a government's policy decision to prioritise investment in another, such as education. This would take decision-making on the basic policy agenda and priorities away from an elected government, counter to fundamental principles of democracy;

— decisions on the best means to realise progressively these rights are essentially policy choices which do

> not lend themselves to justiciable procedures. Some people may judge that the realisation of these rights requires targeted interventionist policies. Others may judge that the best chances for improvement come from allowing the market, and broader economic policies, to advance the economic environment within which people can achieve these rights.

To illustrate the point, it is common sense that the right to adequate housing is not the right for everyone to have a house provided by the government. For some people it may mean being provided with access to shelter when they have no means to provide it for themselves. But for the majority of people it means the government providing an economic environment in which they can earn sufficient income to be able to afford accommodation.

The measure of an individual's right to housing might therefore come down to a test of governmental economic policy at least as much as its application to the individual's circumstances; and many of the rights are themselves not unambiguous standards. This would include the right to the 'highest attainable 'standard of health, or to an 'adequate 'standard of living. This raises questions about how courts could decide what in each individual's case is the 'adequate standard 'or the 'highest attainable standard', given that these standards may well vary between individuals.

These concerns make it clear that not all economic, social and cultural rights lend themselves directly and suitably to justiciable decisions and procedures, as well as raising questions about what role the courts should play. While therefore some states have chosen to incorporate economic, social and cultural rights into their domestic law, the UK Government is not convinced that this can be done in a meaningful way within the British legal system.

The UK Government's view is that there is little point in directly incorporating the Covenant if it is unclear that it will lead to meaningful and beneficial outcomes. The UK Government does not believe, however, that these concerns rule out entirely some degree of justiciability. Some economic and social rights can be incorporated into domestic law (for example, those related to trade union organisation and membership).

The UK Government's policy has therefore been to take legislative measures within the scope of each right where these will meet its obligations under international human rights law and have practical and beneficial effect. For example, rather than have a single 'right to education', we have a number of policies, programmes and legislative measures-like the Education Act and Disability Discrimination Act -which are designed to help people enjoy that right.

Democracy, good governance and the rule of law therefore are important elements in ensuring the realisation of progressively implementable rights. Individuals are able to demand better policies in all fields from their governments when they are able to choose their representatives, and hold them to account for their actions and expenditure. Freedom of association and expression play a crucial role in this, as do many other rights. Participatory and accessible governance means that people are able to play a key role in decisions that affect their lives and deliver progressively the kind of outcomes that economic and social rights are meant to underline.

The rule of law is an important element in making sure that democracy and good governance extends beyond merely holding elections, since it ensures that policymakers cannot ignore the laws they legislate. The UK's support for Partnership for Principle 10 is an important element in promoting this kind of empowerment-based approach to environmental protection, as is, for example, the rights-based approach that underlies UK Official Development Assistance (ODA).

In mid-2002 the body which monitors states 'compliance with the Covenant, the Committee on Economic, social and Cultural Rights, issued a set of recommendations following its consideration of the UK's fourth report to the committee. The committee welcomed measures such as the New Deal programme for employment, the introduction of a national minimum wage and measures take to reduce homelessness, rough sleeping and exclusion from schools.

It also welcomed the UK Government's process of reviewing its reservations to international human rights instruments, with a view to withdrawing those that have been superseded by legislation or practice. It also stated its concerns about a number of areas where it felt the UK could make improvements in its compliance with the Covenant. These included poverty, housing and labour rights. The committee also questioned the UK Government's lack of a national human rights plan and its failure to incorporate economic and social rights into domestic law.

Subsequently, a UK parliamentary select committee, the Joint Committee on Human Rights, has started an inquiry into the UK Government's handling of these recommendations. The Minister responsible for the UK's reporting obligations under human rights instruments, Bill Rammell, will appear before the Joint Committee in

September 2003 to inform the inquiry. UK Government's initial report to the inquiry, Bill Rammell wrote that "the United Kingdom Government takes very seriously its obligations under international human rights law and values the views and recommendations of all the treaty monitoring bodies in their consideration of the UK's reports to those bodies.

The Government therefore welcomes this inquiry by the Joint Committee into the Government's response to the Concluding Observations of the UN Committee on Economic, Social and Cultural Rights (CESCR). In the international sphere the FCO has increased its engagement on economic and social rights. The FCO, in co-operation with DFID and with other government departments, has played a determining role in developing the EU's human rights policy on the right to food.

In June 2002, the World Food Summit, established an Inter-Governmental Working Group (IGWG) to elaborate a set of voluntary guidelines on the progressive realisation of the right to adequate food. The UK Government believes that food security is an important element of wider poverty reduction strategies, and that a rights-based approach to both will lead to better outcomes for the poorest of the poor.

The UK participated in the first meeting of the IGWG from 24-26 March 2003. The FCO, DFID and other departments have been actively contributing to the formulation of the E's contribution to this process. At the 59th Commission on Human Rights (CHR), the UK abstained on the Brazilian resolution on the right to health. The UK had previously supported this resolution but was unable to do so in 2003 because of the emphasis in the text on language relating to violence.

While violence can have a seriously detrimental effect on health, the resolution included links between violence and health which the UK Government felt were ambiguous, particularly where it did not clearly distinguish between state violence which would be considered a human rights violation and violence perpetrated by non-state actors which, when perpetrated by individuals, would be dealt with under criminal law.

The latter point is an important legal and political pillar of international human rights law: some states seek to justify repressive counter-insurgency policies and the evasion of their own human rights obligations by arguing that human rights violations are committed by non-state actors. The UK continues to support the work of Professor Paul Hunt, the UN Special Rapporteur on the Right of Everyone to the Enjoyment of the Highest Attainable Standard of Physical and Mental Health.

At the 59th Commission on Human Rights. The UK played a central role in forging greater north-south consensus on the resolution on the right to development. Some countries have implied that the right to development creates legal obligations on developed states to provide financial assistance to developing states. Some go still further to suggest that developing states have reduced responsibility for securing their citizens 'human rights if they do not receive such assistance. This view runs counter to the very premise of human rights: that they belong to individuals and create obligations between a state and its citizens, not between states.

However, the UK Government recognises that for all governments the availability of resources constrains the speed with which they can advance the economic and social rights of their citizens. The UK is committed to a programme of development assistance to poorer countries. This is particularly aimed at achieving the Millennium Development Goals by 2015. UK development aid aims to mainstream human rights within its programmes - ensuring conformity with, and the promotion of, human rights in recipient countries.

The CHR resolution on the right to development mandates the Sub-Commission on the Promotion and Protection of Human Rights to develop a number of options aimed at improving implementation of the right to development, including the feasibility of those options. Rather than focusing solely on efforts to secure a legally binding instrument on the right to development, the UK helped ensure that the sub-commission would also consider guidelines on how to realise the right to development, and principles for development partnerships, based on case studies of best practice.

Globalisation and Human rights

Globalisation is an imprecise term encompassing a series of economic, cultural, political and technological developments that cut across state borders. The process of globalisation impacts greatly on people's lives -changing the goods we buy, the information we receive, and the ways our children learn. Globalisation will ultimately lead to higher growth in global output and an increase in average per capita incomes.

Global markets mean more intense competition, better allocation of resources, greater stability in prices and rising productivity. By driving down costs for consumers, and opening markets for small and medium-sized enterprises, globalisation has the potential to raise living standards across the world. The UK is committed to making globalisation work for all, including the world's poorest. The benefits of globalisation should be more evenly distributed.

Globalisation is a powerful mechanism to further human rights, whether civil and political, or social, economic and cultural and it is breaking down the barriers between countries and peoples. The international news media allow us to follow events in other countries -often as they occur. In this increasingly open global environment, human rights violators can no longer rely of physical isolation to conceal their policies. Communications networks, and the Internet in particular, are helping more and more people to understand their human rights, and what they can do to stand up for them.

At best, communications can allow civil society to scrutinise the activities of governments and international organisations in fostering such rights. But under all but the most oppressive regimes, people are now able to access uncensored information about developments within their own country, to project their voice and to promote their cause and the cause of human rights in general. It is no coincidence that some of the most repressive governments are also those most worried by the spread of global information communications technology.

Globalisation can also help promote people's economic rights. Much of the growing economic prosperity across the world is a direct result of increased flows of trade and investment. Even in the poorest regions of the world, strong international economic connections can raise living standards and cut absolute poverty, helping people realise their right to an adequate standard of living. Foreign Direct I vestment can play an important role in spreading new technologies, as well as best practice on workers ' rights and environmental standards.

The European Commission has estimated that cutting all trade tariffs in half would increase the income of developing countries by $150 billion a year: this is around three times the annual amount of global aid. The UK is pushing for the EU to adopt a pro-development stance in World Trade Organisation (WTO) negotiations. The UK Government has been in the lead in establishing the Heavily Indebted Poor Countries (HIPC) initiative to tackle the problem of high government debt burdens in 42 of the world's poorest countries.

Left untamed, economic instability can also jeopardise the gains of globalisation. Growing 'interconnectedness 'means that events such as war, terrorism, poor governance and misfortune in one country can have a far more immediate and greater impact than before on other countries. The East Asian financial crisis of 1997 directly caused job losses in the UK. The spread of the Severe Acute Respiratory Syndrome (SARS) virus in the first half of 2003 demonstrated the speed with which increased air travel can produce serious health and economic impacts across distant parts of the globe. Some of these consequences cannot be avoided.

But for globalisation to benefit both the developing and developed world, it is vital to promote economic good governance. Appropriate microeconomic regulation helps developing countries to ensure that foreign investment works to their advantage and allows them to seize the opportunities of globalisation. Good macroeconomic governance, meanwhile, reduces the risk of volatility in capital flows and the possibility financial crises affecting markets around the world.

But good economic governance also needs to be married to good political governance and the rule of law at the national level. Otherwise is difficult to ensure that the benefits of economic growth will be shared equitably and, ultimately, that it will lead to stronger, more stable and sustainable economies and societies. Participatory forms of governance also allow people to demand better economic governance and accountability from their rulers and is an important factor in, for example, combating corruption.

The rule of law ensures that contracts and commitments will be honoured, making states more attractive targets for investment. Lastly, but just as importantly, globalisation will not promote human rights so long as people are excluded from the process itself. Many people in the developing world do not have access to the rapid technological advances that drive globalisation.

In the UK, Prime Minister Tony Blair opened the 6,000th UK Online centre at the e-Summit on 19 November 2002. These centres have opened in libraries as well as in new, dedicated UK Online centres to increase people's access to the Internet. Yet there are many people, in many countries, who do not have access to such technologies. This is largely due to lack of infrastructure and the high costs of access. New technologies can help: mobile telephony provides an easier way to connect rural communities while community-based solutions can spread the cost.

New technology on its own is not enough. In March 2003, the FCO led the second high level seminar on e-government in conjunction with the Office of the e-Envoy, bringing together those people delivering e-government programmes in the Latin American and Caribbean regions. Such programmes increase the transparency of governments and encourage greater interaction between citizens and states, promoting democracy and human rights. There has been much international activity in the past year to promote a more equitable information society across the world. The UK is involved in the preparations for the World Summit on the Information Society (WSIS) in Geneva in December 2003.

The aim of official development assistance (ODA) is to assist developing countries in making best use of their own human and financial resources. ODA promotes sustainable development and people's welfare. The UK is committed to the UN target for ODA to be 0.7 per cent of a donor country's Gross National Income (GNI). DFID believes that untying aid -that is, not making it dependent upon awarding contracts to specific companies or countries -could increase its effectiveness by 20 per cent.

The UK began untying all its aid on 1 April 2001. The World Bank and the UN estimate that an additional $50 billion in aid is needed each year in order to achieve the MDGs by 2015. The EU and US pledged significant increases in aid in March 2002 at the UN Financing for Development conference in Mexico, which could total $12 billion by 2006 and will make an important contribution towards meeting the MDGs.

The International Monetary Fund and the World Bank

The International Monetary Fund (IMF) and the World Bank fulfil important and complementary roles in maintaining international financial stability and improving living standards in the world's poorest countries. Through these roles, the IMF and World Bank contribute directly and indirectly towards people's realisation of many of their human rights.

Worldwide growth and poverty reduction depend on a well-functioning international financial system. The IMF works to increase stability and guard against vulnerabilities through its lending activities, surveillance process and promotion of codes and standards to encourage good practice in fiscal, monetary and financial policy-making.

The international financial system needs strengthening. This can be achieved by putting crisis prevention at the heart of the IMF's work and strengthening the transparency, independence and effectiveness of IMF surveillance. The case for improving the Fund's crisis prevention and resolution mechanisms rests primarily on the need to: promote social justice in the countries worst affected by crises and instability; ensure that economic dislocation is minimised at times of instability; ensure that private sector investors contribute responsibly to this outcome; and ensure that governments get help to manage their economies in a way that promotes the interests of all their citizens.

Macroeconomic stability is an essential pre-condition of economic success for every country, rich or poor. Thus it is important that the IMF promotes macroeconomic stability, sound and transparent institutions and long-term sustainable growth as the foundation for development and prosperity.

The World Bank has helped millions of people realise economic and social rights by supporting primary education, health care and nutrition, sanitation and housing. The World Bank embraced the MDGs and has a well-developed strategy for achieving them. This strategy has two main strands: building the climate for investment, jobs, and sustainable growth; and investing in poor people, empowering them to participate in development and pursue a broader range of human rights and effectiveness of IMF surveillance.

The case for improving the Fund's crisis prevention and resolution mechanisms rests primarily on the need to: promote social justice in the countries worst affected by crises and instability; ensure that economic dislocation is minimised at times of instability; ensure that private sector investors contribute responsibly to this outcome; and ensure that governments get help to manage their economies in a way that promotes the interests of all their citizens.

Macroeconomic stability is an essential pre-condition of economic success for every country, rich or poor. Thus it is important that the IMF promotes macroeconomic stability, sound and transparent institutions and long-term sustainable growth as the foundation for development and prosperity. The World Bank has helped millions of people realise economic and social rights by supporting primary education, health care and nutrition, sanitation and housing.

The World Bank embraced the MDGs and has a well-developed strategy for achieving them. This strategy has two main strands: building the climate for investment, jobs, and sustainable growth; and investing in poor people, empowering them to participate in development and pursue a broader range of human rights. Developing countries constitute the overwhelming majority of IMF and World Bank members and are often profoundly affected by their decisions, yet their ability to influence these decisions is limited.

They should have a stronger sense of ownership in their institutions and policies and must be allowed to develop a stronger voice in World Bank and IMF decision-making processes. All companies, including multinationals, have a responsibility to carry out their business and production processes ethically. They should take into account people's human rights as well as the wider impact a company's operations may have on local communities and environment.

Corporate social responsibility (CSR) refers to the attention companies give to areas such as community development, environment-friendly products and processes and responsible employee relations. Human rights are an integral part of CSR and the private sector has a clear and important role in the promotion of human rights and can play an important part in their observance. Companies are responsible for not acting in a way that impairs the human rights of their employees or of those on whom their activities have an impact, and should act in a way that actively promotes their enjoyment of human rights. It is also often in the company's own interest to work actively on CSR.

Child labour and exploitative wages can tarnish a global brand,reduce sales and harm a company's value. A company ,with a good human rights record is likely to attract quality employees and keep them motivated and to have a loyal customer base. The UK's aim in promoting CSR is to see private and public sector organisations act in a way which takes into account their economic, social and environmental impact, both within their field of operations and more widely.

The UK has taken an international lead in advocating CSR and was the first country to appoint a Minister for CSR in March 2000. The post is currently held by Stephen Timms. The Department of Trade and Industry (DTI) is responsible for leading on issues related to CSR. Internationally, the FCO promotes CSR worldwide as part of its objective of building a secure and prosperous world.

A growing number of Embassies and High Commissions are incorporating CSR into their human rights strategies and into other areas of their commercial, political, economic, development and public diplomacy activities. CSR is also a core element of the FCO's human rights and environment training courses, which are widely undertaken by staff throughout the organisation. The UN Global Compact was set up in 1999. It is based on nine core principles covering human rights, labour and the environment, which are derived from various UN declarations and instruments. It encourages companies to build these principles into their business strategies.

By committing to the compact, a company undertakes to uphold the principles and to make an annual report on its performance. Many UK companies have signed up to the compact and many of the NGO and civil society groups who have been involved with the Global Compact are either based in or have strong links with the UK. The UK supports the Global Compact and the FCO is helping to fund the compact's national learning networks for 2002 and 2003. These raise awareness of the compact and work with companies in developing countries to implement its principles, adapting them to local circumstances.

Together with the Department for Environment, Food and Rural Affairs and other Whitehall departments, the FCO promoted CSR at the World Summit on Sustainable

Development (WSSD) in Johannesburg in August - September 2002. The Political Declaration and the Plan of Implementation resulting from the summit both stress the importance of CSR in achieving global sustainable development and set out an agenda for governments, the private sector and NGOs. The FCO helped to prepare for the Prime Minister's launch of the Extractives Industry Transparency Initiative (EITI)at WSSD.

The initiative aims for greater transparency over company payments and government revenues in the oil, gas and mining sectors. Since the launch, the UK Government has been developing a voluntary compact for host governments and companies to sign to indicate their commitment to provide annual data in a simple, standard template. DFID hosted an international workshop in London for governments ,businesses, NGOs, the World Bank, IMF, and other key stakeholders in February 2003 to develop the initiative further.

The G8 at its Evian Summit in 2003 endorsed this initiative as a key element of its strategy to improve transparency and aid development. Within the UK, the DTI promotes the OECD Guidelines for Multinational Enterprises as a comprehensive code of conduct for international business. The UK expects companies operating in the UK and British companies operating abroad to act in accordance with these guidelines,which reinforce private sector efforts to define and implement responsible business conduct.

The guidelines establish non-legally binding principles on human rights, disclosure, employment and industrial relations, the environment, combating bribery, consumer relations and taxation. The UK and the US jointly launched the Voluntary Principles on Security and

Human Rights for the Extractives Sector in Zones of Conflict in 2000. The principles provide practical guidance to companies on making sure that respect for human rights is central to their arrangements for protecting the security of their personnel and operations in areas of conflict.

The principles were developed in close consultation with oil and mining companies and NGOs working in human rights, labour and CSR. The original participants were from the US and the UK. UK participants are Shell, BP, Rio Tinto, Amnesty International and the Prince of Wales International Business Leaders Forum (IBLF). The Dutch and Norwegian governments joined the process in 2002 -2003 along with several other companies and NGOs from the US, the Netherlands and Norway. In the short term, the principles encourage companies to understand better the environment in which they operate, to improve relations with local communities through dialogue and to uphold the rule of law.

Ultimately, the goal is to create a better environment for sustainable economic investment and ensure respect for human rights. The principles are the first voluntary guidelines for the extractives sector on security and, as such, they are global and generic. They do not focus on a particular country nor do they present a one size fits all approach to preventing human rights violations. They offer guidelines that can be adapted to local operating environments. So far, participants have concentrated on integrating and implementing the voluntary principles.

Many companies have taken significant steps to integrate them into security practices at their headquarters and on the ground. Human rights and CSR groups have given presentations on human rights training, working with local NGOs and protecting personnel at risk. In

Nigeria, Indonesia and Colombia the combination of high levels of foreign investment in oil, gas and mining with domestic tensions has lead in the past to the types of violent incidents that the voluntary principles are intended to address.

Labour Rights

Labour rights are the rights of workers to fair conditions and standards in the workplace. They include the right to work, the right to fair wages, the right to safe and healthy working conditions and reasonable working hours. They are established in the Universal Declaration of Human Rights and International Covenant of Economic, social and Cultural Rights and set out in greater detail in the Conventions of the International Labour Organisation (ILO), the foundations of which pre-date the UN framework.

The UK fully supports the ILO and participates in the ILO conference and governing body meetings, as well as the many sectoral and specialist meetings throughout the year. The UK has ratified all of the core ILO conventions which cover freedom of association and the right to collective bargaining; the elimination of forced and child labour; and ending discrimination in employment.

The UK encourages the private sector to go beyond general compliance with ILO core standards and to lead on issues such as improving employment conditions. Businesses have long acknowledged that by taking a responsible attitude towards labour rights, they can improve their competitive advantage. Many companies see these rights as a necessary part of developing their global operations. Respect for labour rights not only contributes towards sustainable development, it can also enhance brand value. This improves public perception of companies as responsible operators, opens more doors and creates goodwill.

At the 59th session of the UN Commission on Human Rights (CHR) the EU highlighted continuing violations of labour rights as a particularly troubling feature of China's human rights record. The EU tabled a resolution on Turkmenistan expressing grave concern at discrimination against minorities in employment.

The statement condemned attacks against trade union members and called for ILO recommendations to be implemented and measures to guarantee the right to life, physical integrity and the ability to function freely as set out in Article 8 of the International Covenant on Economic, Social and Cultural Rights. The FCO Human Rights Project Fund (HRPF) is supporting a two-year British Council project in China to improve women workers ' rights in the Pearl River Delta.

The project brings together the experience and skills of all those engaged in rights for women workers, and will improve information resources and develop new ways of working with women in enterprises. The project's second phase began in April 2003.

Slavery is one of the worst and most disgraceful examples of man's inhumanity to man. A definition of slavery first appeared in an international agreement in the League of Nations Slavery Convention of 25 September 1926. It defined slavery as "the status or condition of a person over whom any or all of the powers attaching to the right of ownership are exercised ". Contemporary forms of slavery cover a wide range of human rights violations.

A slave is forced to work; owned or controlled by an 'employer ';treated as a commodity or bought and sold as 'property ';and physically constrained, or has his or her movements restricted. In addition to traditional slavery and the slave trade, such practices include forced and bonded labour, the sale of children, child prostitution, child pornography, the exploitation of child labour, the use of children in armed conflicts, and the traffic in human beings.

In many cases there are no clear distinctions between different forms of slavery. The same groups of people are often the victims of several kinds of contemporary forms of slavery such as bonded labour, forced labour, child labour or child prostitution. Extreme poverty often forms the backdrop to many cases of slavery today. In June 2002, the ILO published the report *A Future Without Child Labour* ,in which it estimates that 179 million children are working in the worst forms of child labour -prostitution, bonded labour, trafficking and hazardous work.

The UK is committed to eradicating contemporary forms of slavery. The UK has ratified the key international legal instruments that outlaw slavery; the International Covenant on Civil and Political Rights, the European Convention on Human Rights, the UN Slavery Convention and International Labour Organisation (ILO) Conventions 29 and 105 on Forced Labour; and 182 on the Worst Forms of Child Labour.

The UK has also signed the UN Convention Against Transnational Organised Crime, and the two associated protocols against the facilitation of illegal immigration and for the prevention of trafficking in human beings, especially women and children. There are no short-term solutions to slavery, but by working in partnership with organisations such as the ILO, UN agencies, NGOs and governments.

The Committee for the Eradication of Abduction of Women and Children (CEAWC) in Sudan is a good example of such partnership. CEAWC, which was set up in 1999, works closely with UNICEF and Save the Children UK (SCUK) to identify, retrieve and resettle abducted women and children. Since CEAWC's inception, it has confirmed and documented 1,740 cases of people retrieved from slavery. Information on some of these people show that 244 are now reunited with relatives in north Sudan, 279 with relatives in south Sudan, 142 have been placed in foster care, 164 settled in camps for internally displaced people and 215 are in transit care centres.

In May 2002, CEAWC facilitated the mission of the International Eminent Persons Group on Slavery, Abduction and Forced Servitude to Sudan. At the UN Commission on Human Rights in April 2002 the EU made a joint statement -initiated by the UK -condemning the continuing existence of contemporary forms of slavery and encouraging governments to take action to tackle issues such as bonded labour, forced labour and trafficking.

As part of the Home Office initiative to build a national action plan to take forward UK commitments from the World Conference Against Racism, consultations have continued with a steering group of NGO representatives. Forced labour means forcing a person to work involuntarily, under the menace of penalties such as physical harm, constraint, being indebted to the employer or having identity documents taken away.

Forced labour includes trafficking of women and children for sexual exploitation and labour. The coercive recruitment of forced labourers occurs in many countries in Latin America, parts of the Caribbean, Asia and India. In Europe, trafficking increased dramatically after the break-up of the former Soviet Union. In most cases today forced labour is no longer primarily exacted by states. The main perpetrators are now individuals, organisations and enterprises, feudal landlords and criminals, acting outside the law. Their governments have a clear responsibility to act to eliminate forced labour and punish those responsible.

Many millions of people are held in bonded labour around the world. It is especially prevalent in South Asia. There are bonded labourers working in Pakistan's brick kilns and on farms in Nepal; there are young girls repaying loans to their parents by working in India's cottonseed fields. Bonded labour, or debt bondage, has existed for hundreds of years. Today, it is one of the most widely used methods of enslaving people. A person becomes a bonded labourer when his or her labour is demanded to repay a loan.

The person is then trapped into working for little or no pay until the debt is repaid. Sometimes whole families are bonded. Children may be bonded in return for loans to their parents. Bonded labourers are regularly threatened with, and subjected to, physical and sexual violence. They are kept under surveillance which may include armed guards. The practice of bonded labour is widespread in India with the figures for bonded labourers varying widely from five million to 40 million. This is despite the fact that the practice is illegal -bonded labour is outlawed under the Indian constitution and the Bonded Labour System (Abolition) Act 1976.

Whatever the real figures are, it is clear that bonded labour is a serious problem that affects many people. The state of emergency and emerging conflict over the past year in Nepal hampered any previous progress by the Nepalese authorities in eradicating bonded labour. Despite this, 14,000 bonded labourers received land allocations last year and most of them have begun leading lives that are free of bondage. In January 2003 protests by ex-bonded labourers raised concerns over the size of the land grants; they consider these insufficient to produce a livelihood.

The protesters also called for further identification of more groups of bonded labourers who were not identified in the first registration. The government has responded by organising another registration. Millions of Pakistanis remain bonded to employers through debts they can never clear -a decade after the official outlawing of bonded labour. Most bonded labourers work in agriculture, but also in brick kilns, carpet weaving workshops and the mining, fishing and service sectors. Inhumane conditions are rife.

In Sindh and Punjab, bonded agricultural labourers and brick kiln workers claimed they were kept i shackles at night to reduce the risk of them fleeing. Minority communities are particularly at risk of being subjected to bonded labour; and non-Muslim tribes in Sindh are the most vulnerable. It has been difficult for the authorities to implement the law. Human rights activists point out that the tenancy laws need reconciling with the law on the abolition of bonded labour. Their concern is that tenancy laws permit rent advances to tenants and some landlords use this to legitimise debt bondage of agricultural workers.

The UK was among the first countries to sign the UN Protocol on the Prevention and Suppression of Trafficking in People in December 2000, and encourages other countries to sign and ratify it. To date 117 countries have signed the Protocol, which sets out a framework for dealing with trafficking. This includes criminal sanctions against the traffickers and support and assistance for victims.

In February 2002 in the White Paper Secure Borders, Safe Haven a four-point strategy to fight trafficking, comprising:

— legislation -new criminal offences of trafficking were included in the Nationality, Immigration and Asylum Act 2002, and in the Sexual Offences Bill 2003;

— enforcement -support for the work of the Reflex taskforce tackling the organised criminals who are behind trafficking;

— victim support -making provision for the victims of trafficking to receive support so that they can escape their circumstances; and

— international co-operation -working with international partners to tackle trafficking at sources and ensure effective action against this form of transnational organised crime. British immigration liaison officers have been posted to central and southern European countries on the main smuggling routes and now cover 22 countries.

Their main purpose is to exchange information between the UK authorities and local law enforcement agencies to identify traffickers and their methods. Other EU countries are making similar deployments and British officers co-ordinate locally with their EU counterparts as well as feeding intelligence into Europol, to which the UK has seconded a dedicated liaison officer. EU-wide law enforcement efforts against trafficking are co-ordinated via Europol and the European Police Chief's Task Force. The trafficking of people is a serious and growing problem in Kosovo ,which is both a destination and transit point for the trafficking of women and girls for prostitution.

Implementation of law and order in Kosovo is a key objective to support the work of the United Nations Administration Mission in Kosovo (UNMIK) to prohibit trafficking. Measures include adopting an UNMIK regulation with a penalty of 2-20 years imprisonment. A special unit of UNMIK police, the Trafficking and Prostitution Investigations Unit, has also been set up to deal with the issue. The UK currently seconds 132 UK police officers to UNMIK. In Bosnia ,the UK has contributed 58 police officers to the EU Policing Mission.

In the UK, the Sexual Offences Bill was introduced into the House of Lords on 28 January 2003. It includes proposals for new offences of trafficking for sexual exploitation to replace the stop-gap offence introduced by the Nationality, Immigrationand Asylum Act 2002 of trafficking in prostitution. These new offences tackle the movement of people into, within and out the UK for sexual exploitation, and will carry maximum penalties of 14 years ' imprisonment. The offence relating to trafficking within the UK applies equally to UK nationals trafficked from place to place in the UK and to foreign nationals brought here and then moved around the UK.

Human rights and the Environment

Human beings are at the centre of concerns for sustainable development. They are entitled to a healthy and productive life in harmony with nature. The UK firmly supports Principle 1 of the Rio Declaration on Environment and Development. The Aarhus Convention of the United

Nations Economic Commission for Europe (UNECE), which came into force in October 2001, is related to Principle 10 of the Rio Declaration calls upon governments to provide access to environmental information and to justice in environmental matters and to enable people to participate in decision-making processes that affect the environment.

The UK has taken a leading role in implementation of the convention. Over 100 heads of government attended the World Summit on Sustainable Development (WSSD) in Johannesburg in August and September 2002 -the largest world summit ever held. Prime Minister Tony Blair led a strong UK delegation. The WSSD plan of implementation makes clear that respect for human rights and fundamental freedoms is essential for achieving sustainable development. The plan stresses the importance of action at a national level for successful development. Key components include good governance, the rule of law, gender equality and an overall commitment to a just and democratic society.

Transparency, accountability and fair administrative and judicial institutions must be promoted if sound national policies are to be carried out. The plan also emphasises how important it is to promote public participation in environmental decision making, including measures that provide access to information regarding legislation, regulations, activities, policies and programmes. The plan states that women must be involved fully and equally at all levels of the environmental and developmental process, including those of policy formulation and decision-making. Good governance depends on more equitable, transparent, participatory and just environmental management.

Access to Health and Education

The Universal Declaration of Human Rights makes clear that everyone has the right to a standard of living adequate to their health and well-being. However, more than 25 per cent of the world's population do not enjoy this right. Poor health is both a consequence of poverty and a contributory factor. There is growing evidence to show that better health helps bring greater security, development and opportunities.

Conversely, the HIV/AIDS epidemic in Africa has decimated workforces, has played a part in starting the famine in Southern Africa and is setting back development. Greater national and international commitment, partnership and leadership in health-related issues will make a difference to the health of poor people. The World Bank, UN agencies and other donors must work together by providing the necessary resources to strengthen health systems in those developing countries that have made credible policy commitments.

Through DFID, the UK has provided over £1 billion since 1997 to help countries strengthen their health systems. Communicable diseases are an overwhelming burden for most developing countries. HIV/AIDS, turberculosis (TB) and malaria cause six million deaths every year .At the end of 2002, an estimated 42 million people were living with HIV/AIDS -two million more than at the end of 2001. Of these, 3.2 million are children under 15.

The World Health Organisation (WHO) estimates that TB kills two million people every year and malaria between 1.1 and 2.7 million. Malaria kills an African child every 30 seconds. TB overwhelmingly affects people who are economically active while malaria fatalities are concentrated among young children, particularly those under five. HIV/AIDS is the world's fourth biggest killer and is now the leading cause of death in sub-Saharan Africa.

Millions of people know nothing or too little about HIV/AIDS to protect themselves against it. The fight against HIV/AIDS is a major priority and we have committed significant resources to support HIV/AIDS programmes, including nationally-led, inter-sectoral HIV/AIDS plans, particularly in Africa. The DFID Country Assistance Plan for Malawi, produced in April 2003, included funds for a National Strategic Framework on HIV/AIDS and a strategy to mainstream consideration of the epidemic in all policy areas.

The UK has committed $200 million over five years to the Global Fund to Fight HIV/AIDS, TB and Malaria. This fund was set up following the UN Secretary General's call in April 2001 for the creation of a global fund to fight AIDS. The purpose of the fund is to attract, manage and disburse additional resources through a new public-private partnership. To date, more than US$2.1 billion has been pledged to this fund. Many diseases can be prevented with existing medicines but many people cannot obtain the treatments they need. For example, only one person in three with TB currently has access to treatment.

Around the world, one adult in five is illiterate -most of them women. One hundred and thirteen million children, of whom two-thirds are girls, are not enrolled in school.Most of these children live in Asia, but the challenges are greatest and most complex in sub-Saharan Africa. Everyone has a right to education. Education is an essential part of economic and social development.

Improving levels of education is an important tool in helping to achieve sustainable development and eliminate poverty, preventing conflict and promoting good governance. Education gives people the means by which they can transform their own lives and society. It enables people to use and extend their skills, develop new skills and thereby improve their livelihoods. Equal access to education is critical to eliminating all forms of discrimination. Poverty, conflict, the HIV/AIDS pandemic, gender discrimination and social exclusion are all barriers to achieving education for all.

The Millennium Development Goals set the targets of universal access to primary education by 2015 and gender equality in primary and secondary schooling by 2005. To achieve these targets, governments must make a sustained commitment to sound, long-term policies that recognise the strategic contribution education makes to development. They must tackle the central issues of access, affordability, quality, inclusion and use of modern technology. Gender equality requires major cultural shifts. Often the financing of education is insufficient and inequitable, and the institutions responsible for reform and development are weak.

The World Bank launched an education fast-tracking initiative in May 2002 to provide a financing framework for achieving the goals of Education for All. At the last G8 Summit in June 2002, heads of government agreed to increase significantly bilateral assistance for countries that have demonstrated a strong and credible policy and financial commitment to these goals.

8

Human Rights Education in Universities and Colleges

The human rights movement represents a historical journey that began with the institutionalization of political and social orders. Few phenomena have had such a profound impact on history, and few movements have such a universal presence and powerful potential. The concept of human rights is dynamic, changing as society evolves. The "first generation" rights call on governments not to interfere with the exercise of civil and political rights and individual liberties. Second generation rights place a duty on governments to guarantee economic, social, and cultural rights. "Third generation" rights include the right to self-determination of peoples rather than individuals, to sovereignty over their country's natural wealth, and to development and special protection of disadvantaged groups. Until recently only international lawyers, diplomats, and statesmen were concerned with the study of human rights. Increasingly, however, they are becoming subjects of concern for national lawyers, activists, reformers, policymakers, and other citizens due to the following:

— Governments, activists, the elite, opinion builders, and constitutionalists now realize that most countries' constitutions incorporate provisions of various international covenants on human rights. The Founding Fathers in India incorporated in the Constitution most of the rights enumerated in the Universal Declaration of Human Rights.

— A large number of national and international nongovernmental organizations (NGOs) realize that the concept of human rights can support them in their struggle against injustice and inequality.

— The end of the cold war shifted the attention of human rights activists from serving an ideological cause to fighting for social and distributive justice and checking the ever-increasing power of the state.

— New and powerful movements have emerged for feminism, environmental protection and sustainable development, protection of minorities and indigenous people and their culture, and abolition of child labor.

Education is a powerful means of influencing people and changing their attitudes. Unfortunately, the Indian education system has only recently begun to promote human rights. At the undergraduate level, human rights education is generally conducted as international law and Indian constitutional law (fundamental rights). Only the National Law School of India University in Bangalore, offers a full course on human rights for the Bachelor of Laws (LL.B.) In political science departments, human rights education is still a limited part of the course on the constitutional and political development of India (fundamental rights) and international politics (United Nations). In some universities, human rights education is part of sociology, economics, and modern Indian history.

Human rights constitute only a subtopic of the foundation course, which is compulsory for the restructured three-year bachelor of arts. At the master's level specialized human rights education is given in some departments of law as an optional course. No university offers a master of laws (LL.M.) degree exclusively in human rights law. In departments of political science, human rights are taught as part of one or two courses only. Recently, Central University, Hyderabad, and the National Law School of India University (Bangalore) introduced a master's course on human rights using distance education. A few universities are also introducing a one-year postgraduate diploma course in human rights.

Few doctoral dissertations have been written on human rights. More advanced-degree theses have been written on constitutionally guaranteed fundamental rights, their judicial interpretation and enforcement, and have been, by and large, exegetical. There is no full course on human rights education devoted exclusively to human rights studies, except at the nascent Centre for Promotion of Human Rights Education and Research, Jawaharlal Nehru University. The focus on human rights education in India thus far has been limited, social relevance is not projected, and the humanistic roots of human rights are not emphasized. The reason is that the teaching and learning of human rights in India in the 1960s and early 1970s were linked to the international ethos. Teachers were trained in US and other Western law schools.

Human rights studies in India became more important as increasing violations of human rights, cases of custodial violence, mass detentions without trial, bonded and child labor, and environmental degradation and the like were brought to the public's attention by NGOs, the media, and public interest litigators. The work of the National Human Rights Commission (NHRC) became more high-profile, contributing to this new ethos. Human rights educators believe that a grassroots and indigenous orientation and a focus on local human rights problems are more important than projecting international human rights conventions and norms.

Perspective for Human rights Education

Democracy, development, cultural pluralism, and preservation of human rights are interdependent. Democracy is not a mere form of government: it is a set of values and a way of life that ensures respect for everyone's identity, choices, capacities, and abilities. Development is not merely development of material resources but also the betterment of everyone's quality of life. Development and democracy are also linked to the establishment of a new international economic order and the right of countries to develop their own natural resources and of all states and peoples to self-determination. One of the greatest threats to human rights, democracy, and the rule of law in pluralistic societies such as India is conflict over caste, religion, region, and language. Human rights education should promote tolerance and respect for difference and diversity. Another threat to human rights is the unlawful use of force by the state, resulting in rising numbers of custodial deaths, killings in "encounters," and reports of innocent people killed by paramilitary forces. Bonded labor, untouchability, and sati (widow burning) also violate human rights. Discrimination against and exploitation of women and the prevalence of child labor in hazardous industries speaks volumes about the system's insensitivity and lack of commitment to human rights. Human rights education should not only expose these practices but also re-examine laws that permit indirect violence.

Strategies

Human rights education does not merely impart knowledge in the classroom but also sensitizes students, awakens their conscience, and encourages them to respect human rights. Building strong linkages and networking between colleges and universities and various NGOs and other groups working in the field and community will give human rights education a grassroots orientation. Human rights education must have a strong research component and provide training and public information. Audiovisual aids and distance education should be used, among other tools. Extension work has long been recognized by the University Grants Commission (UGC) as important as teaching and research.

The National Service Scheme, women's studies research centers, adult education, and population education programs, and continuing education are area-specific and, along with field action, should be used to bring human rights programs to the grassroots. Legal aid programs in colleges should be more vigorously used by law schools to help the poor. NHRC has the responsibility "to spread human rights literacy and promote awareness of safeguards." NHRC and universities and colleges should cooperate to promote extension programs.

Human rights education can be pursued by simultaneously —introducing separate courses on human rights, —incorporating human rights issues into courses, and —reorienting all courses so that the human rights component is not just an adjunct to the syllabus. Such a strategy is highly flexible and can accommodate each institution's needs, pace of growth, and extent of commitment to human rights education. If human rights education is to become more popular among university and college students, they should be able to expect decent employment after graduation, but there are few human rights-related jobs in schools, research institutions, and the media. The setting up of proposed human rights courts all over the country could employ substantial numbers of students. Inclusion of human rights as a subject in the national competitive examinations also deserves consideration. Public service providers such as the railways, the post office, telecommunications and electricity agencies, as well as all courts, prisons, and law enforcement agencies, should appoint human rights experts as advisers and trainers.

Scope of Human Rights Courses

Human rights education should be interdisciplinary and incorporate the following:

— philosophical and cultural bases and historical perspectives, theories, and movements (national as well as international); —interdependence of and linkages between human rights and democracy, pluralism, development, ecological balance, peace, and harmony at the national and international level;

— a national perspective-the historical context; colonialism and postcolonialism; post-independence national development; protection for the weak and marginalized groups, including minorities, women, and children; the violation of rights by the state and its agencies (the police and criminal justice system);

laws, bylaws, and rules inconsistent with human rights; violation of rights by armed political groups and terrorists; violation of the rights of the poor and weak by dominant groups; gender inequality, exploitation, and injustice; the role of the judiciary, NHRC, and the statutory commissions on women, minorities, scheduled castes and scheduled tribes, and linguistic minorities; the role of NGOs and the media in protecting and promoting human rights;

— regional perspectives-pluralism, poverty, the colonial past, rigid social structures, mass illiteracy, constant political instability, growing consumerism, and recent economic and structural readjustment reforms;

— emergence of the South Asia Association for Regional Cooperation (SAARC) and the debate over the need for a South Asia charter of human rights, and other regional developments such as the emergence of the European Charter on Human Rights, European Court on Human Rights, European Parliament, and South-South dialogue;

— international perspectives—the study of texts, treaties, arrangements, and structures innovated by the international community after World War II to protect human rights; effect of the cold war on institutions to promote and protect human rights; the end of the cold war and its influence on human rights; the role of developed societies in promoting human rights; the role of institutions such as the United Nations, United Nations High Commission for Refugees, United Nations Educational, Scientific, and Cultural Organization (UNESCO), World Health Organization, and International Labour Organization in promoting human rights; and how these institutions succeeded or failed in promoting human rights.

Some modules for graduate, postgraduate, and diploma courses were suggested in the report of the UGC workshop on human rights education in 1994. Similar modules need to be suggested for short (3-6-month) certificate courses for teachers, law enforcement personnel, and NGO workers. The chair of UGC has recently set up a committee to draw up an undergraduate course on human rights for all universities.

Curriculum Development

Curriculum development should also take into account the changing global, national, and regional socioeconomic and cultural contexts. Textbooks need to be integrated with other materials that refer to local experiences. Preparing, revising, and updating teaching materials is slow, time-consuming, imaginative, and arduous, and entails long-term collaboration among experienced human rights teachers and activists. Above all, the thrust of human rights education is sensitizing the community, changing attitudes, and creating a human rights culture.

Appropriate teaching methods are required for teachers, students, NGOs, other activists, field workers, government personnel (police, army, and other law enforcement agencies), and institutions. The objective could be to disseminate awareness of rights and obligations, or enforce a particular right of a specific group or class, or train law enforcement personnel to respect human rights. Teaching methodology remains neglected in several disciplines. Periodic workshops with interdisciplinary participation, including that of NGOs, could be rewarding.

Holding periodic workshops of those engaged in human rights education in universities, and at the regional and national level could go a long way in building capacities and expertise.

Experiences can be exchanged through a newsletter for all human rights education institutions. Keeping in touch with international developments in human rights education is important. Attending human rights education courses abroad and participating in international conferences and workshops should be encouraged.

Human rights educators should gain field experience to test their methodologies and see for themselves how structures oppress and exploit prisoners, those under trial, children in protective homes, and unorganized and bonded labor. Organizing and mobilizing women against pollution or displacement, or preparing a public interest petition requires innovating strategies and techniques and creating new knowledge. Field experience needs strong linkages between colleges and universities and NGOs and other groups working for justice and human rights.

Training of Teachers

Teachers not only require training in pedagogy, preparation of teaching materials, development of curriculum, identification of projects for study and research, research methodology, formulation and direction of students' activities, and interaction with various agencies, but also in effective communication. Training of teachers should be done through regular workshops conducted with the help of resource persons from various fields, and through application exercises. Help from staff colleges would be useful as would international exchanges and university experience. Departments of social work should identify resource persons from all over the country. NGO and other social activists also require training, perhaps by universities. NGOs should thus be identified, and their profiles prepared and classified.

National and State Human Rights Commissions

The establishment of NHRC and human rights commissions in some states has greatly promoted human rights. Through these commissions' efforts a significant national initiative has been institutionalized. Liaison and coordination are also envisaged among the commissions for women, religious minorities, linguistic minorities, scheduled castes, and scheduled tribes. Coordination of universities with NHRC is minimal but their recent interaction with the UGC has sparked some interest among universities and colleges in promoting human rights education. NHRC could entrust universities and teachers with investigation, collection of data, compilation of study reports, and visits on behalf of the commission. Areas and modalities of coordination between NHRC and the universities should be spelled out.

Human Rights Education Centers and Cells

National coordination and management of human rights education activities is indispensable for the program's success. A human rights center or cell should be set up in the UGC to create a reference database on human rights education, disseminate information, oversee execution of programs and projects, and organize workshops and other meetings. The center should work under a director, whom the UGC may choose from teachers of repute and with standing in the field of human rights. A small committee of people of proven competence and commitment to human rights education should guide the center or cell. The center or cell should be provided supporting staff and equipment by the UGC. In the long run a full-fledged documentation center is needed, and seeking help from global financing agencies to set it up may be viable.

9

Human Rights and HIV/AIDS

The epidemic can be combated effectively on the one hand only with an enabling legal environment, and on the other, societal acceptance through sustained sensitisation and the elimination of stigma and discrimination. Many of the key strategies against HIV-especially those dealing with behaviour change among vulnerable groups-require a set of legal and statutory changes that make it feasible for PLWHA to have a greater voice in decisions affecting their own lives, without fear of being stigmatised and discriminated against. Treating HIV prevention as a core component of the policy framework of human development can help accomplish this task, since the objective of a 'caring society' is common to the concerns of human rights and AIDS activists. Human rights are now widely accepted as being central to any community or nation's effective response to HIV/AIDS. This has been acknowledged both in international documents and national responses. It is important, then, to assess the role and importance of a human rights framework in responding to HIV/AIDS.

Human rights are inherent in and inalienable to every individual. They render the government and the larger society accountable to the citizen. Every individual has a right to live with freedom and dignity and 'citizens' are the 'duty holders' obligated to respect, protect and address this fundamental need. Human rights are not given or bestowed upon people by individual governments or society but are earned by virtue of being born 'human'. As Justice J.S. Verma, former chairperson of India's National Human Rights Commission so aptly put it, "dignity is the entitlement of all as long as life exists." HDR 2000 defines human rights as "the rights possessed by all persons, by virtue of their common humanity, to live a life of freedom and dignity. They give people moral claims on the behaviour of individuals and in the design of social arrangements—and are universal, inalienable and indivisible."

The value of a human rights approach lies not only in principles such as state accountability and popular participation, but also in the normative potential of rights to alleviate injustice, inequality and poverty. The conceptual framework of human development places people at the centre as empowered beings. It embodies a rights-based approach to development that could serve as the appropriate frame of reference for integrating the human rights concerns in the struggle against HIV. Principles of GIPA are, therefore, intrinsic to the human development approach. "The protection of human rights is essential to safeguard human dignity in the context of HIV/AIDS and to ensure an effective, rights-based response to HIV/AIDS. An effective response requires the implementation of all human rights, civil and political, economic, social and cultural, and fundamental freedoms of all people, in accordance with existing international human rights standards...". Addressing the epidemic within a human rights framework involves a strong emphasis on acceptance and nondiscrimination of populations perceived to be more vulnerable to HIV.

The last decade has witnessed the increasing concentration of the epidemic in the developing world where the response needs to not only protect individual rights and privacy, but must also deal with wider developmental concerns like poverty, gender and inequality. Such an approach will encompass the International Covenant on Economic and Social Rights, the Convention on the Elimination of All Forms of Discrimination Against Women (CEDAW) and the Convention on Rights of the Child (CRC). In sum, it will capture the spirit of the Universal Declaration of Human Rights, which talks about poverty being the greatest denial of human rights.

Importance of Human Rights to HIV/AIDS

It has been argued that protecting the rights of those affected and at risk is the best public health strategy to cope with an epidemic. A rights-based approach recognises vulnerability to the epidemic not just in terms of individual behaviour but also the social, cultural and economic conditions that lead to this vulnerability. It also recognises that the vulnerability of women, children, migrant workers, men who have sex with men, injecting drug users and sex workers can be reduced through the protection of their human rights. It is only when the stigma and discrimination faced by PLWHA is eliminated, that they can be empowered to take control of their lives. Protection of human rights helps to create a supportive environment, encouraging PLWHA to access the various health and HIV/AIDS related social services and, consequently, stimulating behaviour change. This position has been vindicated by the experiences of several countries.

The international response to HIV/AIDS has been characterised by two diametrically opposed public health approaches—the isolationist approach and the integrationist approach. The isolationist response proposes three basic strategies for HIV/AIDS prevention: compulsory and universal HIV screening, the disclosure of the HIV status of those testing positive and their isolation from larger society through discriminatory practices. The integrationist strategy, on the other hand, proposes voluntary testing following informed consent, the non-disclosure of a person's HIV-positive status and the equitable treatment of PLWHA in healthcare, employment and all other facets of life. Integrationist policies were based on the fundamental human rights of individuals to self-autonomy, privacy and equality. The basis of this philosophy was that, in the long term, voluntary testing, confidentiality and non-discrimination would encourage people to come out and access health services. This, in turn, would increase the possibility of bringing about behaviour change and instilling a sense of personal responsibility through counselling, thus helping retard the spread of the virus.

The integrationist approach, therefore, sought to battle and reduce stigma whereas the isolationist approach sought to increase it, thus pushing the epidemic further underground. Initially, the isolationist response, requiring as it did the disclosure of the positive status of persons in order to protect the rest of society from the spread of the epidemic, was felt to be most appropriate in South Asia.

However, this approach was given up when it was seen to be violating people's human rights and fuelling stigmatisation. HIV-related discrimination first attracted attention in the region when India announced the testing of foreign students, mainly those of African origin. This was followed by an announcement that certain categories of long-term residents also had to be tested for HIV. Concerns that foreigners might transmit the infection to the local population prompted the preparation of a draft bill prohibiting marriage between foreigners and Indian nationals.

Fortunately, the proposed legislation did not see the light of day. The realisation gradually dawned that the isolation versus integration debate could not be perceived as an issue of public interest versus individual rights. It came to be acknowledged that the protection of the individual was itself in the public interest as it increased accessibility to services and brought the epidemic into the open. This enabled concerted and effective public health interventions that were ultimately beneficial to society at large. An outstanding example of a successful, integrationist rights-based approach is that of the STD/HIV Intervention Project (SHIP) in the red-light area of Sonagachi in the Indian city of Kolkata. The empowerment of sex workers in SHIP brought about significant improvements in their health as evidenced by a drastic decline in STD rates and the marginal rise in HIV infection.

Certain key legal issues arose in the context of HIV/AIDS, which the human rights framework had to consider. The three issues at the core of any response to HIV-consent to testing, non-disclosure of HIV status and anti-discrimination-required that policies be informed by three fundamental human rights—those of selfautonomy, confidentiality/privacy and equality. The issue of consent to testing addressed the question of whether testing should be voluntary or mandatory. Consent, therefore, dealt with the right to selfautonomy, to decide for oneself what can be done to one's own body. The issue of non-disclosure was based on the right to privacy/confidentiality. It was also based on the very pragmatic consideration that disclosure (since that might lead to stigma and discrimination) would make people distrust healthcare and shy away from it, thereby driving the epidemic underground.

Anti-discrimination was based on the fundamental right to equality - that HIV positive status should not prevent persons from accessing services (healthcare, education, employment, insurance, travel etc.) and lead to their being treated unequally from others. These issues also exemplified the famous paradox-that the best way to control HIV/AIDS is to protect those most vulnerable and those affected. Help, support and protection for the infected and their carers has been identified as a key strand of the campaign against HIV/AIDS. "Protecting the groups and individuals at risk is a moral obligation, a priority strategy owed to brothers and sisters because, like us, they are human.

They feel. They suffer. They and their families are cruelly burdened when this infection takes hold, and nowhere more so than in poorer, developing countries where palliative drugs are generally unavailable, social support outside the family, is negligible and where stigmatisation based on ignorance and prejudice is rife. Prevention is not the only strategy." There are certain ethical issues that are important considerations in the human rights-based approach to HIV/AIDS. With the realisation that the denial of fundamental human rights had to be tackled for HIV/AIDS to be effectively controlled, other key legal issues addressing the fundamental right to life required consideration. It was noticed that those most susceptible to HIV/AIDS were persons who were legally and socially disempowered and whose basic rights were denied to them. These groups did not have the basic human rights to lead a wholesome life, which could guard them against public health crises, particularly HIV/AIDS. These populations included injecting drug users, prisoners, sex workers, women, women experiencing gender violence, children, migrant workers and men who have sex with men.

Therefore, it was understood that enforcing positive rights (the entire range of socio-economic rights), law reform and decriminalising behaviours would help in controlling the spread of HIV/AIDS within these groups and, thereby, its spread within the general population as well. In order to achieve this, reviewing and amending laws that prejudice, criminalise and marginalise these groups is essential, and this needs to be supported by changes in underlying cultural and social attitudes. It is important to demonstrate the link between globally recognised human rights standards and the response to HIV/AIDS.

HIV/AIDS and Human Rights in South Asia

Research shows that discrimination is most frequently associated with diseases that have severe (incurable and progressive) outcomes and modes of transmission that are perceived to be under an individual's personal behavioural control. Unfortunately HIV/AIDS fits the criteria perfectly. HIV/AIDS discrimination has led to the use of such terms as 'leper' to label those that are infected with disease as well as to brand them as 'others' or 'deviants'. Metaphors portraying AIDS as retribution or punishment for a sinful life or moral failure are a powerful indication of the stigma attached to HIV/AIDS.

Through stigma, society often blames infected people for being ill and asserts the innocence and health of the stigmatisers". While many serious diseases attract stigma and discrimination, HIV/AIDS is particularly open to generate responses which 'discredit' those who are infected. This is both because the routes of HIV transmission include sexual behaviour and the sharing of injecting equipment by drugs users—behaviours that are considered shameful or illegal in many societies—and because many of the groups that have been most affected are already marginalised and stigmatised within society. This stigma has been compounded by fear due to lack of knowledge within South Asian societies about the modes of HIV transmission. This lack of knowledge is evident even among policymakers and healthcare workers who have often applied unnecessary and restrictive measures to PLWHA, thereby fuelling the misconceptions, fear and stigma relating to the disease as well as violating individual rights.

HIV-related stigma is built upon, and serves to strengthen and legitimise, existing social inequalities. The power imbalances and socio-economic and gender inequalities within South Asian societies combine with taboos around sexuality, fear and ignorance about HIV transmission, to create a powerful stigma attached to HIV/AIDS. Marginalised groups are also stigmatised partly because there is little general understanding of the structural factors that make them vulnerable to HIV.

Therefore, better understanding of the development aspects of HIV would help reduce stigma surrounding them.

Throughout the region, people living with HIV/AIDS (PLWHA) have experienced violent attacks, refusal of medical treatment, rejection from families, communities and from the workplace, denial of last rites and many other rights violations. In Bangladesh, there have been cases of PLWHA being held in police custody, while in India a Supreme Court judgement had "suspended" HIV-positive people's right to marry in 1998, though that right has now been restored. This is happening despite the UN Commission on Human Rights clearly stating: "Discrimination on the basis of HIV or AIDS status, actual or presumed, is prohibited by existing international human rights standards, and the term, 'or other status' in nondiscrimination provisions in international human rights texts should be interpreted to cover health status, including HIV/AIDS".

A recent study of the attitudes and behaviour of health service providers indicates that stigma and discrimination pervades the hospital system as well. The stigma and discrimination attached to HIV/AIDS also hampers prevention efforts, as people are less willing to test for HIV or to admit to their positive status. Many PLWHA, therefore, do not receive the support needed for behaviour change and are not involved in HIV-related responses. This also results in a lack of accurate information about levels of HIV prevalence, making informed preparation and responses impossible. Such denial and secrecy takes place not just at a personal, but also at a social level, with communities and nations across the region refusing to admit the scale of the problem.

Social Violence and Human Rights Violations

The active role of civil society, including that of local decision-policy-makers, in protecting the rights of individual community members is crucial in sustaining the socio-cultural fabric of any community. Given the existing environment of intolerance, stigma and discrimination, societal acceptance is particularly crucial for the effective implementation of HIV-related legislation. There is evidence within South Asia that human rights violations and violence against individuals are often aggravated within existing community structures.

Studies in South Asia reveal that more women die from violence-induced causes than from maternal mortality. The lives of millions of women in this region are defined by traditions that enforce submission to men and endorse unequal treatment. In some countries, it is reported that young girls and women are sometimes killed by their relatives even if they are raped, as they are blamed for bringing dishonour to the family. Women from Bangladesh who have been in the sex trade also fear being killed by their families. Apart from traditional mindset, another reason for such manifestations of violations is the lack of access that women have over familial assets, exacerbating socioeconomic insecurities.

Since young women and girls lack education, there are limited livelihood opportunities available to them, especially since the existing social support mechanism around them is inadequate. Such skewed socio-cultural realities and trends seriously challenge the right to development for many, besides infringing their basic human rights. Women living in these insecure conditions are vulnerable to trafficking and sexual violence and, therefore, to HIV. Gender inequities and stereotypes in South Asia increase the vulnerability of young women, and to a lesser extent young men, to HIV and create an environment in which it is easy for HIV to spread. The taboos around the open discussion of sex and the social value that is placed on the ignorance of women and girls with regards to sexuality, safer sex and relationships creates a situation in which women and girls engage in sexual relationships without the basic information, resources, confidence and skills needed to protect themselves from HIV.

The strong pressure on women and men to conform to widely held gender ideals creates a situation in which it is often socially unacceptable for both women and men to seek information on sex that would empower them to protect themselves from HIV. For women, ignorance of sexual matters is valued as a sign of 'purity' and 'innocence', while knowledge about sex is seen as a sign of 'immorality', making it difficult for them to seek information on sexual matters. Men, on the other hand, are expected to conform to a masculine ideal which values sexual knowledge and experience with a variety of partners, often making it hard for them to admit ignorance on sexual matters and seek information and support. In addition to the existing cultural value placed on sexual inexperience in women, it has been seen that the HIV epidemic can prompt older men to seek ever younger partners who they believe will be less sexually experienced and therefore less likely to be infected by HIV. This makes young women more vulnerable to being infected by older men with wider sexual experience.

Sex between men is common within South Asia, as it is in other societies. However, such sex is generally not viewed as 'homosexual' and those men engaging in it are rarely part of any 'gay' community. Moreover, such activities are taboo and not widely talked about, and are also officially outlawed in most South Asian countries, often by old British colonial laws that have been left in place. Despite this, it appears that in many countries young men have their early sexual experiences with other young men and that many go on to continued bisexual activity in later life. For example, 50 per cent of male university students interviewed in Sri Lanka reported that their first sexual experience had been with another man. While male bisexuality cannot be understood simply as a response to men's lack of access to women, it is likely that restrictions on contact between men and women in many South Asian cultures do play a part in the widespread nature of sex between men as an alternative means of sexual expression.

The Bangladeshi capital of Dhaka found that the rights of men who have sex with men, including male sex workers, were being violated with increasing frequency. The study went on to establish that such violations affected their self-esteem, negotiating power, and ultimately increased their vulnerability to HIV/AIDS. For men, selling sex is both highly stigmatised and illegal in most of South Asia. Although male sex workers are often more aware of their vulnerabilities to HIV and STIs than their peers, the fact that they are an extremely marginalised group, and are forced to operate in circumstances over which they have very little control, makes it extremely difficult for them to protect themselves. It is particularly difficult for young men to negotiate safer sex with older and more powerful male partners, and when anal sex is practised, the unavailability of condoms and lubricants can exacerbate the vulnerabilities that they face. Migration is a survival strategy for many individuals in search of work within South Asia.

The region is currently undergoing major macro economic changes as part of the process of globalisation, which has opened up many avenues for large-scale labour mobility. Poverty, absence of adequate or appropriate livelihood options, depleting rural employment opportunities, caste and gender-based exploitation and oppression, violence and conflict, the hope of finding better opportunities elsewhere and the search for a better life are among the key factors that make people move in search of livelihoods. Migration patterns from the region include internal and inter-country mobility, as well as overseas migration. The migration trends depend upon socioeconomic and geographical factors as well as tradition/past migration experiences in the source community, availability of local livelihood options and proximity to metropolitan cities. According to figures from the Bureau of Manpower and Employment and Training of Bangladesh, the average number of documented migrant workers, both skilled and unskilled, is about 200,000 per year.

In India, according to the National Sample Survey, 24.68 per cent of the population-approximately 200 million people-were recorded as having migrated, either within India, to neighbouring countries or overseas. Recent studies have estimated the annual flow of workers overseas to be well over 100,000, 80 per cent of them from the unskilled sector. Nepal's Department of Labour has registered 52,170 overseas migrant workers, and this figure does not include the vast numbers crossing the open border into India, for which estimates are as high as one million. Figures provided by the Bureau of Emigration and

Overseas Employment of Pakistan for 1999 show 2,790,221 migrant workers working abroad. Its major cities house vast migrant populations both from within Pakistan and outside. Roughly 20 per cent of the population of Karachi consists of individuals who have come from other provinces or are migrants from Afghanistan, Bangladesh, Myanmar, Philippines and the Central Asian states. The total number of Sri Lankans abroad is estimated to be around 788,000, of whom 90 per cent are in West Asia, including Saudi Arabia, Kuwait and the United Arab Emirates. In 1999 alone, almost 180,000 people are recorded as having left Sri Lanka for employment abroad, out of which 64.5 per cent were females. Besides official data on number of departures and arrivals at ports of entry, there is substantial movement by people unofficially, by refugees, immigrants and temporary residents.

A factor that significantly influences the decisions of potential migrants is the narrative of returning migrants, who, in their desire to create a favourable impression, highlight monetary gains and underplay or gloss over experiences of exploitation and abuse. The decision to migrate, therefore, is often based on little more than an ill-defined impression that life will offer more elsewhere, with very little information about the ground realities. Migrants contribute to the development of local economies in both the source and destination countries. Earnings from work abroad are a vital source of income for migrants' families back home. In many cases, the remittances from foreign migrant workers are one of the main sources of foreign exchange for countries in the region.

In Sri Lanka, such remittances form the bulk of foreign exchange earnings. In Pakistan, remittances in 1993 were estimated to be 44 per cent of the total earnings from exports. In Bangladesh, foreign employment is the second highest source of foreign exchange earnings after garment exports. Migrant workers are a source of cheap labour in destination countries, since many of them work for lower wages than the resident workers. It is, however, paradoxical that in spite of this, a majority of these migrants are poor, do not have access to health services and are exploited and neglected. They reside in squatter settlements and urban slums and are employed in the informal sector. Being 'foreign workers', they are often not covered by the same legal protections as their local counterparts, and are generally unaware of their rights as workers. A large number among them have to cope with insecurities in their jobs, unsteady incomes, cultural alienation, lack of access to social support systems and social capital and loneliness. It is these very challenges that make migrants more vulnerable to HIV infection.

However, attempts to establish intuitive links between mobility and HIV/AIDS have often resulted in stigmatisation of migrants as well as restrictions on them, including forced testing for HIV and deportation of those found positive and limitations on the rights of women to move in some countries. The inhumane and exploitative conditions that most migrants face in source areas, during transit and within host communities in destination countries need to be changed and a comprehensive response needs to be developed to facilitate safe migration, thereby reducing HIV/AIDS related vulnerabilities. It must be stressed that migrants are neither 'carriers' of the virus nor are they responsible for the spread of the epidemic. They are often unaware of whether they have been exposed to HIV and of the potential harm this poses to their spouse and unborn children. Most of those returning home because of illness arising from various opportunistic infections are not aware that HIV is the cause of their poor health.

Many, especially those in West Asia, are reported without explanation if found to be HIV positive. In the rare cases where they may have knowledge about their HIV status, the climate of stigma and discrimination makes them reluctant to disclose their status within their communities and even families. Importantly, the female spouses/partners of male migrants are further disadvantaged because existing asymmetrical power and gender equations make it difficult for them to protect themselves against HIV infection. The gender dimension of migration related vulnerability presents a complex picture. The number of women migrating is increasing within South Asia. Globally, the percentage share of female labour in the total agricultural labour force is reported to have increased from 44 per cent to 48 per cent within the last 50 years, in spite of the share of agricultural labour within the total labour force declining by over 20 per cent within the same time period. Such gender-specific trends also give rise to particular migratory patterns, leading to what may be termed the 'feminisation of migration' across the region.

For many women, migration-in addition to being a livelihood strategy—is also an escape route from limitations imposed by traditional societies, oppressive laws and abuse or violence. A study in Bangladesh has shown that families tend to urge women to migrate when they are perceived as being a burden to the family. There are also higher expectations from women to send back remittances, compared to young men. The circumstances of such migration processes, coupled with the limited preparedness, may create conditions that lead to women-especially young girls-being lured with false promises of employment and marriage and being trafficked into the sex trade, slavery and exploitation. Gender biases limit the access of women migrants to information and services that could make their movement safer. These women also lack support mechanisms within their source communities, thus confining their knowledge to hearsay. All these factors exacerbate women's vulnerability to HIV. Women migrants are often victims of violence and harassment. Reports of sexual assault by employers and others are common both within the region and overseas, and legal redress is rarely available or availed of. Further, pressure from the family to send more money may often lead women migrants to supplement their earnings through sex work.

In all of these situations, the ability of women to negotiate safer sex remains low, even if they are aware that they might be exposed to HIV. Contrary to popular belief, the vulnerability to HIV remains high for those migrating with families as well. When men migrate in search of work, women left behind are often exploited including sexually. As sole caretakers of the children and family they are especially vulnerable as the expected incomes from male migrants are often unstable or inadequate.

Apart from women who move, even those whose partners move, leaving them behind, are vulnerable to HIV/AIDS to the extent that they are vulnerable to exploitation and denial of rights. Their lower position in society and their limited control over their lives heighten their vulnerability to sexual exploitation, particularly when debts have been incurred for covering migration costs and remittances fail to come. Where women move alone, leaving their spouse and children behind, the men are often involved in multi-partner sexual relationships and girl children are known to become exposed to situations of sexual exploitation, abuse, rape and incest. The region has several examples of effective responses aimed at reducing the vulnerability of migrant populations. Formal pre-departure trainings in Sri Lanka, initiatives for interactions between returnee migrants and out-going migrants in Bangladesh, multi-sectoral responses to address the broad spectrum of needs of migrants in selected source areas in Nepal and India are some examples. However, there is need for concerted and more comprehensive responses. All efforts to reduce the HIV vulnerabilities associated with mobility need to address the broader issues of poverty, livelihoods, education, access to information and services and the need for a rights-sensitive legal environment. Effective responses would necessarily reflect the voices of migrants and their needs and would involve returnee migrants, spouses, youth, key enforcement personnel, recruiting agencies and PLWHA, addressing vulnerabilities at source, during transit and in destination countries. Most importantly, all efforts to reduce the vulnerability of migrant populations must be careful not to stigmatise the migrants or their families and communities.

Trafficked Women and Girl

For a large number of people in the region, migration has become a key survival strategy. However, the lack of safe, secure and legal channels for migration drive unsuspecting and uninformed women and girls into the hands of unscrupulous agents and traffickers who promise them 'good jobs' and 'safe travel' into sites of work. These are usually young men, themselves from poor families, who are lured into the trafficking networks in order to support their own families.

Because trafficking is an illegal and concealed activity, it is difficult to be precise about the exact numbers of women and children involved. Estimates are based on the reports of law enforcement agencies, researchers and groups working with survivors and communities, and indicate that hundreds of thousands of women and children have been or are vulnerable to being trafficked from South Asia. Sources estimate that 10,000-20,000 women and children are trafficked from Bangladesh every year. NGOs have estimated that 5,000-7,000 girls from Nepal are annually trafficked into Indian brothels. The factors contributing to an increase in the trafficking of women are as follows:

— increased demand and supply of trafficked persons;
— professionalisation of the traffickers and syndicates;
— modern transport, technology and the Internet;
— the growth of sex tourism;
— the feminisation of poverty;
— trading in human organs;
— the changing nature of sex work; and the erosion of social capital.

The all-pervasive neglect, discrimination and sexual abuse of women and girls in the region are responsible for their increased vulnerability to being trafficked, and to HIV/AIDS. Research shows that women and girls often end up bearing the triple burden of exploitation—they are poor, they form a marginalised group and they are women. HIV prevalence rates has been estimated to be as high as 60 per cent in the brothels of Mumbai, India, where condom usage is very low. It is extremely difficult for sex workers who are HIV positive to get medical treatment, and once found to be HIV positive, or too sick to receive customers, they are thrown out of the brothels. This often forces them into informal and unsafe sex work for survival. Significantly, the region is witnessing a dangerous trend of younger girls being trafficked increasingly to satisfy consumer demand.

According to the Coalition Against Trafficking in Women (CATW), the average age of girls trafficked from Nepal into India has fallen over the past decade from 14-16 years to 10-14 years. One common myth fuelling the demand for young girls in South Asia and West Asia is that sex with a virgin girl can cure STIs and HIV/AIDS. This means that the youngest girls, biologically the most vulnerable to HIV infection, are especially sought out for unprotected sex by the men most likely to infect them. Women in Afghanistan have endured a particularly difficult environment, having been, until recently, denied even the most basic rights, including employment and education. The female literacy rate is one of the world's lowest-15 per cent in 1995. Decades of political and civil unrest and conflict had heightened their vulnerability to violence. Emerging information by Amnesty International, indicates that Afghan women and girls had been treated as the spoils of war, and were being systematically kidnapped and raped by fighters. Orphans, women with disabilities, and widows, who are often very young, have been noted as being particularly vulnerable. Poor widowed women with little or no financial support or means of earning a livelihood are forced to resort to beggary to feed their children, thus getting exposed to abuse, including sexual abuse.

In an atmosphere of silence and taboos about sex, this only heightens the vulnerability of women and girls to

HIV/AIDS. Furthermore, there are reports of rising levels of drug use among displaced Afghan men, unsafe sexual relationships, and the migration of male refugees to metropolitan centres, such as Karachi in Pakistan to find work. Many of these men are uninformed about safe sex practices and are themselves vulnerable to HIV/AIDS. On their return, they increase the vulnerability of their wives/ female partners to HIV/AIDS. Trafficking and HIV/AIDS are presenting serious threats to the health, dignity and lives of young women and girls across the region. The nexus of poverty, HIV and the marketing of youth within and across borders is creating ever-widening circles of desperate insecurity and disproportionately threatens the lives of young girls, making poor people poorer through sickness, loss of livelihoods and rejection by society. The epidemic is severely undermining human security and human rights, destroying the lives of individuals and families and posing a serious threat to the social capital and the overall development of the region.

Trafficked persons in South Asia are often discriminated against even by their own communities, once they return or are repatriated from destination countries. The process of re-integration for trafficked survivors is an uphill task, since their communities ostracise them. This is even more pronounced in the case of trafficked survivors who are HIV-positive. Studies in Nepal have documented that HIV positive survivors of trafficking are often stigmatised and find it impossible to re-integrate themselves into their communities. Urgent and integrated action at the national and regional levels is required to address the multiple and complex ways in which the security and rights of young girls are threatened. The integral connection between HIV/AIDS, gender and trafficking through the nexus of vulnerability and sexual violence, can be summed up as follows:

— the factors, which determine the context of trafficking, are also the factors, which are associated with the increased vulnerability of women and girls to HIV/AIDS. Specifically, these relate to gender-related social and economic disempowerment, lack of social capital formation and unequal access to all the indicators of development, including health, information and education. Such circumstances severely undermine the basic rights to social protection and the right to the highest attainable standard of living;

— trafficking is part of a pattern of migration within and across countries, which removes persons from the protection of their communities and severs them from their systems of social support. These very factors are recognised as causes fuelling the continued spread of the HIV epidemic, and which, in turn, violate a person's right to a standard of living adequate for the health and wellbeing of oneself and one's family;

— those caught in the web of trafficking face an increased vulnerability to HIV/AIDS on account of their inability to control their working and living conditions, including sexual relations, as well as their inability to come out of it. Such situations grossly violate a person's right to freedom from slavery or servitude and the right to physical integrity (security of person); and common societal responses to those affected by HIV/AIDS as well as trafficking are strongly influenced by stigmatisation, discrimination and further marginalisation.

These responses, in turn, undermine the basic rights and freedoms of these affected individuals, including the right to mobility and residence, the right to essential services, right to confidentiality, right to free association, and sexual and reproductive rights. It is important to briefly explain the legal frameworks within which most PLWHA in South Asia live. Some of the fundamental human rights are covered under several of South Asia's national constitutions, although the scope of these rights varies from country to country, as does their application in the context of PLWHA. Nations who are signatories to international documents/agreements/ conventions are bound by the standards laid down therein, depending on the binding nature of the document and the manner in which each country codifies it within its national laws. Very few nations in the world-and none in South Asia-have specific statutory laws governing HIV/AIDS or ensuring protections to PLWHA. Fundamental rights guaranteed by national constitutions are, therefore, the prime source of law in South Asia. However, there are also customary and personal laws, particularly in South Asia, that determine the rights of individuals, especially women.

Apart from constitutional guarantees, policies and guidelines on HIV/AIDS drawn up by national governments often become the prime basis on which the rights of PLWHA are defined. However, in India, governmental policies/guidelines cannot be enforced by the courts, though many rights of PLWHA are defined through court judgments as India is governed by the system of English common law. Recently, widely published cases of law enforcement interventions involving harassment of vulnerable group outreach workers created an uproar within civil society in India. Implementation of interventions gets delayed in such a nonenabling environment and lives are lost.

The published cases reveal that national guidelines clash with legislation and law enforcers' instructions. For instance, criminal laws affecting vulnerable populations have impeded sexual health interventions among them. Harm reduction methods like condom distribution and needle exchange programmes could be, and have been, seen as abetting crimes (homosexual sex, sex work, drug use). As a result, their effective implementation has been impossible in many countries. Clearly, clarification, understanding and sensitisation of the particularities of the HIV/AIDS response is needed within law enforcement agencies at first, but also in the judicial administration and the legislature. There has been some interesting development in this regard in India.

Apart from the United States and Australia, the highest number of HIV/AIDS related litigation has perhaps taken place in India. In 1997, the Lawyers' Collective challenged the termination of the services of a worker on the ground of being HIV-positive though the person was otherwise functionally healthy. In a landmark judgement of the Mumbai High Court, the worker was reinstated and paid back wages. More importantly, the Collective was able to obtain an order of suppression of identity because of which the HIV-positive person could sue under a pseudonym.

There are 130 cases handled by the Lawyers' Collective between 1998 and 2001 found that the most important legal issue for men related to employment. In the case of women, the major problem related to maintenance, custody of children and property rights (such as matrimonial or joint property rights). An increase in the number of divorce cases was also noted. It has been suggested that women remain vulnerable within the institution of marriage due to the unjust gender construction of sexuality in various Indian laws. Many of the South Asian countries have undertaken several measures to reform the legal climate surrounding HIV/AIDS. Some of them are:

— organising and training a nation-wide network of lawyers to handle individual complaints;

— providing free legal services;

— organising workshops to formulate policies for the protection of the rights of PLWHA and their families; and

— campaigning for the decriminalisation of homosexuality and sex work and for the formulation of laws covering issues such as HIV testing, confidentiality of HIV test results and discrimination against people with HIV.

Sex workers have used legal redress and access to the justice system to address rights violation, as happened in Bangladesh. The need for legislative reforms has been underlined at regional workshops on HIV law, ethics and human rights organised in the early and mid-1990s by the UNDP Regional Project on Strengthening Responses to the HIV Epidemic in Asia and the Pacific. The issue still remains to be adequately addressed by most countries. In most countries of the region, doctors who wish to prescribe ARVs to survivors of rape find themselves torn between government policy and medical ethics. These drugs are used as 'Post Exposure Prophylaxis' (PEP) for occupational exposure and to reduce mother-to-child transmission of HIV. It has been contended that they should also prove effective for rape survivors. However, many countries limit the use of PEP to occupational exposure and not to rape.

This violates the rights of persons surviving sexual violence, compromises their treatment and care and infringes upon doctors' ethical duties. Moreover, even in countries that have policies for PEP provisions in occupational exposure, there is limited knowledge about such provisions, reducing their operational efficacy.

Reforms concerning gender equality and the empowerment of women do not always receive the much-needed support in male-dominated legislative assemblies. Entrenched conservative attitudes in most countries in the region renders the liberalisation of laws relating to homosexuality difficult. Laws concerning sex work, the availability of condoms in prisons and needle exchange programmes are also treated as being far too controversial by legislators, who prefer to support only what are perceived as 'safe' and conservative measures.

One issue that has dominated the law reform scene in India and Sri Lanka is the proposed repeal of the provision in the respective penal codes making it an offence to engage in "carnal intercourse against the order of nature with any man, woman or animal". This section applies to homosexual as well as heterosexual oral and anal sex, with consent not seen a valid excuse. In 1995, Sri Lanka amended certain sections of the Penal Code and the repeal of the provision dealing with homosexual acts was recommended. In passing the amendment, however, the legislature not only decided to retain the section making homosexuality an offence but widened its scope to cover sexual relations between females by replacing the word "males" with "persons". Such incidences have led to greater harassment of sexual minorities.

A crucial aspect of the human rights of PLWHA is their access to treatment. Denial or lack of such access amounts to a violation of the basic human right to life. The last decade has witnessed a number of significant advances in the understanding of the HIV infection and how it can lead to AIDS. These advances have led to the development of a range of potent drugs to control HIV infection. Both these developments have substantially altered the way in which HIV/AIDS is regarded and treated. The fatal course of HIV infection can now be altered to a chronic manageable condition that allows a person living with HIV to lead a relatively normal life. The drugs that control HIV infection, known as Anti-retroviral drugs (ARVs), are a recent phenomenon and have radically changed the HIV care landscape within a short span of a few years. A combination of three or more different ARVs in various regimens, that as a group are known as Highly Active Anti-Retroviral Therapy (HAART), form the staple of HIV treatment today in developed countries. HIV is one of the most rapidly mutating viruses and its immense capacity for genetic variation enables it to sometimes produce forms that are unresponsive to the drugs that interfere with viral replication. Treating HIV infection with a single ARV drug-monotherapy—quickly leads to drug resistance. The chances of drug resistance are also present in the case of dual therapy. The rule, therefore, is to provide for triple therapy or HAART, where the chances of drug resistance are greatly reduced. In the United States, the widespread use of HAART since 1996 has led to a 50 per cent decline in AIDS incidence, hospital admissions and related deaths.

Developing countries are home to 95 per cent of PLWHA and WHO estimates that 6 million people in these countries are in immediate need of HAART. However, 62 per cent or 500,000 of the 800,000 people estimated to be receiving HAART in 2001 live in developed countries.

Only 230,000 people from developing countries were on HAART in 2002, with Brazil accounting for half this number. HAART reaches only 5 per cent of those who need it in the developing world. In December 2002, around 43,000 people in Asia were receiving HAART, barely 4 per cent of the estimated 1,000,000 who needed therapy. "These drugs have saved hundreds of thousands of lives in Europe and the United States. They could do the same for millions more in developing countries. If we can get cold Coca Cola and beer to every remote corner of Africa, it should not be impossible to do the same with drugs."

There are two perspectives on the issue of access to treatment—the instrumentalist perspective of the human capital approach and the human rights perspective of the human development approach. The human capital approach, with its focus on rates of return and affordability by individuals, is against public provisioning of HAART. This school argues that the efforts to step up access to treatment may dilute the focus on HIV prevention while the high costs of HAART may divert scarce resources away from HIV prevention efforts and other competing requirements within the health sector. In other words, HIV prevention and health priorities such as gastroenteritis, tuberculosis, malaria, malnutrition, and population control may merit greater consideration than the medication requirements of a smaller, albeit vocal, special 'interest group' of PLWHA and their advocates. However, if public health action on HIV especially the care and support regime—is perceived as being an example for other health challenges, then it would no longer be viable to see HIV/AIDS as a special interest of a few people. Instead, the approaches and lessons of the HIV/AIDS strategy would help augment the capabilities of the existing public health system at all levels. Indeed, it would be essential to strengthen the primary health centres and local hospitals even to meet the challenge of HIV at its present scale in South Asia, in addition to ongoing work of the NGOs, voluntary counselling and testing centres etc.

In other words, the agenda for health sector reforms in South Asia would be greatly strengthened by mainstreaming HIV/AIDS. Therefore, there is no unavoidable trade-off between the provision of HAART and other health priorities. The second argument of the human capital school is that HAART involves rather complex regimens of expensive drugs that have serious side effects. HAART, therefore, calls for additional investments in training medical personnel in the long term treatment, monitoring and care of PLWHA. Moreover, HAART has to be taken on a fairly regular basis, life-long, implying regular treatment expenditures for several years. In addition, a person living with HIV has to spend on regular medical evaluation to monitor disease progression as well as on treatment for the management of the side effects of HAART.

In all the countries of South Asia, the cost of HAART is significantly higher than the average per capita income. Access to treatment is, thus, a luxury that most South Asian governments and the large majority of their PLWHA cannot afford. The high cost often results in frequent interruption of treatment, especially among the poorer patients and this could lead to drug resistance. Presently, the private sector is the only provider of anti-HIV treatments that include ARV drugs and, in certain cases, even little understood indigenous preparations. The haphazard provision of ARVs further underscores the urgency for governmental initiatives to standardise HAART, train the health sector-both public and private— and provide affordable treatment.

With South Asia bearing more than one-third of the world's TB burden, comprehensive national programmes based on the free distribution of anti-TB drugs have been in operation for several years. In recent times, TB control programmes have also absorbed the added cost of Directly Observed Treatment (DOT). The TB programmes in Bangladesh, Indonesia, Nepal and Myanmar have made considerable strides in achieving high rates of cure through DOT, thus providing the rationale for considering a similar approach in the case of HAART. Though there are few studies to demonstrate the feasibility of DOT for HAART, the approach can work among some groups such as sex workers or injecting drug users.

The human capital school also focuses on the difficulties in implementing initiatives that promote the use of HAART in a resource limited setting. The majority of the population, its advocates argue, is not literate, and good health is not an immediate pre-occupation of poor households. The problem is compounded when the intervention calls for complex patterns of healthcare, in terms of the timings and dosage of drugs, the need for ancillary services such as periodic medical review, counselling and the management of side-effects. The discrimination against PLWHA even by healthcare providers and the healthcare system in general can greatly complicate access to HAART. This line of thinking can be countered, first, by the public obligation argument. PLWHA may be a small fraction of the total population in the region but, at 4.2 million, their numbers are still large and it would be a dereliction of duty not to address the treatment, care and support of such a large number of people. This argument could also be strengthened if the morbidity and the fatality associated with HIV/AIDS is taken into consideration. Approximately 1,000 people are estimated to die every day in the South and South East Asian region, a number that could be compared to two fully loaded jumbo jets crashing everyday. At 400,000 deaths in a year, the death toll from HIV/AIDS is nearly 400 times the combined annual death toll from railway accidents. Ignoring the requirements for treatment would involve accepting a death toll that would be unacceptable in other contexts. Clearly, then, the 'silent emergency' of HIV/AIDS in South Asia requires urgent attention in ensuring affordable and universal access to treatment, care and support.

It would also be erroneous to look at prevention, care and support as mutually exclusive responses to HIV/AIDS. There is enough evidence from various initiatives to show that the availability of care and support has enhanced the success of prevention. The experience of Brazil shows that a policy of providing free or subsidised HAART to PLWHA has helped destigmatise AIDS and facilitated the mainstreaming of HIV-related care. As a result, PLWHA had the opportunity to access counselling on not only treatment but also on prevention and protection for themselves and their families. This inclusive approach embodies the principle of GIPA, by accepting them as partners with healthcare providers in mitigating the impact of HIV and slowing its spread. The humane approach of providing healthcare and prevention services ensures greater credibility, acceptance, sustainability and involvement on the part of both provider and recipient of care. In the case of SHIP in Sonagachi in the Indian city of Kolkata, sex workers were not approached with isolated messages on HIV prevention, but were simply offered free treatment for STIs. Similarly, the Community Health Education Society (CHES) in the Indian city of Chennai provided STI treatment to sex workers with no mention of HIV unless the women brought it up themselves. Once sex workers found that they could receive care in a non-judgmental and non-discriminatory manner, they developed enough trust in the providers to share their intimate concerns about unsafe sexual practices and HIV.

Condoms, made available at this point, were more likely to be accepted with a degree of understanding of why and how they needed to be used. Providing HAART to those in need, along similar lines, is likely to enhance HIV prevention besides providing care. HAART may also contribute to lowering the efficacy of HIV transmission by greatly reducing the numbers of viral particles in the semen and vaginal fluids. The argument that HAART is beyond the reach of people in South Asia also has its limitations. It is true that the cost of the therapy, multiplied by the total number of PLWHA in the region, appear daunting, more so because these are recurring lifetime costs. However, a careful examination of global experiences indicates that affordable treatment need not be an unrealisable dream for developing countries. The WHO has also made efforts to deal with the issue of access. In 2002, it issued guidelines for scaling up ART in resource limited settings, as part of a commitment for expanding the coverage of ART to 3 million people by 2005. The guidelines were developed through a consensual process of consultations with healthcare providers from developed and developing countries and propose a public health approach to the issue. Such an approach incorporates the following elements:

— the scaling up of treatment programmes to meet the needs of PLWHA in resource limited settings;

— the standardisation and simplification of ARV regimens to support the efficient implementation of treatment programmes; and

— ensuring that ARV treatment programmes are based on the best scientific evidence in order to avoid the use of substandard treatment protocols which compromise the treatment outcome of individual clients and create the potential for the emergence of drug resistant virus.

There are also examples of successful government action to ensure affordable or free treatment from developing countries, notably Brazil. Though Brazil's per capita income is significantly higher than that of the South Asian countries, it is still instructive to see how governments can make treatment available to even those from the lower income groups by according the right priority to treatment. The provision of HAART and care, consistent with the frameworks of human development and human rights, help establish the necessity of ensuring affordable and universal access to treatment, care and support for PLWHA in South Asia. A study by British medical journal, Lancet, comparing the costs of HIV prevention versus treatment reported that for every life-year purchased with treatment drugs, 28 life-years could have been purchased with prevention. The study used Cipla's ARV costing of $350 a patient a year and did not include drug distribution costs. The implication is that the scarce resources available to fight AIDS should go to prevention programmes rather than treatment. Similar arguments that the potential savings of investments in prevention far outweigh the monies saved even with low cost ARV treatment intervention in developing countries, raise serious questions regarding the principles that are needed to guide policy makers in adopting public health strategies.

The global debate on whether to accord equal funding priority to treatment and prevention continues, even as there is emerging consensus that a judicious mix of both are needed to achieve any measure of success in dealing with HIV/AIDS. Meanwhile, a number of field-based studies from developing countries are demonstrating the feasibility and benefits of HAART. They show that treatment and prevention can both be achieved in a simple and low cost manner. Model employer- funded programme for South Africa concluded that a programme that focused only on the prevention and treatment of opportunistic infections would be costeffective for all companies and all grades of workers. If it was to prove profitable, HAART would have to be provided at $500 to $750 per patient per year. With Cipla making ARVs available in Africa for less than $370 a year, the potential viability of such a model is greatly enhanced.

The widespread introduction of HAART in low-income countries is dependent on the provision of generic ARV drugs that are either free or heavily subsidised. Meanwhile, HAART, accompanied by low cost options with regard to the routine laboratory monitoring of CD4 cell counts and viral loads, is already being attempted in some resource-limited settings. In the last two years, small groups of people living with HIV are receiving HAART because of the modest efforts of the few small-scale initiatives that exist in the Caribbean, India and Africa. They serve as beacons of hope for the millions in need of ART in the developing world. The access to ARV treatment is severely limited in developing countries in general and South Asia in particular because of several reasons: lack of proper guidelines on the correct selection and use of drugs, lack of adequate and competent health services, lack of affordable drugs on a sustainable basis, high price of patented drugs and low purchasing power.

There have been several attempts by public-private collaborations to offer ART drugs at decreased prices, the most important of these being the Accelerating Access Initiative. Till March 2002, 78 countries had expressed interest in participating in the Initiative. Each of these countries has committed itself to, and is in the process of, developing national care and treatment plans. So far, 18 countries have actually reached an agreement with the drug companies. While the initiative is a useful attempt to lower the price of drugs, it clearly needs to be supplemented by other measures as well. Patents are a major factor in restricting access to ARV drugs. Pharmaceutical companies in high-income countries develop these drugs after years of research and development at high costs. Patents on these drugs preserve monopoly rights on producing them for a minimum number of years and the selling price includes a premium that helps recoup the research costs. Generic versions of these drugs are much cheaper to produce.

The cost of these drugs in a particular country depends on several factors. Some of these are related to patents: whether the pharmaceutical companies have applied for patents in that country (which, in turn, depends on the size and value of the potential market); whether the country permits product patents on pharmaceuticals; and whether it has the technical capacity, market size and the legal framework to produce generic versions of these drugs. Pricing policies within these countries also determine the cost. India, for example, has been imposing price controls on bulk drugs through the Drug Price Control Order (DPCO), 1995. However, the number of drugs under this order have been steadily decreasing after complaints by the industry over loss in profitability. Combined with the change in the patent regime, this has adverse implications for access to affordable drugs.

Till 1995, individual country patent laws were determined by domestic policy. However, the global system of intellectual property rights (IPR) is today much more structured than before. With the establishment of the World Trade Organisation (WTO) Agreement on Trade-Related Intellectual Property Rights (TRIPS), most countries are required to strengthen their intellectual property laws. TRIPS has profound implications for the availability of and access to medicines for the South Asian countries, especially in the context of HIV/AIDS since most of these medicines are the products of ongoing research, and their supply will be immediately affected by changes in patent laws. The TRIPS Agreement, which came into effect in 1995, requires all member countries to extend intellectual property rights to all technologies, covering both products and processes. TRIPS requires countries to recognise product and process patent rights in the pharmaceutical sector and offer patents for a minimum of 20 years in order to protect the rights of innovators and balance them with the rights of consumers.

India, Pakistan, Maldives, Bangladesh and Sri Lanka together account for 98.7 per cent of all HIV/AIDS cases in the region. All five of them are members of the WTO. Nepal and Bhutan currently have observer status at the WTO. Nepal has begun negotiations for accession and Bhutan needs to begin accession negotiations within the next five years. Iran's application for accession has not been unanimously approved by the WTO General Council, and Afghanistan has not yet applied for membership. Despite their varying official WTO status, all countries in the region are affected by the TRIPS Agreement, since (barring India) all of them lack the capacity to manufacture drugs locally and are dependent on imports from countries that are signatories to TRIPS. The single-most important implication of TRIPS for access to treatment is the impact of patent protection on drug prices. In the case of India, several studies have shown that the introduction of patents once TRIPS is implemented can raise the prices of drugs by as much as 200 per cent. TRIPS also affects the production of generic versions of drugs.

Countries in South Asia have different levels of production capacity. India has innovative capabilities and the technical capacity to produce generic versions of drugs. Pakistan, Nepal, Sri Lanka, Afghanistan, Bangladesh and Iran have reproductive capabilities to differing degrees, since the pharmaceutical industry in these countries can manufacture finished products from imported ingredients only. Bhutan and the Maldives depend entirely on imports to fulfil their drug requirements. TRIPS restricts 'reverse engineering' of patented products and increases the waiting time to market generic versions of these products to the 20-year period of patent protection. The generic drugs industry in India owes its existence to the absence of product patents in the pharmaceutical sector and comprises, along with indigenous research-based firms, up to 74 per cent of the total pharmaceutical market. With the advent of TRIPS, the industry will be unable to produce generic versions of new drugs till the patent term expires or a compulsory license is issued.

Apart from TRIPS, several bilateral agreements between developed and developing countries on intellectual property rights have restrictive clauses that sometimes negate the advantages negotiated under the multilateral framework. The United States and Sri Lanka signed a bilateral agreement in 1991, under which the terms for issuing a compulsory license are significantly more stringent than under TRIPS. For example the government is required to negotiate compensation to the companies in all cases of compulsory licenses except when those licenses are granted to remedy violations of competition laws. Also, all decisions regarding compulsory licenses are subject to judicial review. Such terms make many of the flexibilities negotiated under TRIPS redundant.

TRIPS has serious implications for public health outcomes in poor countries since it not only affects medicines for HIV/AIDS but also research in other diseases. Recognising this problem, the TRIPS Agreement provided for exceptions to these rights under certain specific conditions. However, it became increasingly clear that this was not enough. The exceptions could be challenged under the WTO Dispute Settlement Procedures, and developing countries lacked the legal expertise and the resources to fight these often lengthy and expensive battles. As the implications of TRIPS for HIV/AIDS medicines became clearer in the years since the Agreement was signed, civil society groups and HIV/AIDS activists across the world launched an international campaign against the restrictive provisions of the agreement. Developing country governments also felt increasingly constrained by the TRIPS provisions and demanded more flexibility to address their public health concerns.

In response to these concerns, the Doha Declaration on TRIPS and Public Health was adopted at the Fourth WTO Ministerial Conference in 2001. The Declaration reaffirmed the commitment of the WTO members to public health goals. Specifically, members agreed "that the TRIPS Agreement does not and should not prevent Members from taking measures to protect public health...that the Agreement can and should be interpreted and implemented in a manner supportive of WTO Members' right to protect public health and, in particular, to promote access to medicines for all." While the Doha Declaration was primarily a political statement, it lays down clear legal guidelines for dealing with cases in the dispute settlement process, and is an important and necessary reaffirmation of the precedence of public health concerns over patents. Since the Declaration, however, WTO members have found it difficult to reach an agreement on ways of operationalising it. Following the discussions at the mini-ministerial in Sydney, Australia, in 2002, the chairman of the WTO TRIPS Council released a draft on 19 November 2002 for a decision by the General Council. Most countries agreed with the chair's proposal of a moratorium on disputes regarding TRIPS till the Agreement is amended. However, disagreements remain over certain elements of the solution such as coverage, scope of eligible countries, etc.

The Doha Declaration was particularly important for the South Asian region, because most countries are dependent on imported HIV/AIDS drugs, and, given the low purchasing power in these countries, the cost of drugs is an important concern in the provision of treatment. However, the Declaration and the flexibilities in TRIPS at the international level will only partially help in ensuring access. Eventually, implementation of these provisions will be done through national legislation and appropriate domestic policy. Most WTO members in the South Asian region have already altered their patent laws to make them TRIPS-compliant. India, Pakistan and Sri Lanka have time until 1 January 2005 before bringing the pharmaceutical sector under TRIPS. However, it is not clear if all the amendments carried out fully take advantage of the flexibilities under the TRIPS Agreement and the Doha

Declaration. Maldives and Bangladesh, along with other least developed countries have time until 2016 to implement the patent provisions of TRIPS for pharmaceutical products.

The challenge of providing access to good quality drugs to PLWHA is, indeed, a daunting one, dealing as it does with issues of medical research, pricing and intellectual property rights. However, facing the challenge is an integral part of dealing with HIV/AIDS in a rights-based framework. The Universal Declaration of Human Rights has been recognised as the Magna Carta of human rights all over the world. The basic tenets of this declaration are the right to liberty, security and freedom of movement, the right to work, the right to education, the right to social security and services, the right to equality-equal protection before the law, the right to marriage and family and the right to health. International human rights have been further codified in a number of legally binding international covenants and declarations such as the following:

— International Convention on the Elimination of All Forms of Racial Discrimination (CERD-1965)

— International Covenant on Civil and Political Rights (ICCPR-1966)

— International Covenant on Economic, Social and Cultural Rights (ICESCR-1966)

— Convention on the Elimination of All forms of Discrimination Against Women (CEDAW-1979)

— Convention Against Torture and other Cruel, Inhuman or Degrading Treatment or Punishment (CAT -1984)

— Convention on the Rights of the Child (CRC-1989)

International human rights instruments play an important role in respect of HIV/AIDS and human rights, since their norms may guide the establishment of procedural, institutional and social mechanisms to counter the HIV/AIDS epidemic. In addition to the legally binding instruments listed above, the international community, through its established mechanisms, like the UN General Assembly and the Commission on Human Rights, has issued morally binding declarations and resolutions on emerging issues and interpretations of the codified human rights standards. State parties to most of the human rights instruments need to submit reports to treaty monitoring bodies to receive guidance on more effective implementation. This also serves the purpose of enabling the international community to pressurise state parties to speed up the implementation, by publishing the respective implementation statuses and scenarios.

The treaty monitoring bodies, such as the Human Rights Committee, the Committee on the Rights of the Child, the CEDAW Committee etc. issue comments and concluding observations on the reports submitted by the state parties. June 2001 and the International Guidelines of HIV/AIDS, 1996. There are other important documents as well. As member states of the United Nations, South Asian nations are obliged to promote respect for human rights without discrimination. Moreover, international human rights law and covenants are binding on state parties that have signed and ratified them. Despite South Asian nations being signatories to all of these agreements, the situation on the human rights front is not satisfactory.

In September 1996, the Second International Consultation on HIV/AIDS and Human Rights, convened by UNAIDS and the Office of the UN High Commissioner for Human Rights, led to the formulation of the

International Guidelines on HIV/AIDS and Human Rights. The Guidelines address multisectoral responsibilities and accountability, including improving the roles of the government and private sector. In addition, they stress the duty of the States to engage in law reform and identify legal obstacles to an effective HIV/AIDS strategy of prevention and care. The attendant difficulties in the actual implementation of the Guidelines must now be addressed. The UN Declaration of Commitment is of particular interest since all countries of the region, barring Afghanistan, are signatories to it. The UNGASS was the first event of its kind organised by the United Nations to address HIV/AIDS and included participation by civil society.

The Declaration addresses issues of prevention, care, support and treatment; leadership at the national, regional and sub-regional level; reducing vulnerability; alleviating social and economic impact; research and development; respecting implementation of multi-sectoral strategies; conflict and disaster-affected regions; resources; and follow-up at the national, regional and global levels.

However, the need for a human rights based approach to deal with HIV/AIDS finds only brief mention in the Declaration. Thus, it is not surprising that the document fails to comprehensively address the needs of vulnerable populations such as men who have sex with men, sex workers and injecting drug users. This oversight is of concern to the countries where the promotion of rights of vulnerable populations is largely absent. Empowerment through human rights initiatives has been difficult to initiate due to social stigma and cultural pressures. It is evident that greater international initiatives are required to draw attention to these deficiencies and advocate for human rights protections as part of HIV/AIDS strategies.

The SAARC Convention on Preventing and Combating Trafficking in Women and Children for Prostitution, held in January 2002 marked an important step towards addressing the concerns of gender, sex work and human rights. The SAARC member states—Bangladesh, Bhutan, India, Maldives, Nepal, Pakistan and Sri Lanka—were signatories to the Convention, which requires all state parties to enact legislation that provides punishment for the offence of trafficking, including for keeping, maintaining, managing, knowingly financing, or knowingly renting a place used for trafficking. A major drawback of the Convention is that it considers trafficking solely for the purpose of 'prostitution' thereby limiting the scope of the legislation. Further, the Convention adopts a predominantly welfare-based approach in dealing with trafficking, as opposed to one based on protecting human rights.

The Asia Pacific Forum (APF) of National Human Rights Institutions, a regional network comprising the Human Rights Commissions of Australia, Fiji, India, Indonesia, Mongolia, Nepal, New Zealand, Philippines and Sri Lanka, has a crucial role to play in ensuring respect for human rights in the context of HIV/AIDS. The APF members can ensure the protection of the human rights of PLWHA and consequently the creation of an enabling environment through cooperation; information sharing; training and development for institution members and staff; developing and sharing technical expertise; and benefiting from the 'best practice' experiences of other institutions. At the sixth annual meeting of the APF held in Melbourne in September 2001, the members "committed themselves to combat discrimination and human rights violations on the basis of HIV/AIDS and called upon the assistance of the United Nations, governments and NGOs in the performance of this task".

Sex workers, men who have sex with men, injecting drug users, peer educators and outreach workers make essential partners within national HIV prevention efforts. If they possess accurate information, the means of protection and a supportive environment amongst their peers, family and the surrounding community (including administration of justice and law enforcement agencies), they can contribute effectively to the reduction of transmission of HIV to the general population. The mobilisation and empowerment of women and men working in the sex industry, the MSM community and drug users to access basic services and information has strengthened efforts for the management of the HIV/AIDS epidemic. Such empowerment and mobilisation should be seen as an essential ingredient to an effective. HIV/AIDS response, as it contributes to saving lives. Those within the vulnerable and marginalised groups who are working to this end are actively defending human rights and principles.

The international community has, in recent years, established that human rights defenders deserve recognition and protection by the state. This responsibility is outlined in the General Assembly resolution, 'Declaration on the Right and Responsibility of Individuals, Groups and Organs of Society to Promote and Protect Universally Recognised Human Rights and Fundamental Freedoms'. It is, therefore, critical that all governments embrace this responsibility and protect those key partners in the response to HIV/AIDS. The legislatures and judiciaries in South Asia have had an uneven record in protecting human rights of PLWHA. This partially reflects the lack of understanding of the epidemic within these branches of the government themselves. It also highlights the additional challenges that face PLWHA in countries where the State is insensitive to their needs. Even more worrying are the well-documented incidents of systemic harassment of PLWHAs and designated human rights defenders. The lack of an enabling State structure, along with active discrimination and harassment by officials acts as a further disincentive for people to disclose their HIV status, making it harder to contain the epidemic.

An overview of the legal frameworks in the South Asian countries clearly brings out several lacunae in the law and human rights guarantees that have an adverse impact on PLWHA and those most vulnerable to the epidemic. Certain unequivocal measures, therefore, need to be taken at the policy and legislative level to effectively control the spread of the epidemic. It is clear that all South Asian legal regimes criminalise those most vulnerable to the epidemic. It is because of the legal sanctions and social marginalisation and stigma that these groups face that they find themselves vulnerable to public health crises such as HIV/AIDS. Removing these legal sanctions will go a long way in addressing the problem of vulnerability and stigma faced by these groups and will check the spread of HIV/AIDS not only in their communities but in the general population as well. The empowerment of individuals is the best way to reduce vulnerabilities to HIV/AIDS and this can be done not just through the provision of information and education but also through the guarantee of legal protection.

Protecting the human rights of those most vulnerable to HIV/AIDS-a central component of an effective control strategy-will firstly require the decriminalisation of vulnerable groups through a serious and committed attempt at law reform and sensitisation of law enforcement, healthcare and other authorities. However, this should only be a first step. In addition, it will be necessary to endow these communities with the range of positive rights that allow for the full realisation of human potential. These include rights that guarantee life and liberty in all its varied forms, equality and non-discrimination, employment, access to services and freedoms of speech, expression, movement and organisation. However, any attempt at decriminalisation must be sensitive to the differences among the various groups vulnerable to HIV/AIDS, as a universally applicable approach is not possible. Additionally, there is debate within these communities and groups on the appropriate legal response to their situation. Any effective legal response, then, must be undertaken after consultation with the stakeholders from within these communities.

The exercise of collective power by sex workers can be one strategy that can successfully minimise HIV/AIDS vulnerabilities and human rights violations, as can be seen in the case of the SHIP project and Durbar Mahila Samanvay Committee (DMSC) in Kolkata, India. The argument that sex work should be decriminalised stems from rights-based and public health perspectives. Fear of prosecution has been seen to inhibit sex workers from accessing information and services including healthcare and HIV/AIDS information. Further, the illegal status of sex work makes negotiation with clients difficult. It also makes sex workers vulnerable to abuse both within the sex work setting (madams, pimps, brothel operators and owners) and outside (clients, law enforcers, lawyers, the magistracy etc.). Decriminalisation implies that sex work, including soliciting and earnings from sex work, must not be considered criminal in so far as they pertain to consenting adults. There have been growing demands for this from sex workers' collectives, organisations working with sex workers, HIV/AIDS intervention groups, public health specialists and rights activists. Such demands have come in contexts where sex workers have been able to present their perspectives and where the adverse public health implications of criminalisation of sex work have been recognised.

There are other perspectives on the question of decriminalisation of sex work, including the view that sex work, but not the sex worker, should be criminalised. These ideas largely arise out of the view that sex work itself amounts to exploitation of women. It is not clear how sex work can be criminalised without having an adverse impact on the lives of sex workers. The primary issue in advocacy around these issues is the involvement of sex workers in the decision-making processes. This itself is bound to be a difficult task, considering that there are a wide range of contexts in which sex work is carried out in the region and even within countries. Decriminalisation, however, seems to be a prerequisite for the participation of sex workers in such decisionmaking processes. It is important to note, however, that decriminalisation of these groups does not mean ignoring the root causes which put people in positions of vulnerability (such as the mafia behind the trafficking of humans or smuggling of narcotics). It only means that laws must begin to target those who are, in reality, behind the crimes.

Until the time that a human rights friendly legal regime is put into place, it will be necessary to introduce legal provisions that will allow harm reduction programmes (providing clean needles to injecting drug users and condoms to sex workers and men who have sex with men) to be carried out among vulnerable groups. In the absence of legal provisions, such programmes could easily be interpreted as abetting crimes, as they already have been in India, despite government support of such interventions. Even here, law reform must go hand in hand with the sensitisation of state machinery. Such law reform will require that NGO and community-based organisations working on harm reduction through advocacy, education and counselling be allowed to function outside the purview of criminal laws such as those relating to obscenity and public nuisance. Such harm reduction programmes must, however, lead to the ultimate goal of law reform to decriminalise the behaviour of various vulnerable groups.

As has been observed earlier, legal regimes in South Asia that guarantee equality apply only to the public sector. As a result, private healthcare or employment falls outside the scope of the nondiscrimination legislation and they are, therefore, free to refuse treatment or jobs to PLWHA. PLWHA, therefore, have no legal recourse when they face such discrimination in the private sector. This is a huge lacuna in the law that requires to be filled urgently. Apart from specifically protecting the rights of PLWHA and those most vulnerable to HIV/AIDS, it is also necessary to ensure that appropriate and accessible legal remedies are available to them. This can be done by inserting relevant provisions in the respective constitutions and the civil and criminal laws, where such safeguards and remedies do not already exist. To ensure that the rights of PLWHA are protected and they are able to take recourse to legal remedies, it is necessary:

a) to ensure that the rule of law exists; and

b) to build an enabling environment so that fear, discrimination and stigma do not hinder access to the judicial system.

There are certain other rights of people that may not be fundamental rights, but are legal rights or civil rights conferred by a statute, e.g. custody rights, maintenance etc. Such rights are enforceable through the civil courts in the country. Therefore, if a private employer discriminates against a PLWHA, then, subject to the existing laws, the employer can be taken to court for the violation of the rights of the employee. Persons who have been illegally and unlawfully dispossessed from their homes can file a suit for repossession. Similarly, issues relating to land, property rights, tenancy, maintenance, custody, divorce, dues from the employer, etc. can find legal recourse through the civil courts. The penal code and other penal statutes lay down acts or omissions that constitute an offence. Once a complaint is made and is recorded as cognizable or non-cognizable depending on the gravity of the offence, investigation and trials follow. A person is considered innocent until proven guilty. Victims of violence, persons who have been thrown out of their house because of their HIV positive status, individuals from vulnerable groups who are being extorted, exploited etc. can file a complaint in the police station. If the complaints are not registered at the police station, they can send written complaints to the senior officials and also make a complaint to the magistrate.

These have not yet been accessed by PLWHA and their networks. Their usefulness for issues relating to PLWHA needs to be explored. While commitment at the international and regional level is extremely crucial in initiating debate and setting guidelines for building a human rights framework, their implementation can be ensured only when backed by effective legal mechanisms at the national level. National human rights institutions are one such mechanism. These are independent bodies established by the State for the effective promotion and protection of human rights issues that arise in the context of HIV/AIDS. In his address to the international meeting of human rights institutions in Geneva in April 2001, the Executive Director of UNAIDS identified five practical ways in which national human rights institutions can strengthen their work regarding HIV/AIDS:

— by investigating violations of human rights that occur in the context of HIV/AIDS;

— by conducting public inquiries focusing on these violations;

— by receiving and, where appropriate, redressing complaints of HIV/AIDS related human rights violations;

— by providing advice and assistance to governments in the area of human rights and HIV/AIDS; and conducting human rights education in the context of HIV/AIDS.

These commitments require the integration of HIV/AIDS-related human rights into institutional strategies and programmes at the national level. In India, the National Human Rights Commission and the State Human Rights Commissions are empowered to inquire into complaints of violation of human rights either suo motor on a petition by a victim or someone acting on his behalf. They can also inquire into instances of negligence in the prevention of such violation by a public servant. The Commissions have powers to review the safeguards provided under the Constitution or any law for the protection of human rights and recommend measures for their effective implementation. The Commissions may undertake research in the field of human rights and take measures to promote awareness of human rights among all sections of society.

In Nepal, the Human Rights Commission Act (1997) established an independent and autonomous National Human Rights Commission for the effective enforcement as well as protection and promotion of human rights conferred by the Constitution and other prevailing laws. Bangladesh has also initiated moves to constitute an independent Human Rights Commission. The law, justice and parliamentary affairs ministry is in the process of finalising a draft legislation, which will also fix the terms of reference of the proposed commission. According to the draft, the commission would investigate the allegations of human rights violation and take necessary actions as per the existing provisions of law.

Since 1986, the Human Rights Commission of Pakistan (HRCP) has played a leading role in providing a highly informed and independent voice in the struggle for human rights and democratic development in the country. It is an independent, voluntary, non-political, non-profit making, non-governmental organisation. One of the main functions of HRPC is to work for the ratification and implementation by Pakistan of the Universal Declaration of Human Rights and of other related charters, covenants, protocols, resolutions, recommendations and internationally adopted norms. The poor development of social capital in South Asia has severely limited the progress with regard to dealing with HIV/AIDS, as societies remain entrenched in gender inequities, caste and class-based violence, religious fundamentalism, violations of the rights of marginalised populations and an overall environment of intolerance.

Provisions for strengthening, for example, educational systems, infrastructural facilities and local governance mechanisms would contribute significantly to enriching the social, cultural and economic environment of communities. This, in turn, would have a favourable impact upon the indices for development at macro levels. Parliamentarians can play a key role at the local, national and regional levels in initiating dialogue and legislative action on HIV/AIDS and human rights issues, as well as mobilising financial resources to support HIV/AIDS programmes. They can work at several levels. As political leaders, they can influence public opinion, and can increase public knowledge of relevant issues. As legislators, they vote on acts of Parliament and can ensure that legislation protects human rights, and advances effective prevention and care programmes.

As advocates, they can mobilise the involvement of government, private sector and civil society to discharge their societal responsibilities in responding appropriately to the epidemic. As resource mobilisers, they can allocate financial resources to support and enhance effective HIV/AIDS programmes that are consistent with human rights principles. An important regional initiative is the setting up of the SAARC Medical Parliamentarians, which held a meeting on reproductive health, STDs and HIV/AIDS in Kathmandu, Nepal, in May 1998. The meeting issued a Declaration on the Prevention and Control of HIV/AIDS. The Declaration asked parliamentarians to take a stronger role in advocacy at the regional, national, and community levels. The meeting also recommended the establishment of a regional forum of SAARC Parliamentarians and mechanisms to review and reform national laws and policies.

Democratically elected parliamentarians are in a unique position to influence public opinion and lead their constituents towards attitudes that are supportive of an effective national and regional response to the epidemic. Political commitment is an essential ingredient to a rights-based response to HIV/AIDS and to the allocation of adequate resources to implement it. The impact of the epidemics of HIV/AIDS on individuals and communities has thrown light on the complex intersections between human development, human rights and health. While these domains are organically intertwined, there has been a tendency to lose sight of this interdependence.

10

Defining the Scope of Business Responsibility

One immediate distinction which limits the scope of business responsibility is the distinction between 'immediate responsibility' and 'collective responsibility'. Immediate responsibility is the responsibility which stems from the activities of a particular business, such as a factory using child labour.

The concept of collective responsibility arises from the participation of businesses, as a collectivity, in an inequitable global economic system which engenders severe disadvantages for many groups and societies. It is the role of governments to address and regulate macro-economic or wider social problems that arise from the collective activities of business. In most cases, asking individual businesses to solve 'collective' problems which belong to the global market as a whole is unreasonable and effectively asks them to commit commercial suicide.

Human rights often come under the misconceived heading of 'all things good for human beings'. This is, however, a mis-perception, and one that must be dispelied before we can expect businesses to address human rights issues without fear of opening a Pandora's box of well-meant aspirations. Human rights are in fact defined almost as tightly as any other legal area: not just in the numerous 'bills of rights' expressed in constitutions which inform the decisions of courts throughout the world, but also in international treaty laws and conventions. For example, The Universal Declaration of Human Rights, The International Covenant on Economic, Social and Cultural Rights, and The International Covenant on Civil and Political Rights set down and define human rights standards.

In addition to these universal documents, there are numerous other instruments, some which relate to specific rights, like The Convention Against Torture and Other Cruel, Inhuman or Degrading Treatment or Punishment; others which are limited geographically such as The American Convention on Human Rights. These documents comprise and inform a highly detailed and intricate human rights system which operates at the international level, some with the force of law, which contain enforcement measures; others with a lesser, recommendatory status. The vast resource of human rights law is often overlooked by business because the laws are written for governments, not companies. But there is much which recommends them for use, helping businesses to conceptualise and frame their responsibilities. The laws are 'tried and tested', having proved their practical, as well as theoretical, worth in the political realm. They have been drafted for an international forum, and accordingly are able to reflect the particular cultural perceptions of rights in individual countries. With existing human rights laws at once so reliable and flexible, we recommend that businesses use these as the central platform of their individual policies.

It is a fundamental principle that a 'right' created for one person gives rise to a corresponding 'duty' for someone else. In the first instance, the duties imposed by international human rights law fall to governments and it is their responsibility to uphold and protect rights. Governments are required to act in accordance with human rights themselves, and to ensure that other members of society do likewise. For example, international human rights law stipulates that people have a 'right to free speech'. The government must respect that right when enacting censorship or related policies. It also must set out laws which prohibit others in society from abrogating that right—such as prohibiting powerful individuals or businesses from forming media monopolies. In this manner, non-state entities—including businesses—become duty-holders as well.

Corrupt or weak governments may, however, fail either to recognise their own primary responsibility to respect international human rights law or to undertake measures which delegate that responsibility to other members of society. That does not, however, nullify the existence of these rights, or the necessity that companies operating in such societies respect and uphold their corresponding duties. The human rights duties of business can be identified using a traditional dissection of human rights law. Most human rights give rise to four complementary duties: respect, protect, promote and fulfil. As an illustration these are applied in the figure on the opposite page to 'the right to adequate housing', set out in Article 11 of The International Covenant on Economic, Social and Cultural Rights. Governments are burdened not only with the passive, 'negative' duty to avoid violating the right (i.e., to respect), but also with the active, 'positive' duties which under certain circumstances require the provision of essential services (i.e., to protect, promote or fulfil). When a Special Rapporteur assigned by the UN Commission on Human Rights or other human rights monitors go into a country to assess whether a government is acting in compliance with its obligations, they will look at all four of these areas. In contrast to the extensive responsibilities incumbent upon governments, businesses as well as individuals have their human rights duties framed primarily in negative terms; that is, to refrain from violating the rights of others through their activities. With regard to Article 11 in the example opposite, a business or an individual should 'respect' people's right to adequate housing and therefore should not impede access; but neither a business nor an individual has a duty to protect, provide or fulfil the right to adequate housing.

'Positive' Duties of Business

Some human rights activists would certainly claim so, based firstly on the fact that businesses are members of society, and as such should participate positively in that society, and secondly on the immense power of businesses. But there are reasons to challenge both these claims. Businesses are certainly community members and will often contribute to that community through the provision of community centres, etc. But it is important to define duties in terms of what should be strictly required, not what would be ideal in the perfect society. Other members of society are not burdened—legally, or through social pressure—with positive obligations to actively promote human rights; only to refrain from violating them. Businesses should be subject to no more, and no less, responsibility. As for the power of businesses: in the modern world it is true that businesses can be more powerful than governments, and are often in a position to exercise immense power over the government. But power does not necessarily imply equivalent responsibility. The natural extension of such an argument would lead one to the very nonsensical position of maintaining that a stronger individual has more duty than a weaker individual, and that a larger company or government has a greater duty than a smaller one. We must not confuse 'can' with 'must'. Should businesses have any positive responsibilities in relation to human rights? In four significant areas are given below:

— In relation to their workers: Businesses control workers in the sense that they not only have the capacity to exercise authority over workers, but also that the structure of business is such that the authority is routinely exercised. So long as they exercise this level of control, businesses should act like a government in relation to the workers who are, in effect, their 'citizens', and promote, protect and secure their rights. Health and safety regulations are a good example of the application of this concept of fuller duties in relation to employees. For example, under most national legal systems, a business must not only refrain from abusing its workers, but it also has a 'positive' responsibility to make sure a worker is not abused by a co-worker.

— Businesses have a duty to ensure that their products are not used in the violation of human rights. This comprises responsibility to take reasonable measures to prevent both the intentional mis-use, and the unintentional wrongful use of the product. For example, a chemical company has a responsibility both to avoid selling toxic chemicals to an oppressive government which is likely to mis-use them and to inform users of any safety precautions which must be taken before using their chemicals. Given the ability of human beings to harm other human beings through the ingenious use of any manner of products, this responsibility must be limited. It is suggested that responsibility should only extend to what a businesses could legitimately be expected to foresee as a potential wrongful use or mis-use of its products, to avoid the imposition of unrealistic responsibilities.

— A business should assume positive responsibilities in relation to anyone residing on its land. Particularly this applies to indigenous peoples and disenfranchised minorities. The company then has a responsibility to negotiate and to take into account the wishes of the group on whose land it resides. This includes the 'positive' duty to keep the people informed of changes in the plans to use the land, to give the people a voice in those changes, and to ensure that the 'voice' of the people, i.e. their leaders, is actually representative of the majority will.

— Companies should incur positive duties when they de facto replace the government. Sometimes when a company moves into an area, the government allows it to effectively take over that area. The company will build up the land, create roads and transportation, infrastructure, utilities, etc. The government, particularly one which is unstable or geographically remote, will simply step out of the area, leaving a vacuum of governance there. The company fills that vacuum, thus becoming the only authority in the area. When this happens, the company should take on some of the positive responsibilities of government in respect of human rights. That includes making sure the population in the area is safe, secure and that they have adequate provisions for their livelihood.

Complicity in Human Rights

It is clear that the four areas of more extensive responsibilities identified previously derive not from the power of businesses per se, but rather from the requirement that businesses ensure that the generally more far-reaching effects of their operations do not negatively affect people or communities. These negative effects—or rather, the proximity of the company to these effects—should also be of central consideration in determining the degree of responsibility of a company for any particular human right. The proximity of a company to human rights violations can be viewed on three levels: direct, indirect, and no connection. 'Direct' entails a distinct, clear and unbroken connection between the activity of the company and the human rights violation. Examples include a company discriminating in its hiring practices, or locking the doors on workers to prevent them from running away. In such cases, the company has a straightforward and immediate responsibility to do whatever is necessary to mitigate, or stop the violations.

'Indirect' entails a violation which the company contributes to, but does not directly initiate or perpetrate, by enabling an abusive practice to be established or continued. For example, companies will sometimes buy from suppliers or producers that violate human rights in their operations. Or, a company might undertake a joint venture with an oppressive government. In such cases, the company still has some responsibility to take action to ameliorate the harm, but the action should be proportionate to the nature of the link between the company and the violations. 'No connection' is exactly what it implies. The company has no direct or indirect relationship to the violations, and therefore no responsibility to take action. This category is of the greatest significance where a company is located in a country with an oppressive government. It has been argued, that responsible companies should never operate in China. However, while the company is not facilitating the violations in any way, it is difficult to see why responsibility should be established simply on the grounds of location.

Of the three categories, the most difficult to establish will always be determining what is an 'indirect' connection. In the modern world, the decisions taken by a business can have major implications for lives and communities geographically and culturally remote, so businesses do have to be discerning in identifying their indirect connection to violations. For example, in the early 1990s several international oil companies undertook a joint venture with the Burmese government and the state oil company, Myanma Oil and Gas Enterprise (MOGE). MOGE assumed responsibility for providing labour and security for the construction of a gas pipeline for the project. Allegations later emerged that forced labour and child labour were used to construct the pipeline, and that other violations, including torture, and forced relocation, occurred in MOGE's operations to clear the area and provide security. Although the main Western partner, Unocal, did not directly carry out these purported violations itself, because of its involvement in the project, its liability for acting in concert with the Burmese government and MOGE in breaching universally recognised human rights standards is now under consideration in the United States District Court of California. Businesses must, therefore, be alert to the extent to which they can be indirectly complicit in human rights violations.

In recent years businesses have been the target of consumer action and human rights campaigns to make them more responsive to human rights concerns. Many of these campaigners have targeted the business world because of the immense potential of business to bring about change. While these campaigns have undoubtedly been founded on good motives, sometimes their effects have been destructive, due to unreasonable demands. As a result the real responsibilities have been left unfulfilled in some cases. By defining the minimum responsibilities owed by businesses operating abroad, the Human Rights and Business Project aims to go some way towards ensuring that these minimum responsibilities will not be ignored. Some companies will want to go beyond that minimum—because it's good for public relations, because their customers want them to address these rights, or because they are guided by an ethical, social or religious tradition which demands more of those who have the power to effect change.

11

ICTs in Support of Human Rights, Democracy and Good Governance

The common ground upon which information and communication technologies (ICTs) and human rights can be analyzed was forged two years ago at the United Nations Millennium Summit, which resulted in a declaration that affirmed common global commitments to the protection of the vulnerable, the alleviation of poverty, and the rectification of corrupt structures and processes—particularly in those countries in which there is a dearth of 'rule of law'. The world's leaders resolved to "spare no effort to promote democracy and strengthen the rule of law, as well as respect for all internationally recognized human rights and fundamental freedoms, including the right to development." The current period of preparation for the upcoming World Summit on the Information Society (WSIS)—in which the International Telecommunication Union (ITU) has a leading managerial role—offers an excellent opportunity to address tensions that exist between national, regional and global models of governance—particularly where hotly debated topics like human rights draw to the forefront of discussion key issues like transparency, accountability, and the universality of human rights principles.

This matter will analyze human rights and governance issues as they pertain to ICTs for the WSIS forum, with a focus on the role of those who protect human rights and foster good governance. Various players are increasingly leveraging and applying ICTs amidst various contending national, corporate and supranational interests, and this represents a significant change for traditional distributions of power in the international system. The way in which new communication technologies may be able to help realize some of the goals of the 2000 Millennium Declaration will be explored in this review. The goal of such analysis is to adopt a rights-based perspective on major development goals—specifically encompassing the protection of human rights—that are to be realized through the Declaration. It is where international institutions and their national/civil society counterparts meet and leverage electronic communications networks, that various UN-defined development goals and resolutions have the potential to be realized. Indeed, this is exemplified in part by the fact that "... as human rights groups form international linkages [for instance through the use of ICTs], their frame of reference shifts from national law to international human rights".

ICTs and the Information Society

The convergence between telecommunications, broadcasting multimedia and information and communication technologies (ICTs) that is driving the development of the global 'Information Society' is responsible for the transformation of a variety of economic and political sectors, as well as the socio-cultural strata of nations around the world. The benefits of information and communication technologies (ICTs) lie not purely in the range of their functionality, but in the variety and versatility of their application. Much has been written about the potential of ICTs to 'revolutionize' society, particularly in the context of their role as catalysts of the 'Information Revolution'. This 'revolution' is often juxtaposed with its predecessor, the Industrial Revolution, usually for the purpose accentuating the idea that communication networks are as integral to the process of development as was the birth and development of industry in the 19th century. Among the most important yet sensitive areas affected by ICTs are those of human rights and governance, thereby revealing the big question: what are the true benefits and changes that communications technologies can provide for everyone? While the conventional wisdom is that new technologies contribute to economic development, and that this in turn trickles down to the whole of global society, it is relevant to bear in mind that such diffusion depends on relatively equal patterns of income distribution, as well as a variety of other variables that are not necessarily prevalent in the developing world.

The subject of how modern communications alter the way in which various entities of the private sector, the public sector and civil society interact has spurred much debate. More specifically, such discussion targets the underlying theme of whether they are conducive to fundamental shifts in the distribution of power towards the dissolution of strong, centralized political hierarchies. ICTs include the workings of all digital communications networks (principally the Internet), wireless networks, and radio broadcast networks. Across different phases of policymaking and information dissemination, they can be applied in various forms as database technologies, decision support technologies, networking technologies, and personal identification and tracking technologies. One key to uncovering the complexities of the relationship between ICTs and social change—in a human rights context—may lie in the assessment of the degree of functional interactivity of a given technology. "A relatively high level of functional interactivity of networked electronic media confirms the presumed suitability of those electronic media for multi-directional communication processes", which support the idea that ICTs, in the process of empowering people to exchange information, may help to effectuate change by supporting decentralized, participatory development. Conversely, lower levels of functional interactivity are more likely to render a technology supportive of more centralized power structures.

The idea that new communication technologies may bring about social change— here defined as the enhanced awareness and protection of human rights in the international system—is "... one of the theoretical underpinnings of the positive perspectives on the benefits of the communications revolution." At the same time, it appears that a decisive factor in the way human rights are asserted and protected lies in the way power is governed and managed by those who control and regulate various communications apparatus.

ICTs have indeed permeated the structural workings of the international system, often challenging (though not necessarily undermining) top-down 'command and control' power hierarchies by facilitating the de-centralization of information vital to the workings of national and international governance. Vertical relationships between governments and society are being replaced by horizontal network relationships between public, semi-public and private agents, and ICTs (through their control, surveillance, communication and knowledge management potential) are revolutionizing the internal workings and external relations of public administrations. This is in part because information has become itself a resource and commodity, surpassing its traditional role as mere facilitator to political and economic decision-making. In many ways, the sensitivity of governments to the potential use of information and communications systems against them is itself a sensitive subject area, in part because historically, the deployment of telecommunications networks and informatics have been closely related to the workings of the military complex and the realization of political, ideological and military goals.

The realm of communications has been seen "... as having a hypodermic effect in international politics, bringing their favoured ideas of capitalism and civil society from the West...". In light of this generalization, it seems that where the lines of the dissemination of information, the diffusion of culture and activism, and access provision to new markets cross with those of national security, it is vital that 'Information Society' imperatives are treated with paramount diplomacy. It goes without saying that communications networks facilitate the broadening of scope and perspective in a way that empower all those who utilize them, and a realistic vision and discussion of the Information Society must be inclusive of this phenomena. Held is indeed one author who argues that nation-states are drawn together by complex processes of interdependence on problems such as AIDS, migration, human rights, crime, trade, environmental pollution, and new challenges to peace, security, and economic prosperity which spill over national boundaries.

In the human rights arena, "... there has been a clear shift in attitudes towards human rights protection by Member States. Once considered to be the sole territory of sovereign states, the protection of human rights is now viewed as a universal concern, as evidenced by the recent conviction for genocide, rape, war crimes and crimes against humanity handed down in the International Criminal Tribunals..." The rise in transnational human rights networks (comprising both public and private actors) has been referred to by some as the 'third globalization'—and has helped to develop a global civil society capable of working with governments, international institutions, and multinational corporations to promote internationally accepted standards of human rights and democracy. Examining the economics and politics of ICTs is an integral part of understanding the broad development agendas espoused by a variety of institutions, and a rights-based approach to this development upon the basis of equality and participation is a constructive one.

While the World Summit itself is likely to incite just the beginnings of collaboration and cooperation between the 'powers that be', it is possible that through it, global civil society and international organizations may together successfully emphasize "...the relationship between the global citizenry and the state, whereby the former is seen not as the passive object of the latter's machinations but rather as an active participant in shaping not only immediate policies but also long-term parameters of legitimacy of the state."

While indeed the private sector and governmental institutions are vital to any study of the international system, and while the roots of state-centered governance are alive and well, due attention must be directed towards those which comprise the key component of civil society—

"... the national and international NGOs... extended the range of citizen action beyond the institutional parameters of the sovereign state". The broad array of nongovernmental organizations, clubs, societies, trade unions, and political parties that are the domestic counterparts to transnational networks, have a vital role in illustrating how new transnational networks of common interest are effectively leveraged. They often represent the social interests of individuals and the protection of basic human rights, and are usually not motivated by profit or power. Civil society uses the same tools that commercial organisations and mass media institutions use to influence their audiences: publishing technology, mailing lists, collaboration technologies, conferencing, virtual communities, and electronic polling and surveys. Examining the resonance of such voices in global fora is vital to the appraisal of shifting power dynamics in the international system. "The emergence of an international civil society seems to be taking place due to the so-labeled 'democratization' movements in Eastern Europe, Latin America, Africa and Asia... and new international communications technologies seem to be giving the promotion of these ideas more force than might have been the case 50 years previously."

Overlooking the importance of this group of stakeholders risks compromising not only the richness and integrity of the 'global knowledge networks' facilitated by ICTs, but also their ultimate utility and purpose. This is true only if indeed, "...the advent of technology must be seen as an absolute advantage in terms of the potential that it opens up for individuals." The consultative status of various non-governmental organizations (NGOs) at high levels in many international organizations ensures their participation in processes and institutions of global governance, and the fact that they spill across national boundaries forces a certain recasting of general notions of political participation and citizenship. The practice of the accreditation and participation of civil society in UN conferences and special sessions has evolved and developed during the 1990s, when many of the major UN conferences took place. In the Millennium Declaration and its follow up resolution, enhanced partnership and cooperation with civil society as a whole was called for to ensure its contribution to the implementation of the Declaration. "The United Nations has had a relationship with civil society since its establishment.

The main kinds of issues upon which international decisions are made lie upon the horizontal axis, while the main types of decision-making process lie upon the vertical axis. As new governance arrangements are forged in conjunction with more traditional arrangements (which tend to be generally founded upon the principle of national sovereignty), partnerships are developed between various private and public entities, and the increasing role of non-governmental fora emerges strongly. NGOs are indeed among the newer players with clout in the international arena and continue to be a major reason why ICTs have emerged to challenge existing development and power paradigms.

While on the macro level there continues to be debate vis-à-vis the ultimate cost effectiveness of ICTs in development given other contending priorities, on the micro level, there appears to be near-universal acceptance of the fact that development strategies should be based on partnerships between government, the private sector, and civil society as well as the creation of human capacity (i.e. which some refer to as 'social capital'). Despite 'revolutionary' notions associated with ICTs, there appears also to be a collective acceptance of the fact that governments should be the appropriate policy-makers and leading users of ICTs.

The Millennium Declaration

The Millennium Declaration was adopted by 147 Heads of State & Government members of the United Nations in September 2000, with close consultation and collaboration with the UN, the World Bank, the IMF, the OECD, and other regional experts. The Declaration sought to identify and document 48 social and economic indicators, listed by country and spanning a twenty-five year period, giving each country a profile of progress towards development and the eradication of poverty. "The Declaration acknowledged that progress is based on sustainable economic growth, which must focus on the poor, with human rights at the center"; indeed, social, cultural and economic rights are at the heart of its goals. The power of democracy to effect change and the empowerment of the citizenry, and reaffirms the need to work collectively for more inclusive political processes, with genuine political participation. Strategies for moving forward include the fostering of national human rights institutions, support for the practical application of a rights-based approach to development, the provision of electoral assistance to help the consolidation of new and restored democracies, and progress toward the implementation of democratic principles through institutional reform programs.

They also incorporate encouraging the continued ratification and implementation of the Convention on the Elimination of All Forms of Discrimination against Women, working to protect the rights of migrants and their families, and helping to ensure the freedom and independence of the media. A very basic critique of the Millennium Declaration touches upon the question of credibility: how much can credit can it be afforded, given that in the past 55 years and countless declarations, half the world's population continues to subsist on less than $2 per day? The Declaration sets out to attain several specific human rights objectives, including upholding the Universal Declaration of Human Rights. And yet, of the 190 UN member states, only a few over a hundred have signed the existing protocol to the International Covenant on Civil and Political Rights. This chasm between the Declaration's espoused values and reality is a troubling one.

According to the "Road Map towards the implementation of the UN Millennium Declaration", all human rights—civil, political, economic, social and cultural—are universal and interdependent; they comprise the foundations of human dignity. Human rights are a central part of UN reform, which emphasizes the centrality of human rights in all activities of the system. "People throughout the world remain victims of summary executions, disappearances and torture. Accuracy on numbers is difficult to ascertain because violations take place in too many countries of the world and are rarely reported." Where there are major violations of human rights, there is also often a lack of democracy, poor governance, negligible rule of law, as well as general conflict and injustice. Pervasive poverty and broad disparities in the distribution of power also often go hand in hand with human rights violations, which include transgressions against cultural, socio-political, economical, and civil rights.

A major area of debate over the past several decades has been the conflict between the two major perspectives on human rights: the universalist and the cultural relativist. The former holds that an individual is a social unit, possessing inalienable rights and driven by the pursuit of self-interest. In fact, universalism is used by many Western states to negate the validity of more 'traditional' systems of law, and posits that more 'primitive' cultures will gradually evolve to espouse the same approach to rights and law as Western cultures. In the latter cultural relativist model, a community is the basic social unit, and concepts such as individualism, freedom of choice, and equality are relatively absent. Cultural relativists tend to believe that a traditional culture is unchangeable, and implicitly that there is no unanimity across the determination of that which represents the rights of all individuals everywhere. As an approach, it appears to be in itself a rather arbitrary idea, as cultures are rarely unified in their viewpoints on different issues. Needless to say, however, sensitivity to the imperialism of western conceptions of human rights is high in nations that embrace it.

Human rights and the International arena

It has become evident over the past several decades how mechanisms of supranational governance and intergovernmental collaboration have facilitated progress towards a universal system of human rights. The recent adoption of the International criminal court in June 1998 is an important step in the direction of enforcing and promoting the values agreed upon by the member nations. International organizations/committees "... are responsible for using the implementation of the international system for the protection of human rights—it is through them that it is possible to invoke a state's obligations under international law in order to obtain a formal or official response to allegations of torture and obtain some form of remedy." The International Bill of Human Rights is comprised of the Universal Declaration of Human Rights (UDHR), the International Covenant on Economic, Social and Cultural Rights (CESCR), and the International Covenant on Civil and Political Rights (CCPR). The Commission on Human Rights—a prime example of a non-treaty mechanism/body—drafted a preliminary international bill of human rights in 1947.

The Commission consists of the participation of about 3,000 delegates from 53 member and observer States and from various NGOs. Originally, the Commission on Human Rights sought an International Covenant on Human Rights (CHR) in order to vivify the Universal Declaration of Human Rights; many drafts of this document were created in the nearly two decades between 1949 and 1966. Ultimately, however, it was decided in 1966 that two specialized treaties, the CESCR and the CCPR, would exist instead of just the CHR; over 130 countries have since ratified them.

Universal Declaration of Human Rights

The Universal Declaration of Human Rights came into existence on December 10, 1948, born in the aftermath of WWII, prior to which human rights were in large part considered a subject of domestic concern. The Declaration's thirty articles universalized global concern for a set of inalienable human rights, including the basic right to life, to safety from unfair persecution, to the freedom of thought, expression and religion, and to more culturally based rights pertaining to marriage, employment, education and shelter. Although adoption of this Declaration was limited to the UN General Assembly and has thus been non-binding and un-enforceable, the document itself has served as a basis for the development of other regional human rights agreements.

As a yardstick for addressing democracy in a given society, Article 19 of the Universal Declaration of Human Rights is particularly important to note in understanding global human rights. It states that everyone has the right to "... hold opinions without interference and to seek, receive and impart information and ideas through any media regardless of frontiers. It was further stipulated that news personnel were to have the right to "... the widest possible access to sources and information, to travel unhampered in pursuit thereof, and to transmit copy without unreasonable, or discriminatory limitation, [and] should be guaranteed by action on the national and international plane. Needless to say, NGOs played an important role in the development, adoption and publicizing of the UDHR, starting with the International League for the Rights of Man (now the International League for Human Rights), one of the earliest NGOs to practice the tactic of 'shaming' of totalitarian regimes, military dictatorships and even democratic societies.

The main purpose of the International Covenant on Economic, Social and Cultural Rights (CESCR) that came into force in 1976 was to further clarify rights declared in the Universal Declaration, protecting specifically the rights of workers (to choose one's job, fair wages and appropriate conditions) and families (to paid leave for working mothers, and protection of children, etc.). Broad rights to health, to protection from discrimination (by race, color, sex, language, religion, political or other opinion, etc.) and to an adequate standard of living were also a major part of this covenant, and are monitored by the Committee on Economic, Social and Cultural Rights. The International Covenant on Civil and Political Rights (CCPR) came into force on March 23, 1976, also clarifying rights stated in the UDHR, and elaborating upon new rights associated with the protection of the sanctity of life, rights protecting accused persons and criminals, mobility rights, and civil rights. These fall into the realm of the right to be free from capital punishment (except under very grave circumstances), the right not to be unfairly arrested or detained, the general right to free movement, the right not to be tortured; and the freedom of thought and expression. The CCPR bounds signatory countries to the protection of their inhabitants, and is monitored by the Human Rights Committee established in 1977.

Human Rights Violations

On the international level, there are a variety of predominantly non-violent means employed by the United Nations to deal with violations of human rights among member nations, the majority of which tend to fall under the category of 'sanction'. These include suspension (deferring the privileges of a member state), embargoes (limiting or halting a country's economic activity or communications flow), expulsion (leading to the forced withdrawal of a member state from the United Nations) and force (military action used as a last resort against an offending nation).

A significant portion of the work of the UN Commissions on Human Rights now takes place on the margins of formal sessions, in informal networking among governments, and between NGOs and other stakeholders. Other UN bodies, such as UNICEF, UNIFEM, and the offices of the UN High Commissioners for Refugees and Human Rights often seek out the counsel of networks of likeminded governments, NGOs, and regional organizations such as the European Union, the OSCE, the Council of Europe, the Organization of American States, and the Organization for African Unity. The Paris principles, which were endorsed by the Commission on Human Rights in 1992 and the General Assembly in 1993, have become a particular reference point for UN activity in the area of human rights. More than 50 national human rights institutions have been established according to them, and nearly 40 countries have undertaken the process of adopting national plans for human rights. Up until the present, most members of the United Nations have become either participant or signatory to existing major human rights conventions. Indeed among the most important milestones in advancing human rights through the United Nations system occurred at the World Conference on Human Rights, held in Vienna, Austria, in June 1993. Here, as previously, NGOs played a crucial role, organizing an effective worldwide campaign to ensure their participation; along with governments, they were able to achieve a number of major breakthroughs, including winning unanimous endorsement for the creation of a UN High Commissioner for Human Rights and a declaration reaffirming the universal nature of human rights.

The use of ICTs in the realm of human rights can be broken down broadly to four main realms whose level and quality of interaction—amongst themselves and with one another— has been vastly heightened as a result of the deployment of communications networks. Individuals, NGOs, national governments, and supranational institutions have all been empowered insofar as they have the means to effectively communicate their stories, agendas, laws and agreements, respectively and with maximum impact. Indeed, the ICTs like the Internet may facilitate the networking and mobilizing functions of many

NGOs working across national borders, as a countervailing force to the influence of technocratic elites and government leaders running traditional international organizations, and may be even more effective as a force for human rights, providing a global platform for opposition movements challenging autocratic regimes and military dictatorships, despite government attempts to restrict access in certain countries. The evolving relationship of each of civil society entities with one other—as enhanced and strengthened by ICTs—is significant to any analysis of governance.

This changing dynamic has contributed in many ways to the development of a new diplomacy of human rights, which highlights the alleged tension between power and morality, and which supersedes the predisposition of organizations like the UN to focus selective morality on certain areas of the world over others. Whereas national governments and supranational institutions have long been positioned to guide, respectively, the formation of national/international policies through various well-oiled gears of public diplomacy—individuals and civil society representatives have not. While ICTs have contributed greatly to the enhanced transparency and accessibility of information from the 'top', particularly insofar as legal and administrative information is concerned, they have done even more to improve the administrative, organizational and management skills of the 'bottom', and thus to tip the scales of power slightly back toward an equilibrium. A wide range of governments throughout the world continue to utilize a variety of tools, including licensing, limits on access to newsprint, control over government advertising, jamming, and censorship, to inhibit independent voices.

The growth of new, Internet-based media did help facilitate public access to a wide range of information, but some governments continued to develop means to monitor e-mail and Internet use and restrict access to controversial, political, newsoriented, and human rights web sites. Other governments have chosen to prohibit Internet access or limit it to political elites. For those who subscribe to a 'technological determinist' approach, these types of examples are indeed supportive of the idea that communications technologies are fundamental drivers in the transformation of society at every level—including social interaction between institutions and individuals.

The importance of general information sharing and more transparent and accessible knowledge management systems are being emphasized through ICT coordination in the promotion of humanitarian aid. Most notably, the UN Office for Coordination of Humanitarian Affairs (OCHA), which coordinated a symposium in February 2002, has called for: information systems driven by operational needs (particularly in assessments and "who is doing what where" databases); the development of standards of information quality; the identification and dissemination of successful technology applications; the establishment of ways to connect disparate information systems; and general improvement to preparedness, including baseline data for high-risk areas and rapid response humanitarian information centers. The idea that ICTs can help to avoid the duplication of work and enhance the organizational efficiency of those working in the field of humanitarian aid is only just beginning to be explored. Information gathering as far as 'human rights data' is concerned is in itself a tremendous challenge, for prior to the actual sharing of information between various organizations and networks arises the question of how to quantify and represent acts of violence. Only thus can researchers make systematic, comparative analyses of patterns of human rights violations in time and space.

ICTs thus obviously play an instrumental role—not only in terms of spreading 'the word' about human rights violations and protection through communication networks between civil society, national and international entities—but also in terms of formulating what 'the word' is, and determining how real world incidents can be communicated to the realm of factual, accessible information and data.

In an effort to more deeply examine the relationship between ICTs and the Millennium Declaration goals associated with human rights, democracy and good governance, statistical analysis was undertaken to determine whether or not a quantitatively based correlative relationship exists between the deployment of communication networks and the above-mentioned principles across 161 countries. Several dependent variables were tested as proxies for the growth of ICTs, including the year-to-year growth of main telephone lines per 100 people, the year-to-year growth of mobile subscriptions per 100 people, and the year-to-year growth of Internet subscribers. These were run against the weighted rankings of Freedom House, which can be considered as a general proxy for measuring the likelihood of a national environment to be amenable to acceptable standards of human rights protection, given a reasonable ranking of protected civil and political liberties. It is important in such analysis to control for GDP (or GDP per capita) levels, given the strong likelihood of a positive relationship between the wealth of a country and the capacity of its population to adopt use of mobile technologies and the Internet.

Year-to-year growth numbers were used in favor of absolute penetration numbers because of this same issue of high positive correlations; the extremely high correlation between absolute penetration numbers and the GDP variable lends to problems of multicollinearity (and thus to explanatory significance) in the analysis if absolute numbers are used. Running a regression analysis yielded interesting results, which were not entirely surprising. Despite the fact that the data did not yield significant results for the impact of mobile and Internet subscriber growth on Freedom House rankings, the increasing growth of main telephone lines per 100 people—combined with controlling for higher GDP levels—did prove to reasonably explain corresponding lower Freedom House Rankings (for which lower numbers signify higher levels of freedom). It is crucial to bear in mind that Freedom House rankings are reversed such that lower numbers correspond to higher levels of freedom.

ICTs, Democracy and Governance

There is little utility in analyzing the relationships between ICTs and human rights if the key topics of democracy and good governance are not concomitantly addressed, for before one can help to propagate the other, both must be contextualized as the by-products of the same system. The main impact of ICTs [and the internet] "... on democratic life concerns [their] ability to strengthen the public sphere by expanding the information resources, channels of electronic communication, and the networking capacity for many organized interest groups, social movements, NGOs, transnational policy networks, and political parties with the technical know-how and organizational flexibility to adapt to the new medium." For those who are convinced that the ideological role of communications systems is vital to the shaping, structuring or 'framing' of domestic and international relations, examining the role of communication technologies must precede any analysis of democracy and good governance.

Indeed, rights associated with communication have often been viewed as among the primary gauges of democracies (such as 'freedom of communication' or the 'right to communicate'), amidst some broader criteria like individual civil rights, stability, and free elections with opposition parties. Further confirming the integral role of ICTs in international relations is the proposition that the democracies they help to facilitate do not war with each other; this is very nearly considered empirical law in international relations (although this does not take into account the 'covert' activities of democratic states that use journalists and media as tools of destabilization). The extent to which ICTs—since their most basic inception—have been used to fulfill strategic purposes in international relations must not be underestimated.

While ICTs are indeed touted as the tools of bottom-up empowerment and democratization that actively thwart the ability of highly centralized dictatorial governments to take form, it is important to bear in mind the contradictory danger of facilitating a "tyranny of the majority." That ICTs help to lower the 'barriers to entry' to the political marketplace is not enough of a benefit to posit an assumption that equality of representation is the default outcome. In countries—particularly in the developing world— where the tendency toward political factionalism is high, this can provide reinforcement for a political dynamic that is not conducive to development goals and human rights agendas. Indeed, such "weak states are one of the main impediments to effective governance today, at national and international levels alike." Moreover, the capacity for ICTs to mobilize mass segments of a population and to empower all the various players of civil society should not predispose one from recognizing that the pendulum does not always swing towards democracy as a model of governance. Historical references to the various uses of audio/video technologies in various countries can be easily made to reflect this point.

"Mass communication, in a word, is neither good nor bad; it is simply a force and, like any other force, it can be used either well or ill. Used in one way, the press, the radio and the cinema are indispensable to the survival of democracy. Used in another way, they are among the most powerful weapons in the dictator's armory." Nevertheless, there has been a marked increase in the emergence of democracies over the past 20 years, supported by the Commission on Human Rights' articulation of a number of elements for their promotion and consolidation - including fair and periodic elections, an independent judiciary, a transparent government and a vibrant civil society. According to Freedom House, there are more democracies in the world today, and the highest proportion of democratic states (63%), than ever before in history. "States that respect the rights of all their citizens and allow them all a say in decisions that affect their lives are likely to benefit from their creative energies and to provide the kind of economic and social environment that promotes sustainable development."

The nature of political interaction between representatives and their constituents is particularly interesting as it changes through the empowerment of citizens with access to information at everdecreasing costs. Increasingly, electronic communications and networks are playing an important role in facilitating information sharing. Reduction of the opportunity costs of participation is a potential ray of hope for the concomitant reduction of the negative political implications of geographical urban-rural divides. As the number of people with the capacity to have their voices 'heard' gradually increases despite the 'digital divide', so too does the range of considerations for their representatives, who must to a certain extent recast themselves and find balance between their jobs as decision-makers, and their role as active proxies for public opinion. In some ways, representatives in a democratic system risk being marginalized at the hand of new technologies, as the information for which they are 'middlemen' now easily bypasses their filters and in a sense, undermines their position as focal point for their constituencies.

Many hope that the Internet can strengthen the institutions of representative democracy including parliaments and political parties, as well as providing a platform for opposition parties, protest groups, and minorities seeking to challenge authoritarian regimes. Although the Internet does bring an added component of asymmetrical interactivity unmatched by unidirectional radio and television predecessors, assumptions of its impact on political participation must be measured carefully. Basic literacy is naturally a prerequisite for the effective usage of these technologies in the forms envisaged by theorists. Even in places "... where many avenues to political participation already exist, and where the opportunity cost of participation is quite low... the Internet does not provide a sufficient 'added value' to make it a better alternative than more traditional methods of political communication." However conclusive empirical findings supporting the claim that electronic media have contributed to democracy in Africa are undermined by the lack of good aggregated data on the subject, by stagnant literacy rates, and by the fact that private radio and television have only recently been allowed to exist in most places. In other words, the extent to which the 'liberating potential' of ICTs is unleashed is contingent upon the way governments can influence/control the content, direction and nature of information flows. Neither empirical evidence nor theoretical frameworks appear to provide clear answers to this question.

E-Government

E-Government—and specifically the enhanced ability to collect and share information is revolutionizing the way we look at traditional concepts of political legitimacy, representation and ministerial accountability. According to the OECD, the key issues include the necessity of addressing the needs of the polity as a whole, of facilitating the use of e-channels by disadvantaged groups early in the implementation process, and of building trust and confidence in e-services. While ICTs provide obvious access to information about various topics (including justice and human rights), they also touch upon crucial interfaces vis-à-vis the direct participation of voters, thereby contributing to significant changes in electoral systems digital advocacy and lobbying, and online consultation are all part and parcel of the transformations of governance shaped by ICTs. That said, however, it is important to note that these observations are themselves not yet established facts. An OECD study of e-governance, based on a series of interviews with information specialists, public officials and the policymaking community in eight post-industrial societies in 1996-7, presented evidence that the overall impact of the Internet has failed to increase access to policymakers, to improve the transparency of government decision-making, or to facilitate public participation in policymaking.

There has been research conducted that supports the idea that traditional methods like letters, written submissions and informal meeting continued to predominate, and that digital technologies have had greater impact in the dissemination of information to senior decision-makers and policy elites. A key problem is the fact that opportunities for 'bottom up' interactivity in communicating with official government departments are far fewer than the opportunities to read 'top down' information. Government websites rarely facilitate un-moderated public feedback, for example few published public reactions to policy proposals, or used discussion forums, listservs and bulletin boards, although there have been occasional experiments with interactive formats.

Some argues that there are two camps in the arena of e-governance: cyber-optimists and cyber-pessimists. Cyber-optimists are hopeful that the development of interactive services, new channels of communication, and efficiency gains from digital technologies will contribute towards the revitalization of the role of government executives in representative democracies, facilitating communications between citizen and the state. In contrast, cyber-pessimists express doubts about the capacity of governments to adapt to the new environment effectively and with positive result insofar as the questions of access and digital divide have repercussions for political participation. Some countries have already started to draw up principles or adapt existing guidelines for discussion in the online environment, and most have started to digitize information relevant to the citizenry. One important question is how governments are to manage the publication of their information: do they publish only policies that have been agreed upon by parliament, or do they also publish information in the stage of preparation of policies? How complete is that information? The basis of e-democracy, and thus of online public consultations, involves giving the public the chance to consult government information electronically. It is not enough to give formal permission for information to be accessed, which is why a distinction is made between access and accessibility. The former refers to the real possibility of consulting or acquiring government information electronically, while the latter refers to the ease with which one can actually make use of the possibility of consulting government information online. E-governance is taking rapid hold around the world.

Affluent postindustrial societies characteristically have the widest access to multiple forms of communication technologies, and it makes sense that such an environment is most conducive to the spread of egovernance. The United Kingdom is a good example of a country that has been very active in bringing government online. Amidst changing public perceptions and expectations of the British Parliament, and authoritative evidence indicating a decline of public participation in the political process, efforts are being made in the U.K. to leverage ICTs in order to influence public perceptions, help meet public expectations, and facilitate the inevitable transition that Members of Parliament are bound to face as new technologies proliferate amongst their constituencies. As another example, the United Arab Emirates is also investing in ICT solutions toward facilitating egovernment, bringing online and working across over 40 government departments employing 25,000 people.

According to a biannually released survey conducted by the American Society for Public Administration (ASPA) and the United Nations Division for Public Economics and Public Administration (UNDPEPA), the US was ranked first for its e-government initiatives ahead of Australia, New Zealand, Singapore and Norway. In all, sixty-one member state countries scored above the mean global index of 1.62; geographically by region, North America, Europe, South America and the Middle East all registered an index above the global mean, while Asia, the Caribbean, Central America and Africa fell below the index. Of the 190 UN member states, 169 were providing some degree of information online in 2001, although for over 25% of these countries, the content of the websites was deemed to consist of insufficient information less geared toward public participation than to pure public relations. The capacity to conduct transaction of any kind online at the national government level was available in just 17 member states in 2001.

Free Press

The monopoly of or interference in ICTs and media for the purpose of controlling information can be a core obstacle to the realization of the needs of a democratic society, and can be perpetrated by private and state entities alike. In this regard, it lies in the obligation of states "... to guarantee or promote a climate of open and plural public debate, and to correct a situation in which these characteristics are absent or distorted." This obligation has been articulated in the international arena, confirming the right of the public to be informed and to free expression: It has been encapsulated as a basic human right in the Universal Declaration of Human Rights adopted by the UN in 1948, the European Convention on Human Rights, and the African Charter on Human and Peoples' Rights. The European Commission of Human Rights has officially affirmed the duty of the state to protect against excessive concentration of the press, while the Committee of Ministers of the Council of Europe declared in 1982 that "states have the duty to prevent infractions against freedom of expression and information and should adopt policies designed to promote... a variety of media and pluralism in the sources of information..." The United Nations Human Rights Committee has stated similarly that, with the development of modern mass communications media, effective measures are needed to prevent the control of these media that interfere with the right of all to express themselves freely, contrary to the guarantees contained in the International Covenant in Article 19(3).

In many ways, the impact of ICTs in the human rights context is tempered by the same factors that determine the extent to which a free press is able to manoeuvre in those countries where abuses are prevalent. The ability of the media to function unfettered by government fosters the creation of strong social networks, while engaging citizens in public affairs. Arguably, the extent to which there is a functioning free press is indicative of the likelihood that human rights are going to be effectively impacted through ICTs.

Any discussion on democracy invariably leads to the broader issue of governance— incorporating the dynamic of the institutions, the people, and the various types of agency they wield in the process of governing a nation. As ICTs propagate, the power to influence is more increasingly widely distributed, and hence the tasks of governance—on both national and international levels— become progressively more complex and challenging. A wide variety of modern trends are affecting the state-centric system of governance from all angles: these include international organizations like the UN and the E.U., nationalist separatist movements, international terrorist organizations like al-Qaeda, multinational organizations like General Motors, and international NGOs like Amnesty International. The majority of these fall squarely within the confines of the 'realist' paradigm—in part because they are statist in orientation, or because they seek the control of power in the form of land and resources.

The constitutions of national governments and their treaties have been challenged by the demands of increasingly well-defined ethnic and other subgroups, confrontations to traditional borders created by new information technologies, and the globalization of economies. "As power increasingly resides in the people, the world will become more complex, and we will live "in a kind of international democracy." On the other hand, some argues that the nation state retains its power in the modern era and the main trend has been towards the growth of regional blocs, where nation-states remain the primary actors, not the emergence of a new world order that transcends states. In any case, the more information is disseminated in the direction of those who have not been privy to it in the past, the more of a challenge there will be to political 'incumbents'; escalating pressures on governments for attention to freedom and human rights causes are a case in point. According to the U.S. State Department, some of the most successful transnational networks are those that partner with, respond to, or support government initiatives on behalf of democracy and human rights. While there is no international consensus on how best to address the questions of past human rights violations, particularly in the context of complex democratic transitions, a great deal of concrete progress has nonetheless occurred, including the establishment of International Criminal Tribunals. Certainly, no international consensus yet exists on international justice issues, the controversial subject of the International Criminal Court being one example of this debate.

Legitimacy is a cornerstone of good governance, and to a very large extent, civil society representatives like NGOs and the tools they use to heighten global awareness and public sensitivities are indispensable to the solid construction of that legitimacy. "... Citizens express more confidence in the system of government where, according to the Freedom House classification, there are widespread opportunities for civic participation and protection of human rights." It is also extremely important, through the course of a discussion on global governance, to point out that mention of a 'global civil society' in no way implies the obliteration of discord or conflict within its framework—for the rights of individuals can easily come in conflict with the rights of groups, and the means by which entities (like councils in traditional villages) resolve such issues are not necessarily exclusive of violence or power-mongering. The role of violence has indeed been considered central in state-centric politics, and in the process of state formation and evolution of the state system. States are in fact the main perpetrators of human rights abuses within their own borders—with examples of genocide and ethnic extermination rife even in the last fifty years.

Bibliography

Alston, P.: The Convention on the Rights of the Child: A Commentary. Oxford, Clarendon Press, 1997.

Heggenhougen, K. 1999, Are the marginalized the slag-heap of globalization? Disparity, health and human rights. *Health and Human Rights,* 4.

Hendricks, A. 1995, A selected bibliography of human rights and disability. *Health and Human Rights,* 1.

Henkin, L., (ed.): The International Bill of Human Rights: The Covenant on Civil and Political Rights, New York, Columbia University Press, 1981.

Human Rights - Status of International Instruments, New York, 1987, United Nations Publication, Sales No. E.87.XIV.2.

Jabine, T. and R. Claude, (eds.): Human Rights and Statistics, Getting the Record Straight, Philadelphia, University of Pennsylvania Press, 1992.

Maingay, S., Thornicroft, G., Huxley, P., Jenkins, R. and Szmukler, G. 'Mental health and human rights: the MI Principles - turning rhetoric into action', *International Review of Psychiatry,* vol.14, 2002.

McGoldrick, D.: The Human Rights Committee, Oxford, Clarendon Press; New York, Oxford University Press, 1991.

Meron, T.: Human Rights Law- Making in the United Nations, New York, Oxford Uni - versity Press, 1986.

Nowak, M.: Commentary on the U.N. Covenant on Civil and Political Rights, Kehlam Rhein, N.P. Engel, 1993.

Persaud, A. and Hewitt, D. 'European Convention on Human Rights: effects on psychiatric care'. *Nursing Standard,* vol.15 (44), 2001.

Potter, M. In White, C. (ed.) *Law for Northern Ireland Social Workers.* Gill and Macmillan, 1995.

Robertson, A., and Merrills, J.: Human Rights in the World. Manchester, Manchester University Press, 3rd ed., 1989.

Robertson, A., and Mer rills, J.: Human Rights in the World. Manchester, Manchester University Press, 3rd ed., 1989.

Rosenthal, E. and Rubenstein, L.S. 'International Human Rights Advocacy under the Principles for the Protection of Persons with Mental Illness'. *International Journal of Law and Psychiatry,* vol.16, 1993.

Susan B. Glasser, "Rivalries Cloud Afghan Peace - Lawlessness Threatens Northern City's Renewal," *Washington Post,* April 27, 2002.

Symposium: The Implementation of the International Covenant on Economic, Social and Cultural Rights. *Human Rights Quarterly* 9(2), (1987).

Tyagi, Y.K.: The Law and Practice of the Human Rights Committee, Dordrecht, Martinus Nijhoff, 1993.

Vasak, K. and P. Alston, (eds.): The International Dimensions of Human Rights. 2 vols., Westport, CT, Green wood Press; Paris, United Nations Educational, Scientific and Cultural Organization, 1982.

UNDP. 1995-2002. Human Development Report. Oxford University Press. New York.

Verhellen, E., (ed.): Monitoring Children's Rights, The Hague, Martinus Nijhoff, 1996.

Williams, P.: Treatment of Detainees: Examination of Issues Relevant to Detention by the United Nations Human Rights Committee, Geneva, Henry Dunant Institute, 1990.

Index

American Federation of Labor (AFL) 94
Anthrax 18

Bachelor of Laws (LL.B.) 215
Burmese Border Consortium (BBC) 161

Centre for Human Rights and Prevention of Genocide 175
Centre for the Victims of Torture (CVICT) 151
Communication channels 28
Communication technologies 21
Community organization strategies 32
Community-based health education 27
Consumer behaviour theory 29
Consumer Information Processing (CIP) 29

Democratic Republic of Congo (DRC) 148
Department for International Development (DFID) 150
Discriminatory laws 149

Economic and Social Council of the United Nations 94
Economic Community of West African States (ECOWAS) 154
E-health strategies 21
Environmental activities 23
Ethnic minorities 20
European Commission Humanitarian Aid Office (ECHO) 162

Filtering mechanism 100

Geneva Convention 159
Global Conflict Prevention Pool (GCPP) 167
Groupe Islamique Armee (GIA) 172
Groupe Salafiste pour la Predication et le Combat 172

Health education 22
Human Papilloma Virus (HPV) 18

Institute for War and Peace Reporting (IWPR) 152
Institutionalization 214
Instructional activities 23
Interactive health communications 22

Internally Displaced Persons (IDP) 166
International Committee of the Red Cross (ICRC) 161, 169
International Labour Conference 93

Joined-up approach 151

Liberation Tigers of Tamil Eelam (LTTE) 170

Master of laws (LL.M.) 216
Mèdicin Sans Frontières (MSF) 162
Memorandum of Understanding (MoU) 178
Ministry of Defence (MOD) 150
Multicomponent risk reduction programs 32

National Human Rights Commission (NHRC) 217
Nationality Immigration and Asylum (NIA) 164
Non-Governmental Organizations (NGOs) 215
Non-suspensive appeal (NSA) 164

Occupational organizations 108
Occupational organizations 123
Organizational change 22
Organizational efforts 23

Public Service Agreement (PSA) 150

Revolutionary United Front (RUF) 176
Royal Nepalese Army (RNA) 169

Slavery Convention 94
South Asia Association for Regional Cooperation (SAARC) 220
Structural interventions 25
Sudan People's Liberation Movement (SPLM) 178

UN High Commissioner for Refugees (UNHCR) 158
UN Mission to Ethiopia and Eritrea (UNMEE) 179
United Nations Educational, Scientific, and Cultural Organisation (UNESCO) 220
University Grants Commission (UGC) 218

World Federation of Trade Unions (WFTU) 94